Bleats 365

Too Short for a Blog
Too Long for a Tweet
One Sheep to Another

ANDY REESE

WaterPro Books

DEDICATION

To my best friend and wife Susan who is the inspiration for many of these Bleats as we sit morning by morning talking and reading and looking out on the countryside from our cozy nook.

To you Bleats reader. I am embarrassed to admit that I like the "likes" and most of all I love it when someone sends along a note saying I had read their mind, or made their day, or calmed their fears, or made them laugh out loud. Nothing is better for an author than that.

And to the real Author and partner in every Bleat.
Thank you for trusting me.
I will be faithful because You are there.

Bleatmaster Senior the sheep
by Lauren Goodwin Reese
www.laurelandperl.com

Day 1

The Courthouse Plaque

There would probably be far fewer protests if the Beatitudes were put on the plaque in front of the courthouse instead of the Ten Commandments.

Neither you nor I control what is on the courthouse plaque.

But there is another kind of plaque in which I am much more interested – yours and mine.

Paul says, *"You demonstrate the influence of our ministry to you, for you are our epistle not written with ink but with the Spirit of God – not on public plaques but on the tablets of human hearts."* (2 Cor 3:3)

If Bleats has one purpose, it is to encourage each of you to grow into the very destiny God has for you; daily finding His purpose in every encounter and activity; and enjoying forever the love, intimacy and excitement of a life with Papa God.

We each are read by those around us. I am after beatitudes.

I pray that each day, each Bleat will make a small impression for good within you.

May you be blessed in the reading; and may what you read be better than what I have written.

Day 2

Rich

So... it's that time of year again when you might be disappointed with raises and thinking of taxes and those far better off than you.

Here is good news.

I read a study about the very rich and guess what?

Statistically speaking the rich are more likely - scientifically more likely - to violate traffic rules, steal candy from children, lie, shoplift, cheat at games, and to be more tightfisted. Brain scans showed a lesser ability to feel empathy.

In surveys the rich and powerful were as a group far less happy than the middle class or even than the poor.

It seems there is indeed a growing inequality between rich and poor.

The Rich Young Ruler asks what he must do to gain life. Jesus tells him to empty his hands so he can lay hold of it. He leaves sad...sad. And Jesus says, *"Truly I say to you, it is so very hard for a rich man to enter the kingdom of heaven."* (Mt 19:23)

Like any drug it is not the riches but the love of it that is so toxic.

Quitting cold turkey? Not so easy.

The attachment to riches can be like a deadly disease, a huge disability, a debilitating handicap. Possession of great wealth can make one almost pathologically unable to enter into the life of the kingdom - not in the hereafter but in the here and now - the kingdom that is righteousness, joy and peace; is laughter and lightness, is giving and loving, and carefree and trusting.

On the other hand, the poor are chosen to be rich in faith - the currency of the kingdom.

Rich.

...continued

It is a very exclusive club this life in the kingdom thing - a very private one - membership is costly.

Jesus said many of the wealthy cannot afford it.

Is it hopeless for them? Who can be saved from this miserable wealth?

Commenting on the Ruler Jesus answered that question: *"With people this is impossible, but with God all things are possible."* (Mt 19:26)

Here is the cure.

"Instruct those who are rich in this present world not to be conceited or to fix their hope on the uncertainty of riches, but on God, who richly supplies us with all things to enjoy. Instruct them to do good, to be rich in good works, to be generous and ready to share, storing up for themselves the treasure of a good foundation for the future, so that they may take hold of that which is life indeed." (1 Tim 6:18ff)

By the way.

99% of the world think you and I ARE the rich.

Have you taken the cure?

Oh my... it is glorious to watch.

Like Scrooge in the morning breathing in the fresh air of freedom, leaving a blazing wake of blessing wherever they go.

With God all things are possible.

Day 3

Faithful Work

I recently heard this testimony in church:

"I labored forty hours this week, getting up and going to my job and working hard all day. And this Friday I got a paycheck."

Not.

We love to hear about the person who is "depending on God" and finds money, gets an inheritance, or is forgiven of a debt - you know, who wins the "Christian lottery".

In our church world it may be more testimony-worthy, more pop and sizzle - but I'm thinking there is something that impresses Papa more:

"Make it your ambition to lead a quiet life, to work with your hands, just as we told you, so that your daily life may win the respect of outsiders and so that you will not be dependent on anybody" (1 Th 4:11)

"For even when we were with you, we gave you this rule: 'If a man will not work, he shall not eat.'" (2 Th 3:10)

"A man must labor, performing with his own hands what is good, so that he will have something to share with one who has need." (Eph 4:28).

I wonder if the real miracle, the true example of dependence on God; the praiseworthy event; happens when day after day I faithfully work hard and with excellence.

I suspect God thinks so too.

Day 4

Moore is Less

Moore's law says that the capabilities of digital electronic devices:
processing speed, memory capacity, sensors and even the number and size
of pixels doubles approximately every two years. A 256 gigabyte jump
drive!? I can put... well... something in it... LOTS of somethings!

That's a good thing right? Maybe.

We humans have very limited and singular focus abilities, and limited input
jacks - one stereo eye input, one stereo ear port - linked to one storage
node. We have one internal monitor on which to observe all this stuff... and
16 hours a day, 80 years. Maybe.

Our Designer says: *"The eye is the lamp of your body; when your eye is single focused,
your whole body also is full of light; but when it is bad, your body also is full of
darkness" (Lk 11:34).*

*"So take care how you listen; for whoever has, to him more shall be given; and whoever
does not have, even what he thinks he has shall be taken away from him." (Lk 18:18)*

It is important to me to keep my limited inputs and monitor uncluttered
from mental junk food... stuff that's bad for me, beneath me, only an
addictive time waster.

If I do I can be filled with much light and more.

No maybe there.

PS. I have heard that my new model coming out not so far from now is
incredible

Day 5

Too Late Wise

So... my grandfather used to say in his German accent, "too soon alt, too late wise." As I face 60 I know more than ever that age is unavoidable but wisdom... hmmmm?

God says: *"The fear of the LORD is the beginning of wisdom."* Does that mean when I am afraid of God I "wise up"?

Well, sort of.

The best that personal study of facts and information can produce is knowledge. The best experience can produce is understanding of that knowledge. But wisdom is very, very different from these human-initiated efforts.

The Man said, *"The kingdom of heaven is like yeast, which a woman took and hid in three pecks of flour until it was all risen."* (Mt 13:33)

Wisdom is like yeast in the good sense. You can mix all sorts of things into the loaf - all sorts of study, experiences and life events. Even nuts.

But only the yeast has the life to cause the whole thing to rise and become fit to eat. And only God supplies the yeast.

Wisdom grows when I make a practice of listening to God's commentary on life's events.

So... wise up.

Day 6

Ready for My Father's Business

So... Paul had a 14 year career as a tent maker in Damascus.

Moses had a 40 year career as a shepherd. Abraham too... and David, each had long "careers" that were not really careers at all.

Jesus at 12 was a precocious child, astoundingly brilliant, filled with knowledge, and impatient to be about His Father's business.

His spirit had come into possession of His soul and He felt ready to go. Even a bit of cheek to mom.

Then he had an 18 year career as a carpenter in a small town. Then... He was actually ready to be about His Father's business.

It maybe takes that long to become demagnetized... neither enamored by the opportunity to be important, nor repelled by the many encounters with the failings of humans... many His followers.

Not to swing at the bad pitch of Satan;

acquainted with the feel of the yoke.

"God is not unjust so as to forget your work and the love which you have shown toward His name, in having ministered and in still ministering to the saints. And we desire that each one of you show the same diligence so as to realize the full assurance of hope until the end, so that you will not be sluggish, but imitators of those who through faith and patience inherit the promises." (Heb 6:12)

Day 7

Parallel Universes

So...I am on a conference call with two firms,

...wanting to convince them to put us on their team to go after a very interesting and prestigious project in Austin TX.

I am thinking it would take a miracle but why not try?

We chat for a while; I try not to appear over eager. The president of the firm seems remarkably friendly.

Probably just a nice guy.

At the end we are invited into an exclusive professional relationship with their firm. I am pleased and just a little amazed.

In closing he says, "oh, by the way, I love you book Freedom Tools... our Sunday school class is studying it. See you soon brother."

I think I do believe in parallel universes and wormholes... and in Papa's crinkly smile!

Day 8

Remember One Thing

So... Susan's birthday card: *"At your age it's important to remember one thing."*

Open card

"And if you can remember two things you are way ahead of the rest of us."

And this morning...God's birthday word reminding me of Psalm 37 which I posted all around the perimeter of the land we now live on 20 years ago:

"Trust in the LORD and do good;
Dwell in the land and cultivate faithfulness.

Delight yourself in the LORD;
and He will give you the desires of your heart.

Commit your way to the LORD,
trust also in Him, and He will do it.

The steps of a man are established by the LORD,
And He delights in his way.

When he falls, he will not be hurled headlong,
Because the LORD is the One who holds his hand."

And turning the page... is the one thing to remember all you youngsters.

"I have been young and now I am old,
Yet I have not seen the righteous forsaken."

I think Susan and God are saying the same thing... like always!

Day 9

Just Right

Alas... I am a man of weak faith.

Try as I might, and despite the spate of books to the contrary, I simply cannot become an atheist. I do not have enough faith. I cannot believe that everything had no beginning or just spontaneously appeared. No matter how far back, how pre-big-bang, how pre-physics, I cannot get my head around that fact. It just happened, just right. I do not have the faith for it.

I cannot grasp that life arose from non-life. That the wind and temperature and chemical soup were just primordially right to accidentally mix things in just the right way on just the right planet. There are better odds that a tornado in a junk yard will construct the space shuttle. There are too many "just rights" - about 37 trillion too many. I cannot believe that there is no essential difference of any kind between a rock and a dog except the level of chemical complexity and animation? No difference. The dog is just a more complex version of the rock.

Life is an illusion and the illusion is an illusion. The fact that I am typing this is just the result of the wind being just right a billion years ago - nothing more. It is just one very complex billiard game. Nope. I do not have the faith for it. And, if the first three are not true, then I cannot grasp that all of this is without meaning, without purpose, without intent; just the hobby of some infinite being left on some shelf to rot. If this being wanted to be evil, hateful, and vile then we would all be tortured toast. But we are not. We desire beauty, meaning, love, and eternity is placed somewhere inside of us. Some one very smart and very good exists.

I applaud those who are men of great faith. I know they think those like me are deluded. Maybe so.

But it is a grand and fulfilling delusion and... it is not my fault after all... but that of the breeze and the primordial soup. Maybe we'll all know the truth someday, maybe when things are indeed... just right.

Day 10

Just Doughnuts

So... I have arrived.

Our office had had an early morning meeting complete with gooey doughnuts. Passing through the meeting room I saw the boxes of uneaten sweets and... sort of surprised.

Without any effort or self-denial, no temptation, no saliva - just no desire whatsoever to have one. ...somewhere in my mind I'm sure the quiet voice of Susan Reese spoke encouragement. They looked repulsive to me.

Solomon, who should have taken his own advice with foreign wives, says: "There is a way which seems attractive to a man, But its end is the way of death." (Prov 14:12)

Looks like life. Is death. Doughnuts. But God has a quiet plan of encouragement if I will listen...

"Your ears will hear a word behind you, 'This is the way, walk in it,' whenever you turn to the right or to the left. And you will choose to defile your graven images overlaid with silver and gold. You will scatter them as an impure thing, and you will say to them, 'Be gone!'" (Is 30:21)

There are many deadly things that have this siren song of attraction to us humans. Physical things, soulish things, spiritual things. Power and pornography, gossip and attention seeking, false security and addictive relationships, empty entertainment and empty calories. Many things.

But by listening to the transforming voice of my Teacher, I can have the power to see right through them; see them for what they really are... I can defile them before they defile me (2 Cor 5:17).

They are just doughnuts.

Day 11

First World Poverty

So... six mile hike.

I have choices:
special smart wool socks - check
sun screen - check
Camelback water supply - check
microfiber shirt and hiking shorts - check
wide brim cooling hat - check
hiking boots - check
Cliff bars - check
pointed walking stick - check
map - check
cell phone with GPS - check

African mother going six miles to get water. She has no choices:
water jug - check

God too has choices:

"Has not God chosen those who are poor in the eyes of the world to be rich in faith and to inherit the kingdom he promised those who love him?" (Jas 2:5)

"But God chose the foolish things of the world to shame the wise; God chose the weak things of the world to shame the strong." (1 Cor 1:27)

It is not the poverty in the third world I worry most about. It is the poverty in the first.

"So the last will be first, and the first will be last." (Mt 20:16)

Day 12
You Just Have to Die

My friend Kenny Grindall wrote:

I overheard two kids talking about some video game...

Kid One: "How do you get a new life?"

Kid Two: "Easy. You just have to die."

Easy.

You just have to die.

"Then Jesus said to His disciples, 'If anyone wishes to come after Me, he must deny himself, and take up his cross and follow Me. For whoever wishes to save his life will lose it; but whoever loses his life for My sake will find it. For what will it profit a man if he gains the whole world and forfeits his soul? Or what will a man give in exchange for his soul?'" (Mt 16:24-26)

Day 13

Crash Course

So... I was reminded that a lot of you are changing jobs or locations in the next few months. Here is something I think will help you a lot... it did me.

I was on a plane on fire in an emergency landing at Nashville and God spoke (no my life did not flash before my eyes so I knew I would live) about destiny and purpose and this verse was key: *"we are His workmanship created in Christ Jesus for good works that God has created beforehand that we should walk in them."* (Eph 2:10)

I am specially created – the works are specially planned – I am told to walk in them. One thing.

That means I have to try to miss them (fear, ignorance, or disinterest) because they are hidden for me not from me. They will be perfectly fitted for me. When I simply walk daily alert to what the Father might be doing and say yes to His invitation life takes on a whole new "Easter egg hunt" sort of meaning.

I learned (and now see it in the call of about every old and NT saint) that He never sends anyone anywhere more than He is inviting me to do things with Him not for Him – "I'm going to Africa for a year, want to come along?"

My job is simple – I do not have to figure out my purpose… this is it one step at a time. And as I am older I now realize all the dots were connected into one coherent picture – I only thought I was out on a limb missing it when, in reality, I was connecting dots for a limb I would need someday (like Paul getting about half the New Testament in Damascus).

Anyway, it changed everything about my daily life and made "What" I do a lot less interesting than Who I do it with.

I have never gotten over that rough landing 30 years ago.

Day 14

A Bit Buggy

So...

My IT guy: "Knock, Knock. I need to update your software."
Me: "Again? Thought you just did that... well..."
IT Guy: "Six months ago - you are way overdue."
Me: "What?"
IT guy: "Can't you tell by the way your system is operating?"
Me: "Now that you mention it things do seem to be freezing up, breaking down and slow to engage. A bit buggy."

Slight nudge, slight shift...

Papa: "Andy, you are overdue for an update - some new beliefs and understandings, truer truth."
Me: "What?"
Papa: "Can't you tell by the way you are operating?"
Me: "Now that You mention it..."

IT Guy: "... Andy?...you went away for a bit."
Me: "That's what I hear..."
IT Guy: "??... right... Well, I'll just finish up now."

"And do not be conformed to this world, but be continuously transforming by the renewing of your mind, so that you may prove what the will of God is, that which is good and acceptable and perfect." (Rom 12:2)

A bit buggy.

Day 15

Crash Proof

So... when I was a young pilot I was taught "you can't fly in air above you or land on runway behind you."

Funny how that has guided me so many years.

David was about to come to some angry, quick and opinionated conclusions about the easy life of the boastful rich, the world and even God. He would have crashed had he done so.

But he says: *"I was deeply troubled and agitated; and if I had spoken out rashly then, I would have betrayed your children. But then I gained altitude; I entered Your sanctuary; and I understood... I landed my soul aright."* (Ps 73)

I have learned never to trust any impression, idea, or "inner word" when my heart is agitated, wounded, tossing and turning; when I have already formed an opinion wanting support; when I am afraid; when I am only logical; when I want to judge rather than appraise; never to trust a morning dream when I should be up; or rely on inner guidance when I have something unconfessed or unresolved; when I have hurt someone and know it.

But when I get altitude, enter the sanctuary, find joy, lay down ideas and opinions, clear the air... fly into the air above me. Then I can land the thought safely, right on the numbers of the runway.

The passengers in life with me appreciate the soft landing.

Crash proof.

Day 16

End Times Preparation

So... in most circles it is considered unsophisticated and irredeemably awkward to think or act like we are in the end times, that Jesus is waiting just off stage. Just the sort of thing you would make a mocking reality show about. No one smart expects Him to come back... at least not any time soon. Right?

Think about this. Jesus said, *"For this reason you also must be ready; for the Son of Man is coming when you do not think He will."* (Mt 24:44)

And: *"Know this first of all, that in the last days mockers will come with their mocking, following after their own lusts, and saying, 'Where is the promise of His coming? Ever since the fathers fell asleep, all continues just as it was from the beginning of creation'."* (2 Pet 3:3)

I think the problem is this. If I felt like His return was imminent what would I do? Store up food and ammunition? Move to a remote place? Stand on a street corner with a sign? Talk incessantly about it? Nope. That is crazy, selfish or wrong. It stokes the mockers and puts the church off course.

Jesus, in three parables in Matthew 24 and 25, said to be doing three things: (1) be faithfully serving (the parable of the servant); (2) be being filled with the a "real time relationship" with God (the parable of the ten virgins with oil); and (3) invest the gifts and talents I have given you to steward in kingdom business fearlessly (the parable of the minas).

We will all be surprised when He comes. I want to be among those that are ready.

All the time. Any time.

Day 17

Happy Abba Day

So... God had a lot of choices of names He could have told us to call Him.

In the Old Testament His name was often only a whispered YHWH. He was called Ehyeh (I am) and Adonai (Lord) and Elohim (with a feminine root huh!); and lots descriptors: Jireh (provider), Nissi (banner), Shalom (peace), Kenu (righteousness), Shammah (ever present), Sabaoth (of hosts), Raah (shepherd), and Rapha (healer). He is king, lord of lords, savior, mighty one, and much, much more.

Lots of names. Yet He instructed Holy Spirit to tell us He has a favorite name among His children... one He loves most:

"For you have not received a spirit of slavery leading to fear again, but you have received a spirit of adoption as sons. Because you are sons, God sent His Spirit into our hearts, who calls out, 'call Him Abba' and by whom we in turn cry out, 'Abba!'" (Gal 4:6, Rom 8:15)

God almighty, Lord over all, the One for whom the sum total of all the stars are but dust; omnipresent, omniscient, omnipotent and even omnivorous (He devours Christian and pagan idols equally!)...

That One says this...

"Hey, you the one whose hairs are all numbered; the one whose thoughts are all known before you even think them and whose life was carefully considered before your birth; the one whom I think about more times each day than the grains of sand on the sea shore. That one.

You . . . are My favorite, my sooooo loved child whom I adopted and snatched to my heart... you... call me papa...pops...daddy...Abba. Let's be best friends. Let's be intimate companions. I choose you. Choose Me too."

Happy Abba day!

Day 18

Gift to the Generations

So... every father would like something of himself to outlast his own lifetime in the lives of his progeny.

We fathers look at some of the things in our children that are like us... often to our own discomfort; and know they will probably make better use of that gifting or personality bent then we. Perhaps it will last.

House and wealth too might last if well managed - but mostly it does not. The reality is that our grandchildren may know us somewhat. But their children certainly will not except maybe as some faint grey shadow gone when they were very young.

And their children?

We may be an old photograph in an album; "Oh yes, that is old great great great... don't know much about him". But there is one thing that has the ability to be self-sustaining generation to generation. God speaks of His kingdom as a mustard seed - scattered and small - yet containing life, seed, living and renewing strength (Mt 13).

That life can be transferred undiminished, undiluted generation to generation - to the children's children and beyond (Prov 13:22). This is because it is alive, not a memory. It is now, real, theirs; a life-giving wisdom and a living relationship with the One who makes all things new.

As a father I want to leave much to my children. But most of all - when every memory of me has faded from the earth I want them to know:

"The counsel of the LORD stands forever, the plans of His heart from generation to generation." (Ps 33:11)

Day 19

Truth is Where You Find It

So…In 2 Sam 16 David's men want to kill the mocking Shimei, but David essentially says, "What if the Lord has sent him and I need to hear what he says? Leave him alone."

And all day they endured Shimei's words. Truth is where you find it. Here is some truth, hard to hear, but truth is not always easy:

"I've always said that I don't respect people who don't proselytize. I don't respect that at all. If you believe that there's a heaven and a hell, and people could be going to hell or not getting eternal life, and you think that it's not really worth telling them this because it would make it socially awkward... how much do you have to hate somebody to not proselytize? How much do you have to hate somebody to believe everlasting life is possible and not tell them that?"

Atheist and Illusionist Penn Jillette

There is balance for sure and love and leading must be my guide.

But I asked myself, "When did I last share my faith with someone? Am I afraid to share my belief because it might be awkward? If so, why is that... really?"

"For whoever is ashamed of Me and My words, the Son of Man will be ashamed of him when He comes in His glory." (Lk 9:26)

"We preach Christ crucified, to Jews a stumbling block and to Gentiles foolishness, but to those who are the called is is: Christ the power and wisdom of God. Because the foolishness of God is wiser than men, and the weakness of God is stronger than men." (1 Cor 1)

Truth is where you find it... where anyone finds it.

Share it.

Day 20
Non-responsible

So... someone who can pull my chain asked repeatedly why I didn't seem to be anxious about a certain topic and the persons-of-interest involved who seemed to be heading off a cliff.

They asked, "Aren't you being sort of irresponsible?"

I said, "No I don't think I'm being irresponsible - I think I'm being non-responsible."

I am in a partnership. I am the junior partner. We are engaged in a certain business: God and Sons, Inc. Purveyors of Truth, Love and Service.

A senior associate once said: *"Look at the birds of the air. They do not sow, nor reap nor gather into barns, and yet your heavenly Father feeds them. Are you not worth much more than they? And who of you through worry can add a single hour to his life?"* (Matt 6:26)

And this: *"Very truly I tell you, a son can do nothing by himself; he can do only what he sees his Father doing."* (Jn 5:19)

Many things are not the business of our partnership, and no good will come if I, for whatever reason, try to make them so. Many other things are our business, but the senior partner has them covered. Some I will learn in time, some I will depend on Him to do every time. Others are part of my job description and I go after them energetically and without discouragement.

Conducting business otherwise would be irresponsible.

Day 21

Remove the Plank

So... in light of a number of conversations about and with hurt people I have been thinking about this verse package:

"Why do you look at the speck that is in your brother's eye, but do not notice the plank that is in your own eye? First take the plank out of your own eye, and then you will see clearly to take the speck out of your brother's eye. Do not throw your pearls before swine, or they will trample them under their feet, and turn and tear you to pieces." (Mt 7:3)

When hurt by some organization or group is may be common to use philosophical or theological generalizations to cover my hurt feelings. I might say, "You know the church..." or "The company I worked for..." or "That small group...". And I sound very wise. But I am not.

The occasion of hurt feelings CAN produce real insight into the flaws within an organization. But the occasion can also produce blind-sight. And if I speak out of that blinded place I produce nothing good... because my heart really wants revenge and pity. I want angry allies.

So...of prime importance is to make sure that I myself am full of forgiveness and understanding; that I am not trying to impugn motives and judgments that are misleading or inflammatory. I must remove the plank in my own platform.

When I first do that I am given a gift: clarity of insight, wisdom, God's very vantage point. Real pearls - pearls of great price.

And a second gift is also mine: the wisdom to know when to keep silent, and to sense the occasion to bring the wisdom as healing... not accusation.

Day 22

Breaking the Pattern

So...Is there a pattern of repeated failure or lack of success in some area of your life? After praying with hundreds of people I have found these four areas good checks:

Have I judged or criticized someone related to this area - held them in contempt or ridiculed them?

Follow this: *"Do not judge so that you will not be judged. For in the way you judge, you will be judged; and by your standard of measure, it will be measured to you"* Mat 7:1-2).

Do I have a self-sabotaging ungodly belief about this. Do I think, "right, something always happens to mess things up"; or "I am so stupid..."

Follow this: *"If God is for us, who is against us? He who did not spare His own Son, but delivered Him over for us all, how will He not also with Him freely give us all things?"* (Rom 8:31)

Am I working with all my strength and mind or being lazy?

Follow this: *"Whatever you do, do your work heartily, as for the Lord rather than for men."* (Col 3:23)

Am I going after the wrong thing for wrong reason other than God's leading? Perhaps something I am not well suited for, have no passion for; maybe to please a parent or my friends, out of fear, for selfish reasons or out of greed?

Follow this: *"Do nothing out of selfish ambition or vain conceit. Rather, in humility value others above yourselves."* (Phil 2:3)

Day 23

The Father Debate

So… there seems to be a hot debate going on right now about who can marry who. It seems to me to be a smokescreen, a distraction from the real issue.

This is the real issue:

> *"We know the statistics - that children who grow up without a father are five times more likely to live in poverty and commit crime; nine times more likely to drop out of schools and 20 times more likely to end up in prison. They are more likely to have behavioral problems, or run away from home, or become teenage parents themselves. And the foundations of our community are weaker because of it."*

Barack Obama

"I will restore the hearts of the fathers to their children and the hearts of the children to their fathers, so that I will not come and smite the land with a curse." (Mal 4:6)

God Almighty

Fathers need to help raise children and when they do they provide three things vital to the health and wellbeing of both the child and the nation: provision, protection, and identity. When they don't those things must be foraged for by abandoned children…and the results are almost always negative dysfunction.

I am mostly on the sidelines on the marriage argument …

…but I am all in on the father debate.

Day 24

Coincidence?

So... is it a coincidence that social security and Medicare could both be saved if the babies aborted in America were alive and paying into the system?

Is it a coincidence that the tithe that should have been given voluntarily to care for the poor equals the percent of our income tax given involuntarily to them instead?

Is it a coincidence that the number of illegal immigrants just balances the number of low wage workers our country desperately needs and should have welcomed legally?

When certain tribes wanted to shirk their duty to the nation's needs, to avoid responsibility, to get their own and keep it, Moses said,

"If you do - be sure your sin will find you out." (Num 32:23).

Be sure.

A nation's sin, a company's sin... my sin. It will find me out and it will extract everything owed; every penny. Every time.

And it will extract it later - so much later I would normally fail to see the sowing and reaping connection (Gal 6:7). I may be partial to me and my kind. God is not.

"For he who does wrong will receive the consequences of the wrong which he has done, and that without partiality." (Col 3:25).

I have a chance to give willingly; act righteously; live honestly.

A chance. Be sure.

Day 25

Thunk

So... I am sitting in Capital Park in Sacramento.

The Trees are amazing - huge, old, and - what's this?

An orange tree and oh my. I stare up like an awe stuck tourist, surreptitiously throw a rock, non-nonchalantly bump the tree... I WANT an orange.

Nothing. So I sit. And sit. Almost give up.

Then... THUNK!!

…continued

Mmmmmmmmmmmmmmm

So much better than canned. The juice ran down my beard onto my dress shirt. So? I can change for this.

Then… when Jesus rebukes Satan at the temptation He misquotes scripture saying, "Man shall not live by bread alone, but by every word that comes from the mouth of God." While the Hebrew he quoted implies the ancient written scripture for "word" Jesus here uses the Greek "rhea" the spoken, just now, real-time voice and word of God.

You see, the sweetest, the best, the freshest and most refreshing word from God is that which falls from the tree just for you, that you pick up yourself and peel and eat.

You can say, "In this book I read…", or "The preacher once said…"

But unless God breaths into it, it is second hand, canned, preserved, one off.

It cannot make your heart beat faster, cannot turn you head, cannot warm your soul with the sure knowledge that God has spoken to you, just to you, one on one, heart to heart, just now. And you have heard. And you smile the smile of one well loved.

Throw rocks, bump the tree. Wait for it. *"You will seek Me and find Me when you search for Me with all your heart."* (Jer 29:13)

You can change for this.

Day 26

Killing Prophets

So... today by the fire.

Andy: "Susan I think prophesy is like about everything else in the kingdom. It tries to gets pushed into one ditch or the other. Either it gets theorized out of existence or redefined as simply teaching or encouragement; or it gets spirit-silly making God our prophesy-look-alike bell hop where God is just about to do something amazing and everyone will touch the nations; stand before kings (when do the few kings left have time for all this?!); or be princesses riding white horses."

Susan: "Was it different in the Old Testament do you think?"

Andy: "Well, at least if they were wrong they got killed."

Susan: "Or if they were right."

Pause

Andy: "You are wiser than I am - I just talk more."

Susan: "More coffee honey?"

Day 27

Grand Conspiracy

So... what if it's not a grand conspiracy?

What if there are not a bunch of corporations, socialists, capitalists, liberals, conservatives, hipsters, terrorists, governments, or police planning to gain supremacy and control me in some way.

What if it is just "death" working through and in the principalities of this earth, those intended to serve man, actually now having become perverted to control and dominate him instead.

What if it is the very thing Paul means when he talks about death "reigning" in the earth (Rom 5). What if greed is simply the principle of death working through corporations, control through governments, power through tyrants, violence through terrorists?

What if the only way I know that I have passed from death controlling me to life flowing through me is that I really love others (1 Jn 3:14).

What if I can avoid coming under the system by giving in the face of greed even if I work for a big corporation; serving even if I control policy?

What if the only way to live is to lay my life down and to be in the world but not of it?

Day 28
This Can't be Good

So... sitting in the Nashville airport and hear over the public address system, "Andrew Reese, Andrew Reese please report to the check in desk."

This can't be good.

"Mr. Reese, I hate to ask you this but can you do us a favor."

Nope this can't be good.

"We overbooked for some reason and now we're in a fix. Its to help us out. We just sort of chose you for no reason. Would you be willing to travel first class out to California?"

OK... this can be good... real good.

"God has called us and saved us with a holy calling, not according to our works, but according to His own purpose and grace which was granted us in Christ Jesus from all eternity" (2 Tim 1:9).

This can be good... real good!

Day 29

A Sure Reward

So... I am in Connecticut and take a day from vacation to try to market several local cities. I spend lots of time studying their laws, issues, and players. I know a ton. And, all for naught. Every appointment was a dud. No gain.

But I learned this long ago: *"Whatever you do, do your work heartily, as for the Lord rather than for men, knowing that from the Lord you will receive the reward of the inheritance. It is the Lord Christ whom you serve."* (Col 3:23)

I am sitting back in New Haven. A bit dejected. Then... Papa winks...

My cell rings. It is the Connecticut administrator for the very thing I was studying, "Andy, I am on the senate floor about to propose a bill - I need your help - I know you know nothing about our state law and stuff but can you talk with the senator who has some questions?"

Me: "I am in New Haven, just spent hours on this, what do you need?"

Long pause. "That is... well, amazing huh? What in the world? Can I call you next week about all this? We may need you up here."

Work hard when someone is watching, when a reward is sure. Work even harder when it seems no one is. For then the One who holds all meaningful reward in His hands is the only One who CAN reward. And He loves to do so.

Others can only pay wages. Only He gives inheritance. A ton.

Day 30

Secrets

So... Giulio Andreotti has died. So?

He was three time prime minister of Italy. He had his secrets, suspicious partners, questionable decisions. But there was also one other secret he kept well hidden. He attended daily mass and on leaving invariably gave money and called by name many street people. He was their friend. He kept a secret closet in his office stocked with food; and often he would personally leave to take food to the needy.

The prime minister.

Jesus did the same thing - often and regularly gave to the poor (Jn 13:29). Personally. So did every saint you can read about. Every one.

I have seen that among the righteous and stable rich there is a habit of giving to the poor, personally intervening in crises, paying for college, buying food, rebuilding a burned home for someone, giving time and resources. All the time. They have their secrets.

I can say with great conviction that no matter who I am, I need to give regularly and personally to meet the needs of the poor around me. And if I know none? Then work with those who do. Give time. Give money. Give.

In so doing I will not solve the problem of poverty. I will probably not even solve all that individual's problems. But I will solve my problem. You know the one. You know (Mt 6:2 19:23, 25:37, Jam 5:1).

And... I will have my secrets... worth having... worth keeping. Eternally worthwhile.

Day 31

Heavenly Economics

So... I rarely read about the stars - movie variety that is.

But today I saw that Kathleen Turner, fat from arthritis medication said, "I never valued myself for beauty - its suffocating." Jon Hamm of Madman said, "I am not curing cancer or anything important. The best thing I could probably do is be the dad that tells Bieber 'NO!'" George Clooney is marrying an Oxford educated lawyer primarily because of her intense work against injustice. And comedian Louis C.K. said he tries all his jokes out on his girls to see if they are OK.

Made me think. Nice. What if all honored people gave of their honor in that way?

Here's what.

God has a meta-economic system that works like this: "From everyone who has been given much, much will be demanded; and from the one who has been entrusted with much, much more will be asked" (Lk 12:48).

If you do the math you will see that if all the rich individually dedicated some of their lives to targeting their money efficiently to address social ills every problem would be solved - at least financially.

It is not just money - honor and fame are a commodity to be spent well: *"The members of the body which we deem less honorable, on these we bestow more abundant honor, and so they become more honorable. God has so composed the body, giving more abundant honor to that member which lacked"* (1 Cor 12:23ff). *"Live in harmony with each other. Don't be too proud to enjoy the company of ordinary people"* (Rom 12:16).

If everyone with abundance of some sort (money, fame, time, land, you name it) took a minute to recognize God's demands and requests on them and obeyed, every ill in the world would be met, every problem resourced. Every person has enough abundance of something to give.

If I don't horde. There is enough to satisfy every need.

Enough.

Day 32

Why I was Born

"The two most important days in your life are the day you are born and the day you find out why."

Mark Twain

"Man's chief end is to glorify God, and to enjoy him forever."

Westminster Shorter Catechism

"For all these things the nations of the world eagerly seek; but your Father knows that you need these things. But seek His kingdom, and these things will be added to you. Do not be afraid, little flock, for your Father has chosen gladly to give you the kingdom." (Luke 12:30-33)

"More than that, I count all things to be loss in view of the surpassing value of knowing Christ Jesus my Lord, for whom I have suffered the loss of all things, and count them but rubbish so that I may gain Christ." (Phil 3:8)

Seems logical enough.

I think I'll try it.

Day 33
Hail Mary

Hail Mary full of grace... and enigma.

When He thought He was ready and she knew He was not she reeled Him in (Lk 2:46). When she though He was ready and He felt He was not He obeyed anyway in a small favor (Jn 2:1). When she seemed ready for unwarranted attention and position He did not give in (Mt 12:48).

Sounds like many mother-child relationships I know.

But two thing stand out - vital to know, to remember, to do.

When He was born she sensed His gifts, calling and character and she treasured Him and them in her heart - she treasured her Son... treasured (Lk 2:19). He knew He was her treasure and it made all the difference.

And even when He was dying, and perhaps had other last words to say, He made sure she knew she too was His treasure and He cared for her, made special provision for her (Jn 19:27).

Mothers. Treasure your children - their character, calling, hearts. They must know they are your treasure. But hold them with open hands so that they may fly. They will return.

Children. Treasure your mothers - no matter what. And hold them with strong arms especially near the end when they need to know their treasuring of you made all the difference. Return.

Often.

Day 34

No Uniform or Anything

So... not paying attention and accidentally booked a return flight on the wrong day.

Just needed to change the date. Needed to get home from Augusta, GA. My own fault. My fault. Mea maxima culpa. I needed help. Today.

Desk agent: "You gotta pay $500 to start all over."
Silver elite agent: "Policy is $600 + $100 change fee."
My travel agent: " Our policy is $200 change fee plus fare difference."
Friend: "You should rent one way to Atlanta and then try from there."
Augusta gate agent: "Well, I'm not sure what to tell you, you booked it and that is our policy.

Sooooooo mad at myself and everyone else. So hard. I hate that airline.

Then... an old black woman, like Momma from The Shack, who had been watching all this quietly motioned me over. I didn't even think she was an agent - no uniform or anything.

"Come ova here honey - let's jess fix dis lil thing for you."
And she did. No fees. No criticism. Perfect connections. First class upgrade. I love that airline. I'll fly it next week if I can.

Paul says, *"Do you not know that it is the kindness of God leads you to repentance?"* (Rom 2:4)

"But encourage one another day after day, as long as it is still called 'Today,' so that none of you will be hardened by the deceitfulness of sin." (Heb 3:13)

When someone around me breaks a rule and it hurts them. Let the mistake do the teaching. It is God's kind intention expressed though me that will lead to restoration, reaching the destination, and even a first class upgrade.

No uniform or anything.

Today.

Day 35
Bait

So... recently there have been several viral web events that have given me pause.

The story line in each is similar: accusations of anti-Christian conspiracy by the government or media. Then the backlash police go on high alert, crazy things are said, they go viral, the truth is little to be found, and outrage is all the rage. Later and quietly, saner voices give a fuller picture and saner folks shake their heads at the fuss. It becomes "a tale told by an idiot, full of sound and fury, signifying nothing." It does God and the godly no favors.

What up?

Nehemiah was working hard for things of the kingdom, good things; God appointed things; things that made for justice, peace and safety for immigrants and refugees and war victims. Sanballat and his crew repeatedly attempted to bait Nehemiah, distract him, intimidate him. Their real goal was to stop the real difference-making work and deflect it into pretend work, self-defeating argument, fearful self-protection.

Into nothing.

Nehemiah responded, *"I am doing a great work and I cannot come down. Why should the work stop while I leave it and come down to you? Should a man like me flee? And could one such as I go into the temple to save his life? I will not go in."* (Neh 6:3)

It is bait... bait and nothing more. When I take the bait I become less and say less than I can say and do - I transform the conversation into accusation - and all the sound and fury expended does... nothing. Like Nehemiah I want to say: "Should a man like me really get involved in this?"

Should one such as I not be *'quick to listen, slow to speak and slow to become angry, because human anger does not produce the righteousness that God desires'* (Jas 1).

Look twice - and if it has a hook in it swim away. Let evil catch... nothing.

Day 36
I Like the Odds

Me, "Not sure if we should go out - there is a 60% chance of rain."

Susan, "Doesn't that mean there is an 40% chance of sunshine and fun?"

Me, "... I guess that is true."

Susan, "I like the odds."

Today - I have a very good chance of glory, fun, God being with me, and some of those "works prepared from before the foundation of the world" lying in wait to ambush me with meaning, laughter and good.

Today I have a 100% chance of watching as I go for the pre-paired opportunity - me and it paired by Papa to create a win-win since eternity.

Don't need no ticket to board the train, no reservations necessary.

I have no reservations.

I like the odds.

Day 37
A Praying Man

So... there is something rather amazing about being ready to go into arthroscopic surgery and having the surgeon walk in and say,

"Are you a praying man? (nod) well then... Lord Jesus only You can make this go perfectly no matter my skill and my brother's need.

So we declare our reliance on you and thank You that every time we call on You You answer, and we are confident of Your love and care here and now. OK brother see you after surgery."

Then everything sort of fades away... and fades back 45 minutes later.

And how did it go?

You need not ask... because my surgeon already did the asking.

I love it when a great and highly skilled man is also humble and knows full well that while he kicks and strokes vigorously it is God who keeps him afloat.

But this God, like this man, prefers to remain humbly behind the scenes even if all those around Him think He hung the moon.

Cause maybe he did.

Day 38

Change the Conversation

So... having a conversation with the pastor of a mega church about their struggle to articulate a stance on homosexuality. It's a tough one.

Here is a thought.

In the Old Testament there are maybe 28 crimes for which death (normally stoning) is the punishment. The sexual ones include: adultery, rape, men having sex with men, bestiality, premarital sex, and some incest.

I bet 75% of those reading this should be stoned.

I should be.

When someone was brought to Jesus who had committed one of these crimes - adultery in this case (Jn 8) Jesus did a wise thing.

He changed the conversation.

He ignored the argument baiting, accusing, punishing one they wanted, and articulated one that looked honestly and mercifully at the failures of everyone standing there... everyone; and the work of God in healing the hearts of everyone standing there... everyone.

He always changed the conversation when confronted by someone wanting to draw a line and force some to be on one side or the other (paying taxes, the sabbath, where to worship, etc.).

He went for the heart.

Would He have acted differently if it had been another one of those items?

Maybe mine? Maybe one I personally loathe?

... *continued*

I'm thinking not.

I personally hope not.

I have never convicted anyone of sin, or made them change. Only God can do that.

The best I can do is to invite the broken and hurting and shame ridden (whether they know it or not - and I rarely get it right anyway) into relationship; serve them; and demonstrate a God who said that none of us are qualified to throw stones, none of us are righteousness enough to judge and condemn.

All we like sheep have gone astray; all have sinned and fallen short.

Everyone.

When I focus on calling others to be their very best selves and love them all the way (letting them love me too) I bet it becomes easy for them to let God make the changes in them He desires.

Change the conversation dear ones.

Day 39

Seeing Treasure

So... I almost threw away a treasure... a small plastic bag of old cilantro.

Just as I was putting it in the trash Susan says, "No, save that, I am composting." I look at her, at the bag, and glance outside at the million tons of greenery visible from our kitchen window and am about to laugh.

Then Papa God, who rarely misses an opportunity to correct one whom He loves says, "Never look with eyes that can only see what eyes can see. The widow's copper coins were worth millions to Me - much, much more than the Pharisees trumpeted tithe."

In Mk 12:42 Jesus speaks about Papa's appraisal of worth, of value, of what turns His head... catches His eye, causes a smile and a warm heartbeat. And it can rarely be seen with eyes that look only at what eyes can see. There are no insignificant acts of kindness, no small people, no worthless gifts and talents, no silly dreams of goodness, no overlooked righteous purposes. He values intention and heart - small hidden faithfulness.

The size of the act is of no consequence. An honest and good heart IS the result He is looking for. He can accomplish everything else Himself, but will never force my heart to be a treasure to His heart. But He intensely desires and loves such a heart... such a person.

His eyes are on the sparrow - you and I are worth far, far more than that (Lk 12). Nothing that I have done secretly is hidden from His sight. To the wicked this is a fearful thing.

But to the one who may feel like their life right now is a small hidden thing, worth little - a "copper coin" life - to you I must say... don't throw away the treasure.

You... you are that treasure.

Day 40
Risk Free

So…want to live risk free?

In statistics the terms "uncertainty" and "risk" have very different meanings. In life they do too... and it makes all the difference. Uncertainty means I do not know exactly what will happen - but it seems workable, doable. Risk means that there is a chance something random, unknown and irrecoverably bad will happen. Out of control.

God allows uncertainty. Not risk.

The three in the fiery furnace in Daniel 3 were uncertain of the outcome but they perceived no risk... none. God is trusted. Their outcome was rescue. Paul was also uncertain of life or death (Phil 2:17), but felt no risk. He was calm and joyful. He did not risk his life... he gave his life. Even Jesus in the garden was uncertain of the exact outcome ("If it be thy will...") but did not imply risk in God's response ("nevertheless thy will be done."). Trusted. Gave his life too.

When I confuse the two I can begin to fear uncertainty and to mistrust God when I see seemingly hard outcomes around me. I do not like it - I like predictability, safety, security. And God does not offer that to His children. He rarely tells us what our future holds. But He does guarantee His grace will be more than enough (1 Cor 10:13, 2 Cor 12:9); and that He will be with us in the midst - like the fourth figure in the furnace; and that the risk of forever loss is zero...zero.

He holds the future.

And we, like Paul, can say: *"I know whom I have believed and I am convinced that He is able to guard what I have entrusted to Him unto that day."* (2 Tim 1:12)

God is offering a "risk free when-in-trial" offer. Risk free.

Day 41

Hunted Down

There are at least two things that hunt us down... find us out. They are diametrically opposed to each other.

The first is sin, low living and death. "Be sure it will find you out" (Num 32:23) says God. There is a prowler lurking around looking for some sheep far from the herd, far from the shepherd. Its intent is to destroy you (1 Pet 5:8).

The second is destiny, meaning and life. You and I were created for it, for it to find us. Hard to avoid: *"For we are God's handiwork, created in Christ Jesus to do good works, which God prepared in advance for us to do."* (Eph 2:10).

How do we avoid the first and find the second? Easy. But so backward sounding to most ears: *"If you try to hang on to your life, you will lose it. But if you give up your life for my sake, you will save it."* (Lk 9:24)

What? Hanging on to my life, trying to "get all I can" or "experience everything" is a sure way to lose it and to fall prey to the first hunter. It doesn't LOOK like that is what I am doing. It just seems reasonable after all.

But giving up that life, laying it down, setting my dreams aside in favor of simply listening to and trying to please God. It seems unreasonable, overly sacrificial, religious, out of step.

And then I slowly become aware of something... wonderful

... well, well, well.

Look what I found!

Day 42
Illusions

So.. so, so

"The greatest enemy of knowledge is not ignorance. It is the illusion of knowledge."

Astrophysicist Stephen Hawking

I am an Ivy League scientist and should agree, but I don't think he got it quite right.

The greatest enemy of truth is not the lie - it is the illusion that all truth is found in science... in logic... in man.

"Knowledge makes arrogant, but love edifies. If anyone supposes that he knows anything, he has not yet known as he ought to know; but if anyone loves God, he is known by Him." (2 Cor 8:1)

"Thus says the LORD, 'Let not a wise man boast of his wisdom, and let not the mighty man boast of his might, let not a rich man boast of his riches; but let him who boasts boast of this, that he understands and knows Me, that I am the LORD who exercises lovingkindness, justice and righteousness on earth; for I delight in these things,' declares the LORD." (Jer 9:23)

I want to study hard. Keep learning. Always. Every day.

But more than that I want to seek to know God and know that I am known by Him.

Day 43
Paraclete

So... one striking feature of the Boston Marathon bombing discussion was the fact that it happened at the finish line - the very place that the runners said they most wanted to hear the voices of friends and loved ones cheering and urging them on.

That is just evil.

In ancient times a marathon runner often chose a close friend or family member to be the "paraclete" - which literally means "along side caller". Their job was to call out encouragement to the exhausted runner to help them finish the long race.

This is the name given to the Holy Spirit three places in the New Testament. And that Paraclete looks at me and asks if He can use me to be the "paraclete" to others": Pursue love, and desire earnestly that you may prophetically speak exhortation to men (παράκλησιν - paraklēsin) (1 Cor 14:3).

When I look around I see many marathon runners: the young mother holding the family together, the handicapped trying to make it, the one out of work struggling, the aged facing the end, the young visionary feeling disappointed, the cancer patient fighting, the student not making the grade.

To some of those I have been privileged to be the paraclete - to call out encouragement and truth; to remind them of the greatness of their quest, that they are not alone, that they can make it.

You and I are equipped by God with words of life, hands of service, a smile of love.

That is just good.

Day 44

Choosing to be Glad

So... yesterday was Friday the 13th and today, today is Valentine's Day the 14th. Interesting juxtaposition huh? Universal dread and universal attraction - luck and love back to back. Such very different days...at least on paper hanging on my wall calendar.

I awoke this morning far from my love and the (almost) first thought was: *"This is the day that the LORD has made; I will rejoice and be glad in it"* (Ps 118:24).

I recall many years ago papa Don Finto saying this: "How most days turn out is decided between the bed and the breakfast table." That determination is made by me... not by fate, not by circumstance, not by bank accounts, jobs, my current situation, or relationships or non-relationships felt most keenly on this day. And I believed him.

Good day or bad. That decision is mine alone. Mine. There is Another who can actually do something about whether it is Friday the 13th or Valentine's day and He says: *"For I know the plans I have for you,' declares the Lord, 'plans to prosper you and not to harm you, plans to give you hope and a future'"* (Jer 29:11).

An old embittered grouchy and despondent person did not start out that way. But day after day, between the bed and the breakfast table, they unwittingly let circumstance and thought habits make a decision for them... and they slowly by slowly talk themselves into bitter hardness and despair.

"Take care, brethren, that there not be in any one of you an evil, unbelieving heart that slips away from that One who wants to lift you up. But encourage one another day after day, as long as it is still called 'Today,' so that none of us will be hardened by the deceitfulness of sin. For we have become partakers of that One. Today if you hear His voice do not harden your hearts" (Heb 3:12-15).

Today... this day... between the bed and the breakfast table declare; "THIS is the day the Lord has made, I will rejoice and be glad in it." You may have to slip back into bed and start over. No problem! I can change my life by making a small but important one minute decision to change today.

And today I will be glad.

Day 45

The Four Issues in Life

So…no matter how complex a problem seems on the outside; how many logical reasons, excuses, explanations, conjectures and diagnoses; no matter the pathology, I have come to see that most every major issues is motivated by feelings of discomfort, of pain, of being trapped on the inside.

And those inside issues are of four types… four only and these are spoken of by Christ in the singular parable in four parts in Luke 15:

- the lost coin,
- the lost sheep,
- the prodigal son
- the older brother.

First: Someone is wounded deeply, rejected, abandoned, hurt. It is not their fault though they always feel it is. They are that lost coin – dark, abandoned, but with the image of the king and value stamped on them. The problem is Wounding.

The solution is to find that person, clean them, give the pain to God, receive love, shine light on the lies that entrap, bring them into healthy relationship and celebrate them to remove their shame. You, like the woman, can shine that light, help them feel clean and valuable again, and celebrate them.

Second: Someone has naively gotten themselves into a trap, a situation, a snare. They wandered into it, made a bad deal and now are hopelessly, fearfully, stuck. Drugs, relationships, organizations, contracts, vows, soul-ties, habits, judgments, unforgiveness. The problem is Entanglement. They are that lost sheep, never meaning to go so far and be in such trouble.

The solution is to track them down, get to the bottom of the problem, give the mess to God and receive something He comes up with in return, return them to sound relationships, honor them, and celebrate them to remove their shame.

... *continued*

You, like the shepherd, can commit to help them to see the source of the issue, give it to Jesus to carry (he bore those things), and let them receive something real in exchange to help meet the legitimate need illegitimately met.

Third: Someone has chosen the wrong path and it has almost destroyed them. It is <u>Sin.</u> It is stupidity fueled rebellion, unrighteousness, crime, dishonesty, perversion. They are that prodigal, willfully sinning but now needing rescue.

The solution is to let them come to the end of themselves, be there for them when they are ready, ask them to really repent, give the burden to God and receive unconditional forgiveness (the sin did the teaching), bring them into healthy relationship, and celebrate them to remove their shame. You like the father can offer a robe (restored right standing), a ring (restored authority), and sandals (restored purpose).

Forth: Someone is trying very hard to do everything perfectly... but perfectly burned out following all the rules but never being in a loving and intimate rest relationship with Papa God. They have all the answers but have stuffed all the questions. They are harboring <u>Ungodly beliefs</u>. They are the older brother, sad and angry.

The solution is to gently help them to see the belief system that is killing them, invite them into relationship with God, help them to change over time, and ask them to only work WITH Him not for Him from now on. Ask them to celebrate someone else with God. You, like the father, can help the person to understand the relationship, intimacy, and generosity of God the Father.

Look around. Look for WESU – step in as a spiritual/emotional first responder. You are now armed and dangerous.

"It was for freedom that Christ set us free." (Gal 5:1)

Day 46

Knowing Fully

I have often wondered why it is that God seems sort of different to each individual. Each stresses something about God that seems sort of unique.

Of course this is great fodder for non-believers about making God in our own image, having Him be what we need Him to be.

I think there is something to that... but not like they might accuse.

I sometimes think of humans as sort of like chicks inside a shell. At salvation three things happen: the yoke inside the shell comes to life; the evil snake ready to eat the egg is held mostly at bay; and the warm incubating light of God surrounds the shell and chick inside on all sides.

Then the chick begins to peck at the shell - becoming more free of its constraints and stronger with the effort. As its beak punches holes in the shell light streams in - and wherever the light enters the chick sees that part of the full glory of God; and says to itself, "God met me in the midst of that struggle - I just know that God is like this... and this... and this."

"Now I know in part, but then I will know fully just as I also have been fully known" (1 Cor 13:12).
"We know that when Christ appears, we shall be like him, for we shall see him as he is" (1 Jn 3:2).
"And we all, who with unveiled faces contemplate the Lord's glory, are being transformed into his image with ever-increasing glory" (2 Cor 3;18).

Someday we will know fully, see clearly, our 360 degree God.

Until then you tell me what you see, and I'll tell you what I see - and through each other's eyes we'll all see.

Day 47

Multi-colors of God

So... I guess I belong to the First and Third Apostolic Free Evangelmatic Catheterian Bapticostal Church of Christ God Incarnate.

I've been everywhere man. And I've seen this.

The Christian church is like the pure white light of God refracted through a prism into many colors - each beautiful, each incomplete. Peter calls it the "varicolored" grace of God (1 Pet 4:10).

But I may have little idea of this reality. "I'm pretty busy with my own flock you know. After all, isn't indigo the right color to be? We are comfortable as indigos, God is using us to..."

I may pay lip service only to the others but actually secretly and subtly judge, ignore, smile benignly. If I am honest with myself I may find I feel a bit superior, more enlightened, more modern, more relevant.

My treasure is THE treasure; my truth THE truth.

To the extent that I, from my strength, judge another's weakness... to that extent I am deprived of their strength to heal my own weakness. And so my body suffers a sort of self-limiting spiritual vitamin deficiency... rickets, health problems, issues.

Of course each body is better at something. But that better is given as a gift to be given away freely, accepted freely. God has so composed the body of bodies (not just individuals) that no one gathering can say to another, "I have no need of you" or "I am not needed by you".

God calls us to go to the light - the full light - to let our deficiencies be exposed and healed.

Day 48
WWJD

So... in the spirit of WWJD... was Jesus a pacifist?

He did say turn the other cheek and not take my own revenge. He was led meekly away to be killed.

One might draw that conclusion.

But think about this. This is the guy... one guy, one whip weapon, hundreds of money changers running for their lives. That is the very picture of violent zeal.

This is the guy who said; " *'I know I said all along to not worry but tonight sell your stuff and buy a sword.' They said, 'Lord, look, here are two swords.' And He said to them, 'It is enough'* " (Lk 22).

This is the guy - to update the translation - who said: *"It would be better that you shoot the man than to allow him to abuse a little child."* (Lk 17:2).

I think non-violence is the right way in opposing your government (like Gandhi); it is the right way when espousing something right and being personally attacked; minimal force is to be used as necessary (ask any cop about their training) to stop unfocused and evil personal physical attack by an individual on me and the innocent and defenseless; and the right of a nation is to defend itself against aggressors... with minimal force and after other options have failed.

I think maybe He was a godly and wise pragmatist.

Though I am not sure.

Day 49

Tolerance

I am told I need to be tolerant of those who do not think like me, are unlike me.

No way!!

How does it feel to be tolerated? You want to be tolerated? Would Jesus just tolerate?

I think He tolerated government because He had better things to do but people... nope. People He loved, befriended, spoke with, lived with... well except the religious ones. The sinners knew Jesus before He became a Christian... and maybe He was a lot more relevant then.

I want to be hospitable, engaging, interested. I want to know about those very different from me and not just to correct them... I bet some fishermen could have instructed a bunch of Pharisees. If my life in Jesus cannot be lived comfortably and well with those unlike me then maybe I am too unlike Jesus in the first place (Mk 2:15-17).

Then if I have something true to say I can say it, really say it, mean it... and it will be listened to because I listened, cared, and loved well.

Be more tolerant?

Such a weak answer to the world's problems... and my own.

Day 50

Things Multiplied

So... I just realized something.

Jesus, the best picture of God ever taken, only multiplied three things, creating more and more and more:

wine (Jn 2:10),

food (Mk 6:41), and

brothers and sisters (Heb 2:10).

Kinda makes me happy to think about being with a God like that forever.

Puts being "godlike" in new light. Think I'll try to be like Him.

You?

Day 51
Don't Play in Traffic

So…I sometimes think we believe God is playing a game of gotcha.

You're a homosexual…GOTCHA! You're greedy…GOTCHA! Maybe we have it all wrong. Let's say, for example, that someone insisted on playing in traffic. Again and again he was saved from it. At some point a parent might say, "go ahead and see what happens." The parent is not playing gotcha he or she is simply saying, "In the world of physics when a car hits a body the body loses."

In my 60 years of life and in counseling hundreds of individuals I have come to see that certain decisions tend to have consequences and it is not "God" who is causing them… they just happen. Stealing has consequences; multiple sex partners has consequences; child abuse has consequences; arrogance and greed has consequences; and so on.

And I have found the bible to be a very good moral guide on which things tend toward ruin (please don't quote an Old Testament ceremonial law OK?). In our own arrogance or desire for independence (pick one) we decide which things we believe have negative consequences and which don't.

We think we have a fairly unerring knowledge of good and evil. And when someone says, "look out that is unsafe (or "wrong")", we get mad at them and think they are judging. Maybe they are, in fact, judging (and that is a big problem).

A Christian who might think that the bible is a pretty good barometer on what is life giving and who is really not judging is in a pickle when they want to say something like, "I think this is going to be bad for you - I love you - choose life."

In today's society unless it is simple physics to some people it ALWAYS seems like judging.

Maybe it's just a friend saying, "don't play in traffic."

Day 52

What I Control

So…there is a lot of talk about our society, how to stop this and that, what to say. What am I, as a Christian, responsible for? What do I control?

Paul says:

"I wrote you in my letter not to associate with immoral people; I did not at all mean with the immoral people of this world or with the covetous and swindlers, or with idolaters, for then you would have to go out of the world. But actually, I wrote to you not to associate with any so-called brother if he is an immoral person, or covetous, or an idolater, or a reviler, or a drunkard, or a swindler—not even to eat with such a one. For what have I to do with judging outsiders? Do you not judge those who are within the church? But, those who are outside God judges." (1 Cor 5:10)

I am NOT responsible to judge or condemn the behavior of those who are not voluntarily under my authority and part of my local congregation. Rome was far worse. When I start to do that I begin to play God... and nothing good comes from that. God rarely starts to influence a person on the basis of sin but on the basis of need. I just mess that up when I judge.

I do have the right to require compliance with God's laws of love for those who are under the authority of the organization I lead (like ANY organization). And habitual disregard for that means someone does not want to be part of... so they are asked to leave... like in any organization.

I do have the right to let my voice be heard and to be active in the political realm just like any other voice - unashamedly advocating and voting for the things I believe in - all the time rendering to Caesar. As a tax exempt organization I cannot advocate for specific candidates... or I can pay taxes and advocate for anyone. And I can help get laws passed that are constitutional that I can support.

And finally I have the responsibility to insure that my participation in developing laws does not negate my responsibility to the law of love shown to all men at all times.

Day 53
Just as I Am

So... it kind of works like this... says my friend David Kyle Foster. Had to share it. As a child I was mostly ignored, criticized, and non-affirmed. So I do not know who I am. I have little identity on which to rely for life choices and changes. I adopt an identity as a teenager based on my unmet needs - normally it contains a good bit of self-loathing, self-disregard and addictive behavior. After all, I am probably flawed, second hand goods; and feel a desperate but submerged need for affirmation. "Will somebody tell me who I am and that that person is lovable and good?"

The addictive behavior is a sure reward, a pleasurable distraction... and deadly destructive of my true identity and destiny.

But it is my best choice it seems, among a number of not so good choices. And so... *"I was dead in the way I walked according to the course of this world, according to the spirit that was working in me. But God, being rich in mercy, because of His great love toward me right where I was, made me alive together with Christ, and raised me up and gave me an honored seat with Him so that in the ages to come He might show the surpassing riches of His grace in kindness toward me."* (Eph 2).

Then it hits me that this verse is talking about me... me... the real me... just as I am. There must be something about that "me" that the only One who really knows thinks is wonderful, attractive, even worth dying for. And now He is here... right here. He does not leave the room when I sin... does not turn away... but even comes closer.

He patiently demonstrates and shows me who I really am to Him and what I was made for (identity and destiny) as a good father should... and I believe Him.

And soon... me... the real me... just as I am... knows I have better things to be, better things to do.

Because I believe Him.

Day 54

Tikkun Olam

So... Tikkun Olam

No it is not the latest song from Lion King II but is actually an ancient Hebrew thought process, philosophy, belief and life.

It can be literally interpreted as "suture the world". Stitch up its wounds, apply salve, stop the bleeding, help the breathing.

We each slowly construct a philosophy of life as we grow. Can't help it. Often those philosophies are simply the untended outgrowth of experience and internal juvenile interpretation of events. Sometimes the smallest thing becomes a plank in our platform. If our life is hard then our bent is naturally toward self-protection, getting what I can, what I need... and maybe more, much more. If it was filled with love then our natural direction is to also give love, to relate, to be at peace.

But at some point it dawns on each of us that we have the opportunity to choose what kind of person we will be, how we will live, what will be the guiding ideas. Not to choose is to choose to wander, to let our lesser selves dictate moment by moment. Not to choose is to drift with wind and tide. To wash up on a shore not of our choosing.

But to choose... that gives us legs, sets our sails despite the gales. Even if we don't know the destination - and no one ever really does - the journey takes on meaning that can fuel joyful purpose for a life.

On the verge of the land of promise Joshua set the decision before the Hebrew tribes: *"This day I call the heavens and the earth as witnesses against you that I have set before you life and death, blessings and curses. Now choose life, so that you and your children may live"* (Deut 30:19).

I can think of no better choice of life than this - Tikkun Olam

Day 55

A Casual Relationship with Reality

So... I was accused of having "a casual relationship with reality" by a secular friend of mine.

I thought, "If He only knew what goes on inside !"

Jesus said, "Repent, for the kingdom of heaven is at hand."

I used to think that meant that I should confess my sins, live a good life, and go to heaven. No longer. My honey and I were talking about that this morning and she said, "I think it means that I need to change my mind about how I see reality - like the servant of Elisha whose eyes were opened to see the angels everywhere in the hills around (2 Kg 6:17). I can simply reach out and poof... the kingdom is right there... at hand."

I live in another world too, and that world is bigger than this one, eternal, and easily influences this one. Jesus said healing is the kingdom being at hand, driving out demons... ditto (Lk 10:9, 11:20), hearing God, knowing things I should not know... but I do.

Right... there. Within reach when I need it.

One day it will appear as it is as the veil is ripped away and... poof... right at hand. There all along. And we might say, "how could I not have seen it!?"

So today I listen, today I watch that other kingdom... right here, at hand...

and poof...

Day 56

Ligaments

So…young 20 and 30 somethings are leaving the church in droves for… coffee, craft beer, and expensive whisky and cigar houses. Why is that?

Context, context, context.

In Ephesians 4 Paul tells us the one thing that will cause the body of Christ to grow big and strong; and it is not great preaching. That may be a proper role for the pastor and teacher, even the prophet. Great speaking will increase attendance at the weekly Sunday lecture, but it may do little to actually grow and hold together the <u>body</u> of Christ.

On the contrary, Paul says it is the proper working of "ligament relationships" that build the body (vs. 15-16). Beyond preaching truth, He says that leaders must equip us to be better friends, initiating, taking time, sacrificing convenience, bringing encouragement - especially to the least. Most young people are not in the lecture-hearing-habit... they are in the connection habit. Create that culture.

Ligaments are flexible but unbreakable, like leather not like rigid steel or fragile gossamer threads. It is through those unconditional channels that life flows, love knows, growth shows. For the individual (which we all are) "truth in love" does not mean kind preaching - it means an individual life laid down for an individual person. I will be there for you. Maybe no preaching at all.

If I abrogate my responsibility to live in relationship with you then I forfeit my right to speak truth to you.

In a body there is no such thing as dis-fellowship... only dismembering.

Day 57

Listen to A Different Game

So... I was once wondering how some people can be so joyful in the midst of...well...crap. A sudden memory came from that place where memories that are more than memories come from.

As a child I was at a Vikings game during the time they lost <u>every</u> game. The crowd was somber and stoic (as Minnesotans are wont to be). Suddenly, for no field-apparent reason, many began to cheer and back-slap. The snowshoe grog went up and down the row shared by all.

I asked my dad...

"Andy, the Twins just won the second game of the world series... the fans are listening to a different game on transistor radios... and we won."

Listening to a different game... and in that very real game we are encouraged, things are secure, sure, safe, eternally good... we win. It is ultimate reality.

"For our citizenship is in heaven, from which also we eagerly wait for a Savior, the Lord Jesus Christ; who will transform the body of our humble state into conformity with the body of His glory, by the exertion of the power that He has even to subject all things to Himself." (Phil 3:20,21)

Dear ones... listen to a different game with your good ear. And with the other one... be in the game on the field... but be of good cheer.

Our team wins the "other world" series.

Day 58
God Speaks

So... as the old joke goes, a man asks the doctor how to tell if his wife is losing her hearing. Doc tells him to start distant and ask the same question several times as he walks closer to her.

So he starts 50 feet away, "What's for dinner honey?" He tries it again at 40 feet, 30, 20, and finally right next to her, "What's for dinner honey?" She finally turns to him and says, "Henry, for the fifth time... chicken!"

I have often heard, "God is not speaking to me, I keep asking but..." The answer is often, "wait on Him." And that is right. But maybe the answer is also, "maybe you are not listening, not perceiving, not attuned, or not alert."

In Job 33 he says, *"Why do you complain against Him that He does not give an account of all His doings? Indeed God speaks once, or twice, yet no one notices it."*

He speaks of events and dreams and hardship as some of the ways God intersects with men.

God is not human and His first language is not English... even Hebrew. His ways of speaking are designed to draw us into alertness... into closeness... into a dawning awareness of relationship that is far far superior to just speech. He engages us at a visceral, emotional, full-person-contact level; all around, active, but also hidden.

Sometimes when I want to know what God is making for dinner I just need to catch the scent, then draw close and "taste and see that the Lord is good!"

Day 59

Always Good

I have always said that God is good.

Always.

And when I was much younger I could tell you specifically how He would be good to me, in most situations, in detail. He would protect me, give me favor, prosper me, find me a wife, get me a job, keep me healthy, cause my team to win. Always.

Recently one of the wisest people I know came very near death - mere minutes away. He said that he was not sure he would live, in ICU connected to tubes and monitors. And he told me something, "It was like I was plunged into a pool of grace. I do not know how but I was filled with overwhelming thanksgiving, peace, and joy. I did not know exactly how this would turn out - but I knew I would be OK, even if I died, I would be just fine, my family would be fine. And that God is good. So good."

David says, *"Precious in the sight of the LORD Is the death of His godly ones."* (Ps 116:15)

That day, precious to God, is a sure thing.

Now that I am much nearer that precious day than when I was young I have stopped telling God how to be good to me... well, almost.

But far more I am simply content with the sure, sure, sure knowledge that He is good, that I have been immersed in a pool of grace, and no matter what it is OK, no matter what.

Always.

Day 60

Go and Sin No More

So... I really like the part where Jesus says to the woman caught in adultery, *"I do not condemn you"* (Jn 8:11). Change the conversation.

And I like to think that demonstration of mercy is how we all should act toward all sinners - all who would have been stoned to death under Old Testament law. Jesus getting to the heart of the matter again. We all gather around and support each other in such behavior. It is so current, so millennial, so radical right. Yes !!

But that is only half the story - only incomplete mercy... unfinished business.

So... the other half of Jesus' statement to the woman is, "Go and sin no more."

Downer huh?

It is not mercy to give children all the sweets they want to eat, even if it is kind to give them a treat now and again. Bodies suffer when we do. It is not mercy to let someone fill their mind with violence, sexual perversion, and silly twaddle no matter how their darker nature craves it. It is not mercy. Minds suffer when we do.

And it is not mercy to ignore behavior that God would call sin, in myself, in those I love, or in those over whom I have authority... in my nation, my city, my family. Similar to the body and mind, when I make a practice of doing the things that God has labeled sin I have found (from sad experience) that I end up dark, wounded, less a vibrant person, slimed, twisted, and furtive.

God too takes that responsibility very seriously: *"God deals with you as with sons; for what son is there whom his father does not discipline? But if you are without discipline, of which all have become partakers, then you are illegitimate children and not sons"* (Heb 12:7-8).

Do I want to duck discipline, correction, taking responsibility for God-defined right living? Fine. But I should not be surprised if I feel, deep on the inside when I am honest... illegitimate.

Day 61
How Am I Doing?

So... had a crazy thought. So I did it... so unprofessional.

I called a manager of a small office simply to tell him what a great job two of his people did for me. Long pause... then a shaky voice trying to maintain control, "Thank you so much, how I needed that - you made my day... maybe my whole week." So unprofessional. Such life.

It took two minutes.

New York Mayor Koch was famous for asking, "How am I doing?" We all want to know the answer to that... long to know it... it is like oxygen to our souls.

And guess what? You and I carry the oxygen for another right here - right in our mouths, our heads, and our hearts... plenty of it. But it is not for us; we can't easily get to it alone. It is for another.

"Therefore encourage one another and build up one another, just as you also are doing"
(1 Th 5:11).
"But encourage one another daily, as long as it is called 'Today', so that none of you may be hardened by sin's deceitfulness." (Heb 3:13)

How? Easy.

Thank someone for what they have done or who they are. Tell someone what you like about them, what you see in them. Ask about their dreams and encourage those. If you are stuck ask Papa... He has lots of ideas, lots to say.

Change a life today...today. Two minutes.

Day 62

The Source of All Comfort

So…God won't allow something I can't handle right? Such a heart rending question from someone who just lost someone so very dear. I wouldn't touch that one right then with a ten foot theological statement. But this IS what God seems to say about temptation and tests darkly designed to bring us to sin he says:

"No temptation has overtaken you but such as is common to man; and God is faithful, who will not allow you to be tempted beyond what you are able, but with the temptation will provide the way of escape also, so that you will be able to endure it." (1 Cor 10:13)

Limitation on evil's access to me… guaranteed. For persecution and its attendant sorrow and suffering and pain He seems to say (the context is "you will be scattered and afraid"):

"These things I have spoken to you, so that in Me you may have peace. In the world you have tribulation, but take courage; I have overcome the world." (Jn 16:33) *"He is near to the brokenhearted."* (Ps 34:18)

Grace, nearness, and comfort (not wordy justifications and explanations)… guaranteed. And the ultimate? About every person described in Justin's Book of Martyrs relied on this in the end. He says through Paul:

"We were so utterly burdened beyond our strength that we despaired of life itself. We felt sentenced to death. But that caused us to rely not on ourselves but on God who raises the dead." (2 Cor 1:9)

… who raises the dead… eternally. I win. Guaranteed.

Just like we can somehow miss the grace in time of temptation and fall, we can also miss the grace in time of sorrow or agony and equally suffer needlessly and alone; not turning to the One who can both fully feel and know our pain and actually do something very, very real about it - the source of all comfort the source of all truth.

Day 63

Change the Equation

So... outside grocery store - three cute and very insistent girl scouts, three moms - one me not wanting cookies - only four dollars each. That was the equation. Simple addition (or addiction). Or so it seemed.

Passing by and then... a nudge, a wink and godly mischief is in the air!

"Tell you what... I want to buy three boxes of cookies... three!"

"Pick me, pick me!!"

"Here is what I want to do. Each of you pick one box, pick your very favorite kind. OK? got it? Here is the money."

Puzzled looks all around.

"Now, sometime today or maybe tomorrow in school I would like each one of you to give that box away to somebody who you think would love it, or somebody who can't afford one, or somebody who is sad and just tell them this is for them. Can you do that for me?"

Puzzled looks, then one…then three excited grins, three nodding moms. Three boxes of cookies on course to change the world just a bit.

One smiling Papa.

Multiplication.

I can change the equation in my world today.

Day 64

This is America

So…I married up. Way up.

Andy: "Why is that billboard in Spanish?. This is AMERICA!"

Susan: "This is America."

Andy: "…oh"

"You must regard the foreigner who lives with you as the native-born among you. You are to love him as yourself, for you were foreigners in the land of Egypt; I am Yahweh your God." (Lev 19:34)

Day 65
Talking to Myself

So... I am sitting in a basement by myself working off a TV tray and speaking to about 500 people in a webinar.

Such a strange feeling, like I am talking to myself even though I know a lot of people are out there.

Wonder if that is how God feels sometimes.

"Why do you complain against Him that He does not give an account of all His doings? Indeed God speaks once, or twice, yet no one notices it. In a dream, a vision of the night, when sound sleep falls on men, while they slumber in their beds, then He opens the ears of men, and seals their instruction... Man is also chastened with pain on his bed, and with unceasing complaint in his bones... Or there may be an angel as mediator for him, one out of a thousand, to remind a man what is right for him... Behold, God does all these oftentimes with men, to bring back his soul from the pit, that he may be enlightened with the light of life. Pay attention...". (Job 33)

Day 66

The Top Five Values

So…according to a UCLA study, the top five values emphasized in television shows popular with children who are now teens were:

- fame,
- achievement
- popularity
- image
- financial success

According to a King David (KD) study in Psalm 5 the top five values emphasized by the only One who really matters are:

- integrity
- kind speech
- hating evil
- fearing the Lord
- not taking unfair advantage of anyone

I think I live in opposite world.

And funny thing... the cleaned up and made holy version of the things in the first list…

each one…

were attained as a byproduct of the values prized in the KD study.

Day 67
Tend the Fire

So…Maybe the most important thing we do as believers is to tend the fire of the Holy Spirit within and among us.

That fire enlightens; it energizes; and it consumes that which can and maybe should be destroyed. I never can seem to explain or understand the ways and purposes of this fire. But I want to be one who tends my fire well, stirs up its gifting, the heat of its love and passion.

I try to be an observer of it in those around me. In some it is well hidden - a rustle of warm air but far removed. In others it seems more like a gas fire behind glass, decorative. In some places the fireplace seems to be the focus, the mantle, the room, the setting. In some it is a wild fire - and that is not always a good thing - unless there is a littered forest needing to be cleansed. And in those that break my heart it is a smoking wick nearly quenched by wounding and worldliness - longing to be coaxed to life again.

In the ones I seem to love the most it is more like a camp fire - always an element of danger, of unpredictability - yet cozy and inviting. It is full of the fresh-air thrill of being out at night. It warms and lights up the faces of those around, and is the occasion of storytelling… and story making.

Outside where the camp fire is needed there is plenty of wood, hay and stubble needing burning, darkness needing light, and coldness needing the heat of love… fewer worries about ornate furniture; fewer players-with-fire and more users of fire.

Day 68

Core Beliefs, Core Behaviors

So…I think there is a difference between core beliefs and core behaviors. Behaviors are how we express, live out, and demonstrate our beliefs. Only the first is not negotiable.

And I bet you would agree, if it were about another group!

I have been in many churches that have core beliefs I strongly affirm… but express those beliefs in such stylized, inbred, and distracting ways that I cringe with embarrassment for them… and maybe for God.

I know god sometimes offends the mind to reveal the heart… but I want to make sure it is God doing the offending.

My core beliefs can find many expressions that do not needlessly offend, and yet will not be compromised.

When I confuse a non-negotiable belief with a practice I may like I can run into problems… with God.

"For through your knowledge he who is weak is ruined, the brother for whose sake Christ died. And so, by sinning against the brethren and wounding their conscience when it is weak, you sin against Christ." (1 Cor 8)

If someone is offended with me I want it to be because I healed on the Sabbath and not that I insisted on some unique action that in their eyes distracts and steals focus from God onto me and my group.

Day 69
Quenching the Spirit

So... a mature freedom minister friend was rejected from continued working with a large conservative church because of her affiliation with a certain spirit-filled ministry.

They said she greatly helped many and that they would love to stay connected but that the antics of some of this group's leaders/members was causing lots of problems.

At first I was just dismissive of the conservative church. They are just such fuddy duddies and... then... I listened. In 1 Cor 14 Paul says: If we must speak in tongues but no interpreter - speak quietly to self; if we feel moved to prophecy - take turns, yield to another; and the "spirit of the prophet is subject to the prophet." He ends with: *"ALL things must be done properly and in an orderly manner."*

All. All. This Paul is the same guy who told us not to "quench the spirit". Mature Christians are not to offend, not to distract, not to let even the valid and real wild nudges and urges of the spirit within bring negative fruit through unrestrained inappropriate behavior. I said inappropriate not somber.

Peter and John healed the paralytic. He danced and yelled, but they seemingly did not feel a need to do so to make it happen. The power of God was not stopped in the least. I think sometimes the real quenching takes place, the real loss - some of the most powerful and earth changing work of God gets discounted - because of the example of drunken and silly immaturity of the workers.

"We have this treasure in earthen vessels, so that the surpassing greatness of the power will be of God and not from ourselves." (2 Cor 4:7)

First time drinkers may get drunk (witness Pentecost and revivals). Celebration is good. But every teenager must eventually learn to drink responsibly.

Day 70

The Higher Authority

So... airport parking lot, late like usual. I AM LATE. Doesn't the universe know this!? I am running to get to the bus stop.

Why is the parking lot bus just creeping along?

Wait... that's not its normal route. I KNOW they are not supposed to go off course. But he seems to be going in a circle.

Slow, slow, slow... then I realize. They are waiting for me and veering to come my way.

Hurry up.

Jump on bus.

Andy, "Wow thanks I really appreciate this. I didn't think you were supposed to break the rules."

Driver: "I obeyed the one that matters to me."

Andy smiles - you sir will be a bleat today.

"Let no debt remain outstanding, except the continuing debt to love one another, for he who loves his fellowman has fulfilled the law." (Rom 13:8)

Day 71

Co-conspirators

So... it was a conspiracy.

We were checking out at Whole Foods and admiring a young family just ahead with four kids dressed up with sun glasses and cool hats. Dreds. Trying to pick good food for the family.

Then it happened. High alert. The invitation. Co-conspirators with God.

I noticed that they began sadly handing things back to the clerk as they were deducted from their total - they did not have enough to pay for food. Susan and I looked at each other - she heard it too.

I quickly whispered to the checkout guy as he was about to finish, "This is wrong. I'll cover that. Just ring it up".

Surprised look then... he was in. But, "I can't, he has to finish first."

They shuffle quietly to the door, dad looking at the receipt. Done... Hurry !! Cashier rapidly scanning; bagger smiling conspiratorially, quickly packing, glancing over her shoulder. Cashier finishes, he is at the exit door. Stops to answer his phone. Hurry !!

Bagger slips away quietly, we are staring at the ceiling. Dad glances out the door, bagger walks past nonchalantly, and slips bag into cart, and glides past. Perfect!

She comes back and we exchange the kind of secret-sharing smiles only secret co-conspirators know. "That was great" says the cashier.

We go to the lot with our stuff. They are parked next to us. God never misses a detail. They are looking at their bags and bit mystified.

"You have beautiful children" I say. Shy smile. "Thank you."

"For we are His workmanship, created in Christ Jesus for good works which God has prepared beforehand that we should walk in them" (Eph 2:10).

Co-conspirators every one... every one.

Day 72

Sweet Comfort in Sorrow

So... sweet hard life.

Sitting with a dear friend who lost her husband after many years. Such honest conversation and courage about her next weeks. I asked what comforted her the most right now. This was precious to her:

> "In this sad world of ours sorrow comes to all and it often comes with bitter agony. Perfect relief is not possible except with time. You cannot now believe that you will ever feel better. But this is not true. You are sure to be happy again. Knowing this, truly believing it will make you less miserable now. I have had enough experience to make this statement."
>
> Abraham Lincoln

This has been a lighthouse to me for 40 years:

"Do not grieve over those who have fallen asleep in Jesus as those who have no hope. Jesus will bring them with Him when He descends from heaven with a shout and with the trumpet of God, and the dead in Christ will rise first. Then we who are alive and remain will be caught up together with them in the clouds to meet the Lord in the air, and so we shall always be with the Lord. Therefore comfort one another with these words."
(1 Th 4)

Comfort one another with these words - it will hurt less and you will smile again, and we shall always be with the Lord...

always, always.

Day 73

Hail Joseph Full of Grace

Why doesn't anyone ever say a "Hail Joseph".

He gets no beads on the rosary; no large cathedrals; no halo paintings of just him; no Catholic holidays.

Like his life was mostly a hidden secret.

And maybe that's a good thing.

Again and again God says in the Psalms that He resides in a secret place, lives there when He is not out in public.

He says in Mt 6 that when I give, pray, and fast in a secret place He sees (I guess because I bump into Him in the dark)... it is where He is.

In the public eye? It's not His favorite... maybe because it is mostly not real, authentic, and true.

Dear one who feels overlooked? You are not. At least not by the only One who really matters. He maybe has a public face when He goes out. But His face in private is the best... the best.

The secret place is where He mostly is, and if it is where you mostly are too then you are in good company...

...really good company.

Day 74
Pi Day

Soooooo excited. A once in a world celebration of Intergalactic Pi Day.

What you say? Pi is only the most mystical and important mathematical concept ever. It is the ratio of the circumference of a circle to its diameter. And if you think about it for 20 seconds you will see it is ALWAYS the same - 3.141592653 and so on in non-repeating sequences of numbers for infinity...for eternity.

No one has ever found the end of Pi. The numbers go on forever. Yet so simple and basic. Always the same yet ever changing, a circle and a line. Sort of like God if you stop and think for 20 seconds. You can read lots about it but here is a little gem: 1 Kings 7:23, says: *"He made a molten sea of ten cubits from brim to brim and a LINE of thirty cubits did compass it round about."* This implies that pi = 3. Which is not quite right.

However, there is a hidden code. In Hebrew, each letter equals a certain number, and a word's "value" is equal to the sum of its letters. In 1 Kings 7:23, the word "line" is written Kuf Vov Heh, but the Heh is not really needed barely pronounced - except it gives it its "breath". With Heh, the total value is 111, but without it 106. (Kuf=100, Vov=6, Heh=5). If we take exact Pi divided by not quite right Pi and exact Hebrew "line" divided by the not quite right "line" we get the equation: pi/3 = 111/106; solving for pi, we find pi = 3.1415094... This value is the most accurate value for Pi calculated and would be so for hundreds of years.

Who cares?

Well, we bible and mathematics nerds think it is pretty cool. And if you think for a bit more than 20 seconds you might see that that little gem is just like God - seems a bit off at first glance sending scoffers on their way. But if you persist and drink deeply of Him, observing not just seeing, then you will find that nearly everything around you has hidden meaning, secret code, and deep wisdom... everything has breath.

Happy Intergalactic Pi Day - Saturday, March 14th at 9:26:53.

Day 75
Reclining at Table in Eternity

So... it seems like death is all around me these days. Some feels more bearable like the "see you soon" kind. Some not so seemingly well defined.

I had such easy and fine answers on who would be in heaven when I was 20 and it was mostly theoretical.

I love it when Jesus says of a pagan Roman centurion - a good man - trusting the one thing he knew about a God he did not know: *"I say to you that many will come from east and west, and recline at the table with Abraham, Isaac and Jacob in the kingdom of heaven."* (Mt 8:11)

I like what Paul says: *"It is not the hearers of the Law who are just before God, but the doers. For when Gentiles follow their conscience and do instinctively the things of the Law that is written in their hearts they will be justified on that day when God will judge the secrets of men through Christ Jesus."* (Rom 2)

And so I wrote to a fine friend, a really good man with a faith I could not readily define about to step into death:

"I don't suppose any of us know what we need to know about life – and certainly not about 'afterlife'. But If there is such a place, such a thing, such a being, then my prayer for you is that you wake into joy inexpressible surprised by the ultimate goodness of all that is and realize that for a good man such as yourself there is good… for a good, good, long, long time. And if so, save me a place at the table!"

...and feel Papa would make up for all the deficiencies in that... for both of us.

Day 76

Out on a Limb Without a Paddle

The young woman in the small group said earnestly, "You know I love that verse that says when God closes a door He always opens a window." She was so serous.

Ahhhhh... love that one too. Well, except I think it is only the verse of a song.

The Internet, radio waves, and countless pundits and bloggers are screaming streaming meme-ing opinion, wit, and wisdom... and recipes. The daily deluge.

When I put my weight down, when I make life decisions, when I need a lighthouse, a map, a guide those other sources are like junk food... some of it deadly. Most of it attractive as a Twinkie. Truth is where you find it for sure.

But I have found over forty years of trying that there is but one constant and unfailing source that is pure truth backed up by the Guy who wrote all the laws that are actually enforced every time all the time...

"For truly I say to you, until heaven and earth pass away, not the smallest letter or stroke shall pass from the Law until all is accomplished." (Mt 5:18) *"Then the LORD said to me, 'You have seen well, for I am watching over My word to perform it.'"* (Jer 1:12) *"Every word of God is tested; He is a shield to those who take refuge in Him."* (Prov 30:5)

The one who <u>chooses</u> not to read and order their life by that lighthouse has no advantage over the one who cannot.

I want to take time to surf the bible. Don't wanna be out on a limb without a paddle!

Day 77
Logic and Reason

Adam's failure, his sin, was to decide to rely on his reason and intellect as the final arbiter of action. Sure God could advise, be a voice, an influence, but the final decision was Adam's. And he would figure it out.

It is not the ability to think that sets us above the animals, that says we are made in God's image. Crows, dolphins, and even dung beetles can reason within their realm of existence. They are self-aware, can figure things out, and act. Sure we are better at it; but it is a matter of degree not of kind.

Maybe there is a part of us, the wild unreasonable part, the imaginative part, the lavishly creative for beauty's sake part that is most like God. There logic and reason are the servants - carrying out what the intuitive, revelatory, even childlike part of us knows.

Of <u>course</u> it can look illogical, even silly sometimes. Maybe that is part of the point. What did the angel mean when he said to John, "come up here and I will show you..." (Rev 4:1)?

I think God in His "god-ness" is most like the visually overwhelming, only semi-logical book of Revelation... less like Leviticus. And when I say I am made in His image I am saying that that chip lies within me too and I can decide to put more weight down on it, more reliance, than on reason alone.

I want to live a life that communes with a God who says, "come up here and I will show you..."

Day 78

The Stranger Among You

So... when do we begin to recognize that the disregard for the heart and principles of God is a two-edged sword cutting everyone? It is not a political problem.

It is a moral one.

This is God's expressed heart concerning foreign workers who are in our land. It cannot be clearer.

"The stranger who resides with you shall be to you as the native among you, and you shall love him as yourself, for you were aliens in the land of Egypt; I am the LORD your God." (Lev 19:34)

And when this doesn't happen?

Our nation has an unavoidable dependence on migrant workers to harvest our crops; and we need many low skilled workers in many sectors of society.

Yet due to our "all or nothing" way of approaching the problem we have no way to get the job done between willing employers and willing workers (remember capitalism) but to break the law.

It would be easy to provide a workers visa during harvest time, or to allow employers to hire abroad when they have exhausted national attempts (we do so in the medical field) and all would be legal.

A history of steady work for the second category might even lead to citizenship. But we have created a no-win situation for millions including our own agribusiness.

... *continued*

The unintended consequence of disobedience to the command and the heart of God is that it ends up:

- further depressing illegal wages;
- creating substandard living conditions;
- keeping revenues out of the social security system;
- allowing a non-sustainable minimum wage;
- creating split families and children without a home country;
- stimulating a welfare state for those who will not compete with the illegally low migrant wages;
- and, allowing artificially low food prices for us all to enjoy who do not seem to mind profiting on the backs of the poor as long as we don't have to actually see them.

I am not soft on illegality and citizenship should be earned not a circumstance of birth location for non-citizens, but this counter-intuitive system of mindless injustice needs to be changed regardless of the special interests involved - no one is THAT special in God's eyes except the downtrodden.

Love you neighbor as yourself... even your national neighbor.

Day 79

The Death of a True Prophet

So…this week a real prophet died. No, not the kind you are probably thinking of.

was editor of the Atlanta Constitution during civil rights in the 1960's. He offered no simple solutions to the racial problems. Instead, he drew poignant scenes of suffering and loss to condemn violence and miscarriages of justice. And he explored themes of courage and questions of responsibility that went beyond mindless acts of racism to challenge a people with traditions of decency. His most famous, read for Walter Cronkite on the evening news began:

"A Negro mother wept in the street Sunday morning in front of a Baptist Church in Birmingham. In her hand she held a shoe, one shoe, from the foot of her dead child. We hold that shoe with her. Every one of us in the white South holds that small shoe in his hand."

He won a Pulitzer.

He won the south's heart.

And he surely won God's highest award… to speak God's words and call a people to courageous living.

They complained to him one day, "I see what you are trying to do Mr. Patterson, you are trying to make us believe we are better people than we are."

That… that is prophecy.

Day 80
It's all About Behavior

So... I get dragged into a long discussion about liberals and race and work and the poor on plane today (can't he see I am trying to work!).

He is seems fairly conservative, the middle seat person fairly liberal. Me... fairly uninterested. All believers. I finally get inspired.

Look at this, what does it say to you:

"There will be tribulation and distress for every soul of man who does evil, of the Jew first and also of the Greek, but glory and honor and peace to everyone who does good, to the Jew first and also to the Greek. For there is no partiality with God." (Rom 2)

"Men do not despise a thief if he steals to satisfy himself when he is hungry; but when he is found, he must repay sevenfold; He must give all the substance of his house." (Prov 6)

What this says to me is that it is never about race and also never about poverty. It is always about behavior. Bad behavior is never excused by God no matter the circumstance. Never excused.

And racism is never excused by God no matter the history. Never excused.

God is an equal opportunity rewarder and punisher. He does not espouse liberal or conservative views. And His double edged sword of truth cuts both ways... every time.

At least my past scars say so!

That bought me 682 miles of peace.

Day 81

Follower of a Follower

Being a follower of Jesus is very different from being a follower of a follower of Jesus.

Followers of self-proclaimed followers of Jesus have been repeatedly lured into diabolical anti-Jesus missions each one in clear violation of Jesus' direct teaching on honor, service, greed, humility, forgiveness, and much more.

Jesus His Own Self warned of this: *"...an hour is coming for everyone who kills you to think that he is offering service to God. Watch out that you are not deceived. For many will come in my name, claiming, 'I am he,' "* (Jn 16:2, Lk 21:8)

If "followers of followers" would have been simply followers of Jesus' teachings over the last 2000 years, there would have been no black eyes for "Christianity" - no Inquisition, no Crusades, no pogroms, no Holocaust, no religious wars, no catholic or protestant religious persecution, no enslavement of Africans or abuse of native Americans, no stealing of tribal gold, diamonds, oil or other resources.

Simple followers and their bands of co-followers would have drastically changed the whole course of history and led the world along a different path... peace; and not as the world brings it (Jn 14:27).

If I want to be leader in bringing peace...

I must be a simple follower.

Day 82

The Telling of the Old

This juxtaposition of verses is too delicious not to notice... not to digest. Lev 19:31-32:

"Do not turn to mediums or spiritists; do not seek them out to be defiled by them. I am the LORD your God."

"You shall rise up before the gray headed and honor the aged, and you shall revere your God; I am the LORD."

Even if a fortuneteller could say so, it is better not to know the particulars of my future - both the good and the bad. For to know the first is to ruin Christmas and to know the latter is to set fear before my eyes.

But, when I look upon the aged and see they are yet joyous; when I see hoary-headed wise ones living my own distant future with both grace and dignity they become to me a light house of guidance against the rocky reefs of life and a guarantee that darkness is never enough to snuff out even the smallest candle of life and love.

They teach me to know that in the world I will have tribulation and that God is good.

Both are sure.

One will surely kill me... but the other will more surely resurrect me.

I am the Lord your God.

Day 83

Someone from the Future

So... yesterday I met someone from the future.

So did you.

Probably.

They are well disguised; living among us quietly going about their lives... hidden.

But if I look carefully I can see them... though they might deny it and some even try to hide it.

There is an unmistakable clue:

"Gray hair is a crown of splendor; it is attained by a righteous life." (Pr 16:31)

One of them wrote this: *"O God, You have taught me from my youth, and I still declare Your wondrous deeds. And even when I am old and gray, O God, I will declare Your strength to this generation, Your power to all who are to come."* (Ps 71)

Once outed I have found they can be coaxed into telling me about the future... my future. They live there every day.

But I have to give them something first... honor... and time (Lev 19:32).

Day 84
His Delight

So... Susan: "Andy look !!! The dahlia is blooming. I've got to go look at it!"

I smiled at her as she was going to walk outside in pajamas, coffee in hand, to be delighted more close up... sort of silly but cute, so cute.

And then Papa said, "Your silly prayer last night was my delight you know."

What!?

And just like that my whole attitude changed.

I have tended to be someone who is hard to delight. I appreciate, sure, smile, sure, but delighted?

Nah.

And I remembered: "The prayer of the upright is His delight" (Pr 15:8).

His delight? His delight! The almighty God of the infinite, omniscient, omnipresent, omnipotent... and my short whispered prayer before teaching last night was His delight?!

I like that.

I want to BE like that.

Easy to delight.

Hard to disappoint.

Day 85

God the Subject

Nominative, dative, accusative.

Verbs, prepositions, and adverbial prepositional phrases.

Past, present, perfect, participles.

No child would ever learn to talk if they had to first learn all the structures, rules and parts of speech. Never would. No adult either.

Some things I learn by doing, feeling, experiencing, absorbing. Full contact. Immersion. Only later might I try to explain and structure what I know... maybe.

Mathematics, on the other hand, quickly moves to structure, rules, and logic. Some things I have to mostly learn that way. I am lectured to, taught. Study study study.

God is not the later type.

Luke begins Acts with: "The first account I composed, Theophilus, about all that Jesus began to do and teach." Do. Teach. Action... explanation. Experience it... then understand it. "I have shown you the Father."

Shown.

I err when I make God a subject more than a relationship, a sermon more than a celebration. Ear tickling is good. But I cannot know God that way.

Heart burning is better.

Day 86

Old Person Moment

So... there are old person moments and wise person moments. This was the former.

Through security in SFO yesterday: "Sir you have a knife and a fork in your briefcase." "No I don't... in my BRIEFCASE?!" "Yes - you do." Pulls steak knife out, and they are obviously used. A couple other passengers laugh.

I redden. "What!?!"

I am thinking... "The hotel maid set me up... I... who could have done this to me?... um somebody else..." Stew on it four hours SFO-LAX-BNA. How in the world?

I am determined to call the hotel... except for a sudden vague memory. I packed leftover steak to work one day. Used office utensils and then absentmindedly put them in my briefcase... where they sat for two weeks and three scannings until today.

Awoke in the night to this thought: *"What else have you packed away absentmindedly my son whom I love... My desire is to reward you. 'For the ways of a man are before the eyes of the LORD, and He watches all his paths.'"* (Prov 5:21)

I make choices even when I am not thinking I am making choices... with consequences.

Walk aware, choose life.

Though it would have been more funny if I wasn't just 60!

Day 87

Time for Coffee

So... driving fast to airport, late, no time for coffee, San Francisco. NPR story about lost faith in young people... Arabic young man hurting, heavy baggage... unsure, longing.

My heart hurts.

But no chance to help.

Hurrying down concourse, late, no time for coffee. Small, round old woman, lugging a heavy bag... no wheels. Three steps then stop- thee steps then stop. Late too. Can she make it? Unsure.

I smile at her and grab her bag.

She steps back startled.

"Which gate?" "I...I... Arabic... no English... this one." Points to ticket. Number nine - let's go!!

Just in time. Just. Quick smile, light touch, something in Arabic.

Papa smiles: "Just look for the ones carrying heavy baggage around you... where I send you... you'll see if you'll see. That is all I ever ask of any of mine."

My flight is conveniently late. Time for coffee?

Sure.

Just.

Day 88
Deceive

So...three amazing pictures caught my eye all displayed together. A planet, a crazy wall of sand over ice and water, and a beautiful spiral galaxy in the night sky above an old Spanish monastery. You and I encounter ones just like them every day.

"Deceive" means "to cause to believe a lie." The time is coming when the whole world will be deceived (Rev 12:9). I think deception works sort of like three pictures. The first looks real, but is not; an artist's concept of a dwarf star. Not knowing the real I believe the fake. Fears not foundation, faith not fact, opinion not truth. I go with the crowd. It is the pure lie. Take Col 2:8:

"See to it that no one takes you captive through philosophy and empty deception, according to the tradition of men, according to the elementary principles of the world, rather than according to Christ."

The second is a sand storm in Iceland. Sure. Give me a break! Not even a good Photoshop attempt. Well... except it is real. When something does not meet my preformed opinion then I can be self-deceived and reject it, miss it. God and truth often comes and acts in ways I do not expect. He wants to stretch me into His shape. He sends "dust storms to Iceland" and I may say - nope, that is NOT God. I know better.

Take 1 Jn 1:6: *"If we say that we have fellowship with Him and yet walk in the darkness, we lie and do not practice the truth."*

The bottom is both real and unreal. There is a church in Greece and there are the Rose Galaxies... just not together. This is the most insidious kind of deception because each part can be explained as true, even biblical, but the end result is hurtful, harmful, enslaving, misleading. This is the kind of deception the Pharisees practiced, and the Devil tempting Jesus, and religion... not black, not white... just grey. Take Mt 23:2-3:

"The teachers of the law and the Pharisees sit in Moses' seat. So be careful to do everything they tell you. But do copy them, for they do not practice what they preach."

Day 89

Falling Short

So... failed in your New Year's resolution yet?

I was thinking about the story of the woman caught in adultery (not that that was your resolution!). Jesus looks at her and gives her two things: "I do not condemn you" and "go and sin no more."

When He said "I do not condemn you" He was giving her a gift of mercy; forgiveness. But when He said "go and sin no more" He was not tormenting her by setting an impossible standard. He was giving her a gift of grace.

You see, grace is not primarily about forgiveness. That is mercy. Grace is primarily about being given power and authority to "become children of God". The fruit of self-control is mine.

Fruit not effort.

I may think the struggle is all about what I have done. And I try and try not to do it.

That is a mistake. The real battle is all about what I believe about who I am. The dark side tries to make me into a sinner and to say in my heart: "I sin because I AM a sinner."

That was true but no more. God says to me, "My child, you fell short, I will help you because I know who you truly are; I love you; and I am in you."

God says "I AM... and so are you."

Day 90
Whimsy

Sometimes it's not whimsy...

...its revelation.

Day 91

Just Business

On TV Chefs compete; buyers of junk; and bachelorettes fight over the one man on TV. Everything... everything has become a competition. Destroy the competition, demolish them. Cause them to look bad. Fight dirty to make them lose the election... all is fair. We hear all the time: "It's nothing personal... just business."

So wrong.

To God it is always personal... always. He takes my choices and behavior personally ("You did it to me when you did it to them").

He does not let us separate an amoral business life from a moral personal life. *"What does it profit if a man gains the whole world but loses his soul?"* (Mk 8:36).

All the time. Every time.

Such thinking will destroy a person, business, institution or a nation as it has done many times before. It is just thinly disguised idolatry, greed and avarice.

God does endorse one form of competition: *"Outdo one another in showing honor"* (Rom 12:10). *"With humility of mind regard one another as more important than yourselves"* (Phil 2:3).

He shows a "more excellent" way (1 Cor 12:31):

I want to be excellent at what I do and love still more excellently.

So right.

Day 92
Bronze Serpents

In Numbers 21, at the command of the Lord, Moses made a bronze serpent which caused any one who looked upon it in humility and repentance to be cured of snake bite by God.

700 years later Hezekiah had the guts to tear it down as a "high place" because it had slowly become the focus of devotion subtly obscuring and replacing the real-time, one-on-one, face to face, relationship with I AM (2 Kg 18:4).

Should have happened 699 years earlier.

People want heroes and objects of glory. They want kings and security. They want certainty. They want "high places".

Institutions and individuals when placed on high often overreach their authority, expand their role, outlive their purpose and subtly and even unwittingly position themselves between God and men to catch some of the worship, some of the respect, some of the glory.

Anything, even a God originated "thing"; and anyone, even a God anointed "one" that becomes subtly inserted or self-inserted between God and people must be torn down too - regardless of its original purpose, of its initial godly intention.

Because it forgets its purpose (which I will now overstate for effect!) which is to humbly point the people to God, insure the relationship is sound, and to step aside and become irrelevant.

Maybe should have happened years ago.

Day 93
Institutions and Purpose

Steering an institution is a bit like steering a car. Sometimes when I drive I look at the edges of the road and the guard rail as well as the center line. It helps me steer straight. The edges, the boundaries, are good to define.

Every institution must periodically ask itself and God: "Have I strayed in any way into something or become someone that sometimes stands between men and God rather than next with them encouraging and propelling them to godliness and abiding in Christ? Is my example mostly compelling men to chase God and not to be conformed to me and my institution's personality, culture and key messages?"

David asked that question of himself in Ps 139:23: "Search me oh God." Paul too said to examine yourself, test yourself (2 Cor 13:5, Gal 6:4). Even a clear conscious does not guarantee a clear me (1 Cor 4:4).

OK now the other ditch.

We should never drive by looking in the rear view mirror of past failings, nor constantly checking the gas gauge and speedometer of current performance. Keep our eyes on the road, on the prize, on Christ the author and perfecter (Heb 12:1-2).

Or we might well become the centipede:

> *A centipede was happy – quite!*
> *Until a toad in fun*
> *Said, "Pray, which leg moves after which?"*
> *This raised her doubts to such a pitch,*
> *She fell exhausted in the ditch*
> *Not knowing how to run.*

> Katherine Craster

Day 94
God is Watching

This is the best way I know to take spiritual temperature.

Close your eyes and say to yourself, "God is watching."

How does that feel? Really.

There are two kinds of responses to that statement within my heart.

The first is all about wanting to hide, to make things right, to be acceptable, to pretend not to care, avoid, feel like punishment for falling short is right around the corner. It is uncomfortable to think about so I don't think about it. It leads to a distant angry God mentality.

The second is like a picture I saw of a mother and baby owl sitting perfectly camouflaged. Mom looked fierce. Chick looked cute and dumb...and comfortable.

Yes God can see in the dark, fly to kill silently, tear with His beak and grab with His talons. Yes He can hide in plain sight and hear the slightest whisper or grass movement. He is ferocious and feared.

But I am that hatchling of His. And regardless of what I do, WHO I AM never changes in His perfect sight. All those fearsome weapons are used for me not against me - to feed, protect, and teach. I nest with Him, under the shadow of His wings. Regardless of my thoughts or behavior in the moment.

God is watching? That is a wonderfully comforting thing.

Day 95
True Fame

So…. Beate Sirota. Heard of her? Me either. Till I heard her story.

In 1945, at the age of only 22, fluent in Japanese, Russian and German she was asked to be part of MacArthur's staff and to draft the portion of the Japanese constitution which addressed women's rights. Without legal training or background, but with a burning desire to set vulnerable Asian women free, she drafted a framework that even today  provides unprecedented broad civil and marriage rights. It revolutionized the culture; changed the world. She chose never to speak of it for fear some would reduce its scope knowing it came from a woman.

Today she has cast off the last restraints to freedom and soars on angel's wings uncircumscribed by man or means to touch the very face of God. My heroine. God's child. Unknown. Destiny follower. Quiet.

Jimmy Savile. Ever heard of him? Famous, British radio star, loud, larger than life personality, sought… and for 50 years the worst sexual predator of vulnerable women in history. Who knew? He was knighted.

He died too.

"So then each one of us will give an account of himself to God. The sins of some men are quite evident, going before them to judgment; for others, their sins follow after. Likewise also, deeds that are good are quite evident, and those which are otherwise cannot be concealed." (Rom 14, 1 Tim 5).

The invitation of destiny comes to each of us… small or great, hidden or public. It invariably comes disguised as a choice to act in simple faithfulness, steadfastness, self-sacrifice, goodness. Choose it. Choose well. Soar.

Day 96
Ages to Come and Geeky Thoughts

Tens of billions of Earthlike worlds are strewn across the Milky Way, many of them circling stars very much like our own sun, astronomers announced a year ago. Now the estimate is in the millions of "just right" planets. Who knows?

So... think about this:

There will be a new heavens and a new earth. Check.

I will be like Him when I see Him which may mean I will have a body that can rise into space and survive, eat, go through walls, fish and catch fish, appear and disappear in different places instantly and look good. Check.

God is light. What does that imply about travel in space-time? Hmmmmm? Check.

The old heavens just coincidentally has the same number of galaxies as there has ever been people (by 2040). Hmmmm? Check.

God says we will rule over cities but there are not enough on earth so...the heavens seem infinite and eternity is infinite. Check.

God said, *"No eye has seen, no ear has heard, no mind has conceived what God has prepared for those who love him"* (1 Cor 2:9). Check.

I love Him. Check.

"He raised us up with Him, and seated us with Him in the heavenly places in Christ Jesus, so that in the ages to come He might show the surpassing riches of His grace in kindness toward us in Christ Jesus." (Eph 2:6,7) Check.

I can't help but to think this is going to get real, real good.

Day 97
Business by the Book

So... meeting with potential client... big client.

Client: "This is an important project, we had a real good facilitator but their contract ran out and you guys have a lot of capacity on yours... so maybe you can step in temporarily."

Andy: "Why don't we just add this guy to our team and you can use him since the citizens group already likes him."

Client: "But isn't he the competition?!"

Andy: "I don't think so. I think the pollution in the river is the competition. The failing infrastructure is the competition. He is a potential partner to us all."

Client: "Wow... I... well... I like your thinking. That's refreshing. Let's give you $250,000 to work on this and I'll talk to him about working with you. Thank you so much."

Andy: "Wow too - we are honored to be trusted to help you with this touchy political issue."

God to Andy on plane home: "So... I told you that would happen huh?"

"Love one another with brotherly affection. Outdo one another in showing honor. Give, and it will be given to you. They will pour into your lap a good measure-- pressed down, shaken together, and running over. For by your standard of measure it will be measured to you in return. " (Rom 12:10, Lk 6:38).

Day 98
Sure as Spring

So... today I begin to draw military retirement.

Sort of shocked me when a check arriv3ed. I had forgotten.

When I began in 1975 I jumped out of airplanes, worked with many countries, did top secret stuff, encountered spies, shot every kind of weapon the army had... did lots of boring stuff too. Rarely thought of retirement; but I knew it was there and I did not want to miss out.

Now at long last it has arrived... that day.

Jesus was not shy about post-life retirement thinking and the savings plan there for you - where neither inflation nor bank crashes will reduce it.

"Store up for yourselves treasures in heaven, where neither moth nor rust destroys, and where thieves do not break in or steal" (Mt 6:19).

On that day Paul and I and you will say this, *"I have fought the good fight, I have finished the course, I have kept the faith; there is laid up for me the crown of righteousness, which the Lord, the righteous Judge, will award to me on that day"* (2 Tim 4:7-8).

And Papa will say to you, "well done good and faithful child of mine... thank you for your service."

That day is coming sure as spring... that day.

Day 99
Les Miserables

So…my friend and co-author of *"Freedom Tools"* Jennifer Carter Burnett wrote:

To love another person is to see the face of God.

I am pondering Les Miserables tonight.

I want to be a Jean Valjean type of person.

OK with pushing through a sewer to get someone else out to safety.
OK with the stench, the filth, and the lowly place if it means life on the other side for both of us.
OK with helping to lift a heavy burden off another, even if I get a little broken in the process.
OK with helping someone to pay a debt.
OK with releasing someone of a debt.
And OK with acting in mercy and forgiving, over and over again. Simply because I know that I have also been pardoned.

Jean Valjean is the way to go.

But a different kind of revolution.

Not for France. Not even for America.

But for a different kind of kingdom that cannot fall.

A King worth fighting in Love for.

Day 100
Walking with a Bump

So... I got a scan of my once shattered collar bone. No one should be able to see their own bones that clearly! For years it was stuck in a painful limbo - artificially held together with screws and plates. The fourth operation did the trick. Pronounced healed.

But there is a big bump.

Once I noticed it I now glance at it every morning in the mirror – like a magnet for my eyes. The guy with the bump.

God often seems to come to the rescue of my disappointment with perspective. Here is some.

We all have been hurt by someone - let down, or put down. Maybe we were abandoned or rejected, mistreated, abused or misunderstood. Maybe the details are now dim. It swims into our mind unbidden... may even faintly discolor our life and living. It gets triggered.

Draws our eyes.

When I re-encounter or re-image that memory, person or institution – am I healing or is it still painful? Has it gotten worse? Has it devolved into bitterness? Am I held together artificially?

Time does not heal all wounds. Healing comes when I actively seek to gain God's perspective and take appropriate steps such as forgiving or repenting of my part. If it still hurts dear ones know that is not the end God intends. Even if it takes four operations - then take four and do not be ashamed to ask for help. Get it.

And if there is a bump?

So what? Jacob had a limp and it became to him the hallmark reminder of his wrestling and prevailing with God.

Day 101
Tonto

So... sitting in Fore Street the coolest restaurant in Portland, Maine with a business friend finishing dinner. Talking about the Lone Ranger and his faithful companion Tonto... go figure.

Then I hear, "They're trying too hard... Tonto" I turn my head to see what wonderful mischief Papa is up to. Oh!

Young couple is seated at the next table. She sits ramrod straight, smiling aglow in just that way as to say, "please, please know I like being here with you." He touches her hand to see her new pinkie ring. She looks into his eyes. He tries to impress with his knowledge of oysters. She tries to be very impressed. He labors long over ordering just the right wine bottle for her.

Ah... the silver bullet - really? "Got it Sir."

Standing to go I quietly tell the waiter, "I want to buy that bottle of wine for them." Quizzical look. "But you have to say to them 'The One who bought this said you are both perfect - have fun'" Same look. Then a conspiratorial smile. "You got it sir."

I slip out. I love being Tonto. You too.

Hi ho Silver... awaaaaaaaaaaaaaaaaaaaaaay!

Day 102
Just Details

So... the "fear of the Lord" gets a bad rap.

Solomon said this: *"The fear of the LORD is the beginning of wisdom."* (Prov 9:10). At first glance that seems sort of like: "Watch out or God will get you", or: "He is a far, fiery, and fearful being - keep away."

Not at all. I think it is like this:

The sun, when placed in the center of things causes everything, everything, to come into orbit around it and with respect to each other - the important ones all in one plane - the ecliptic. It is a wonderful balanced order, with each one able to still be fully unique, having its own gravity. There are a few hundred million more tiny bits in other orbits but collisions are very infrequent... in a relative way.

Just details.

When I place the fear of, the respect for, God and His words and ways in the center of my life - as a singular focus - then everything, everything, begins to come into proper orbit, to take on appropriate importance, to take its proper place around that center. My view of myself does too.

Doing so does not snuff out my individuality, but rather creates a platform for its full expression. Doing so helps me slowly-by-slowly come into wise and right relationship with, and understanding of, every facet of my life. Everything.

Everybody orbits around something, everybody. Gravity is unavoidable. We only get to pick what. Might be a black hole, might be another person or idea, might be...

Paul says: *"The man focused on the spirit can properly evaluate everything - even though most people don't get where he is coming from"* (1 Cor 2:15).

Focus on one thing puts everything in right orbit. Everything.

The rest is just details.

Day 103
Valuing Truth

Guest Bleat from my friend Hope Seth

If I make judgements regarding the heart of a person or institution early in a relationship, will I then filter their actions based on what we first believed about them, good or bad? I think so.

What if my initial impressions were not the truth and my "pre-judge-ous" cost me the truth. I lost my sense of discernment...like a sense of smell...gone!

I think this is where Pontius Pilate and the culture was when he rhetorically asked Jesus "What is Truth?" Having already judged Jesus as just another Jewish troublemaker he was unable to see anything else. He was unable to discern the Truth standing in front of him.

Without a value for truth wherever it is found there can be little discernment.

This IS the way of the world: *"For even though they knew God, they did not honor Him as God or give thanks, but they became futile in their speculations, and their foolish heart was darkened.22Professing to be wise, they became fools, and exchanged the glory of the incorruptible God for an image..."* (Rom 1:21-23)

My prayer for the next generation is that Truth would be valued and sought after and discernment would be restored.

Day 104
Offended by Me

Guest bleat from my buddy Becca Wineka who lives far more than she ever talks about.

Jesus is talking about John and responding to those sent by him asking if Jesus is really (really) the Messiah. Maybe it is sort of, "Because if you are God, then why am I in prison awaiting beheading. It makes no earthly sense."

Jesus ends His answer in an unusual way. He says, "And blessed is the one who is not offended by me." (Lk 7:23)

In Jesus' life his hometown took offense at Him, the Pharisees took offense at Him, His disciples took offense at Him, His mother Mary and His siblings took offense at Him. An equal opportunity offender.

His gospel is equally offensive:

Where is the wise man? Where is the scribe? Where is the debater of this age? Has not God made foolish the wisdom of the world? For since in the wisdom of God the world through its wisdom did not come to know God, God was well-pleased through the foolishness of the message preached to save those who believe. For indeed Jews ask for signs and Greeks search for wisdom; but we preach Christ crucified, to Jews a stumbling block and to Gentiles foolishness, but to those who are the called, both Jews and Greeks, Christ the power of God and the wisdom of God. Because the foolishness of God is wiser than men, and the weakness of God is stronger than men. (1 Cor 1:20-25).

Whatever it is that I seek understanding on, get this, I may <u>never</u> understand. Demanding to understand, to have God explain Himself <u>is</u> taking offense.

But "blessed is the man who is not offended by me..."

Day 105
Render to Caesar

So...tomorrow we render unto Caesar... smile now.

I read this letter to the IRS: "I have been unable to sleep, knowing that I have cheated on my income tax. I understated my taxable income, and I have enclosed a check for $150. If I still can't sleep, I will send the rest."

Thought you might find these facts interesting to ponder as you consider our land and its people.

After the pain of The Great War came the profligacy and greed of the 1920's, then the inevitable collapse of the inflated stock market and the onset of the Great Depression. The government began to step in and try to care for the poor because others could or would not. This role of the government has been expanding since and has far overtaken that of the church and its people in so doing.

You probably tithe to the poor.

67% of all tax dollars go to a program to aid someone who ostensibly cannot help themselves. If you are married, filing jointly, take the standard deduction and together make $75,000 then you effectively pay 14% of your income to the poor... the extra 4% is government overhead cost (!).

I cannot tell if that is judgment, coincidence, or what.

I do know that Christ, as He considered a corrupt government with outlandish taxes, asked us to pay it anyway.

So I drop my return, with a smile and thanksgiving, into the letter box.

Day 106
Rental Agents

So... Andy "Susan I really do not want to go on this business trip today. It just feels wrong."

Then: flight circling Atlanta - then diverted to Huntsville - missing my next morning meeting in Portland, ME So... "Sir, I need to get off this plane here in Huntsville and just drive back home...'. I call my agent to get a reservation.

Then: Business guy, "Hey can I drive with you" Sure! Then: three youngsters trying to get to KC for a funeral crying, "We need to get a car too." We all go to counter.

At counter, "Sorry we only have one car to go one way."

Andy: "Don't cry, you can all go with me, I'll drive you to Nashville airport. Son, sweet girl - you WILL make it to your brother's funeral - I guarantee it." Hugs and tears. Business man with arm around girl, me with one of the boys.

Rental agent, looking at the hugs, "I'm going to break all the rules right now - take any car you want to get outta here - I'll figure out the paperwork."

More tears, exchanged email addresses, more hugs, business man gives them money, more tears, more hugs... and off we go. I get an hour of free financial advice from the president of a major insurance agency. More hugs, no tears.

It just felt right. And then...I am home. More hugs.

Be careful what you wish for.

He often decides to do more than we ask or think because He loves adventure!

Day 107
You Do It

So... I'm sitting on a conference call with a couple junior folks I'm mentoring talking to a client in another city. I've prepared them and asked them to do much of the talking, explaining, teaching.

They are nervous.

I smile when they squirm giving me a frantic look as I nod and mouth "you can do it - you answer his question". They did great.

Not that I'm God, of course, but I realized this.

God also loves to work in the background, subtly, invisible to those who might not think to look for His hand in something. He enjoys letting me look good, be successful, seem wise.

In Deuteronomy 8 Moses recounts all the ways God helped Israel and then says, *"You may say in your heart, 'My power and the strength of my hand made me this wealth.' But you shall remember the LORD your God, for it is He who is giving you power to make wealth."*

As I walk through life I do my best to remain conscious that I am, in fact, on a conference call with the world and God sits with me saying, "You do it - you answer his question."

Day 108
Watch Over Your Heart

Other than the greatest commandment and the one like it, if there were only one command by which to navigate life this would be it:

"Watch over your heart with all diligence, for from it flow the springs of life" (Prov 4:23).

The word "springs" means the "out-gushings" or the things that propel my life – its motor. The verse asks us to tend our hearts like a well-kept garden. I am what my heart is. I cannot be anything else except to pretend.

So how do we do that? How do I watch over my heart. One way to give legs to that verse is to stop, and in the quietness of a moment, listen to your inside and fill in this blank : "I have hardened my heart toward_____."

Then, take the necessary step to make that place soft: confession, forgiveness, a phone call, a letter, a check, a trip home, truth for a lie, help from another, maybe a cup of coffee.

Not every situation in my life can be fully resolved: *"If possible, so far as it depends on you, be at peace with all men"* (Rom 12;18).

It takes two sometimes to make everything right on the outside.

But on the inside.

But it only takes one... me... to make my heart soft again.

Day 109
One Option

In the early 1500's Hernán Cortés was commissioned to conquer the Aztecs. The morality of such a charge aside, fearing mutiny in the midst of a tough situation he destroyed his ships - reducing his options to one – conquer or die.

So... some time ago I was having trouble with boredom which led to visiting a couple of not-that-great websites. It vexed my spirit, weakened my spiritual ability and created a low grade guilt.

Paul says, *"But put on the Lord Jesus Christ, and make no provision for the flesh in regard to its lusts"* (Rom 13:14).

I saw I had made provision - I left myself the option to mutiny against the King. So I set up my browsers with blocking, closed my eyes and typed in a password I would never know... destroying my ships and reducing my options to one...

God makes very clear there is plundered treasure at the end of that decision... lots of it.

Day 110
Whose Way?

In my experience every leader building something is tempted in three ways - like Christ in Luke 4.

	My Kingdom	God's Kingdom
My Way	"turn stones to bread" My Kingdom My Way	"worship me and get earth" God's Kingdom My Way
	Luke 4: 1-14	
God's Way	"cast yourself down" My Kingdom God's Way	"Spirit power growing reputation" God's Kingdom God's Way

It is all about whose kingdom is being served and whose "way" is being followed:

#1 - "stones to bread" - My Kingdom, My Way - I am deceived into making it mostly about my ideas, my reputation and needs and ego. I choose to make it happen in the way and time of my choosing. It's about using the best the world has to offer to grow my thing. It rarely starts out this blatant - but it is what it is.

#2 -"cast yourself self down" - My Kingdom, God's Way - I think I am doing something for God but it is still mostly about me forcing God's hand to bless my initiatives. I subtly try to game the system of spiritual laws, trying to manipulate God's way of doing things to prosper my ministry, to be blessed. It is subtle witchcraft.

#3 - "worship me and get the earth" - God's Kingdom, My Way - I think I will win the whole world for Christ! What can be wrong with that? I am lured by some "world winning" opportunity and take it. It seems exciting, expansive, big, logical... too good to be true. But in the end it brings ruin and I find I am serving the wrong kingdom.

Lk 14 shows the result of God's Kingdom, God's Way: spiritual power and growing influence. It is organic, mustard seed small, life-filled, humble, spirit led, pure, deeply satisfying, fitting, challenging... right.

Just say "no" to the rest - study Deuteronomy, Christ did and quoted it each time He was tempted - it is all about preparing for conquest.

Day 111
Punch Through

Years ago my son Evan was a brown belt and said, "Dad, want to know how to punch somebody's face in?"

Me, "Sure, who wouldn't want to know that?"

Evan, "You don't punch their face, you fix on a point past their face and punch there, their face is just something along the way to the target."

Now that is something I can use every day. No, really.

It was said of Jesus, "... who for the joy set before Him endured the cross, despising the shame..." (Heb 12:1-2).

Jesus, facing the worst of the worst, looked right through the trial to the joy at the end... and set that before His eyes, that was His target.

He punched through to joy!

Scripture says the exact same thing, repeatedly

"Punch through to joy when you encounter trials because of what they will produce in you..." (Jas 1:2).

"Rejoice and be glad, because great is your reward in heaven, for in the same way they persecuted the prophets who were before you." (Mt 5:12)

"Not only so, but we also glory in our sufferings, because we know that suffering produces perseverance." (Rom 5:3)

I can face a trial or test or hardship far more easily, with greater confidence and better outcome, when I fix on the joy on the other side. What I face is just something along the way to the target. Punch through what I face to joy.

Now that is something I can use every day. No, really.

Day 112
Untouched

So... thought I'd just slip in and prepare something for the bees, no protection... such a bother to put it on.

Ouch!!

Right on the exposed underarm. Burned like H, itched for days. Later that day I made the simple decision to actually put on my bee-armor suit. Result: 30,000 bees wanting to kill and destroy me could not touch me. Not once.

Paul (Eph 6) says that when we put on the "full armor of God", a simple but deliberate choice, we are similarly protected. I have found that God will show you what each piece means in your life. Stop and mull it over.

I stand firm therefore, having girded my loins with the white jumpsuit of truth, and having put on the Dadant bee hat of righteousness, and having my feet shod with the rubber boots of the gospel; in addition to all, taking up the smoker of faith with which I am able to ward off all the stingers of the bee-ones. And take the head net of salvation, and the hive tool of the Spirit, which is the word of God.

Well, you get the point.

A simple but deliberate decision.

Not touched, not once.

Day 113
Principled Passion

This is the first generation in America where large numbers of children have been told "You can do anything, follow your gifting and passion." It would seem SO politically incorrect to suggest otherwise. Evil and downfall lurk on the outer edges of truth - and so too here.

When I follow unmitigated pursuit of passion two things happen.

First, passion works like a drug, like an addiction. I tend to become blinded to other things that may moderate or inform my passionate life - I react against them much like a drug addict reacts against the threat of withdrawal - I become a caricature of my best self.

Second I become self-centered, and devolve to a low state where the voice of my fleshy needs begins to subvert and pervert the gifting and passion within me. *"Like a city that is broken into and without walls Is a man who has no control over his spirit"* (Prov 25:28).

Paul says, *"Earnestly desire the greater gifts, and I show you a still more excellent way"* (1 Cor 12:31).

I must pursue my gifting with passion or my life is passionless.

But rather than take a wrong turn into self-focus, I must choose to use them to serve and love and to make decisions based on truth and principled living.

Then my passion boosts me into the stratosphere of living - fully satisfied, fully alive, fully destined.

Passion is the engine, principle is the track, love is the goal, service is the way.

Day 114
My Grace

I held him while he wept. A shocking loss of a loved one. He cried out, "What will I do, what will I do?" I desperately wanted to speak out some wise and satisfying answer - some reason, to conjure some explanation to sooth his anguished heart. But there was nothing, nothing at all. I just held him feeling inept, empty, answer-less.

Paul was desperately anxious to be freed from some sort of "messenger of Satan" and prayed again and again (2 Cor 12:7-9). Nothing, nothing at all. Maybe he even made up some reason for it all... it does seem a little over the top.

Then God answered. Quietly. Without explanation.

"My grace is sufficient for you."

Sometimes when I am anguished, anxious or even just annoyed I want answers; I want it to make sense... the world to make sense. I want justice or rescue; maybe even a good steam-letting-off argument with God.

But He wisely does not indulge me. He just says the one thing I really need to hear most... "My grace is sufficient for you."

And it is everything, everything at all.

Day 115
Gotcha Covered

So...at combo city hall and post office in Arizona. 108 degrees.

Ready to dash to the car when, like a whisper in my ear I hear,

"You only take cash!? But I have to mail these. I have no cash."

Why not?

Andy: "How much is it? No problem, gotcha covered."

Guy: "what...no...ok but I work at Trader Joes. Ever you come in just ask for Tom. You're beautiful man..."

Postal Lady: "Hey, this is one of them 'pay it forward' things... You know that game"

Guy: "No I think it's a contest or movie or something... Thanks man ... I'm in... My turn. Trader Joes"

Smiles all around.

My mentor says: *"If a man loses his life for My sake..."*

Not sure if it is a contest.

I only know there is a prize for the loser.

Day 116
B+

So... Denver. I walk into a 1,500 person professional convention opening session five minutes before starting. People run up to me, "Where have you been?!?! We called ten times. Another &%$#@# speaker bailed on us - can you give a quick ten minute speech as part of a panel - pleeeeeeese?"

Heart pounds - what!?! OK, gulp. What is the topic... jot a few shaky notes, gathering thoughts, two minutes,

Am introduced ... I walk up a bit befuddled but getting my act together - sit in chair 3,000 staring eyes. First one speaks. Second one speaks. I am ready now. Then... up the main aisle strolls the missing speaker... up on stage and right up to me... 3,000 staring eyes. "Sorry I'm late, I'll take it from here."

Shake hands, fake smile, "Glad you made it" Shuffle off stage, 3,000 staring eyes. Deep breaths, fuming, embarrassed, shaking mad, avoiding eye contact, staying professional... mostly.

Then I hear, "I know how it feels, I'm with you, watching you, this is the test not the speech - you could do that in your sleep."

And I suddenly recall the verse: *"With humility of mind regard another as more important...have this attitude in yourselves... Jesus was God but emptied Himself... humbled Himself by becoming obedient to the point of shame and death on a cross. For this reason also, God highly exalted Him"* (Phil 2:3-9).

Deep breath. One set of eyes. Matter.

"Poor guy must have been embarrassed to be so late," I told the conference chair who ran up to me at the back... and I meant it... mostly.

Maybe a B+

Day 117
Mindfulness

So... the digerati have met again in Wisdom 2.0, the gurus of the gurus in tech, and have issued an apology saying, "People have a pathological relationship with their devices".

Addiction to beeps, tweets, and emails. It is literally rewiring brains to the dopamine rush when the Pavlovian sound is heard, and is shrinking parts dedicated to impulse control, concentration and empathy (!)... much like cocaine... and creating an epidemic of self-absorption.

To try to counter this Google, Facebook and Twitter are teaching mindfulness meditation to their executives...telling them to stop using their own products for a while.

This strange verse now makes more sense: *"For nothing is hidden that will not become evident, nor anything secret that will not be known and come to light. So take care how you listen; for whoever has, to him more shall be given; and whoever does not have, even what he thinks he has shall be taken away from him"* (Lk 8:17-18).

Is that addiction evident in me? The cure? Science says it is "awe and thankfulness" - getting alone in nature, quiet and meditative.

Who better to be in awe of and thankful to than God Almighty?

So... turn off the device. Just say no.

Treat what we listen to like what we eat - healthy and in moderation.

Let's try "organic listening" for a while!

Day 118
Live Bait

God can indue anything with a meaning or a message... any bird flying, cloud sailing, star twinkling, flower blooming, smile, touch, look or book... anything. Even a Bleat. But make no mistake - that is God's prerogative not man's.

Paul says: *"See to it that no one deceptively hooks you through: a new philosophy, old traditions or practices, science and principles of the cosmos, special food or drink, a special day or Sabbath, a phase of the moon, self-abasement, angel talk, or visions he claims to have seen"* (Col 2).

If you have eyes to see you will notice some of these around a good bit.

For example, this week there is a "Blue Moon" perhaps claimed to be rare and special, a time of God's special moving. Maybe it is. But a Blue Moon is simply an artifice of the pagan Julian Calendar we adopted and the fact the moon's phase is 29 1/2 days while the month is 31 days. So every 2 1/2 years or so you get two full moons in a month - nothing more. A phase of the moon.

Next year it will be a Blood Moon. The coincidental lunar eclipse and Jewish holy day spaced six months apart. Interesting that eclipses (due to the moons orbit) and these two holy days (due to God's setting up a lunar-solar calendar for the chosen People) are <u>always</u> spaced six months apart.

Every fish is defined by the bait it will take. Lots of fake lures out there to hook men, colorful, jiggling, lifelike. I want to be sure to bite only on the real thing.

And I want to make sure I use only "live bait" when I am out being a fisher of men.

Day 119
Dependency

There are some things that God ultimately reserves to Himself to give to and "be" to men - two of which are provision and protection. It is within the unenlightened behavior of institutions to unwittingly step into those roles - perhaps supposing they are doing some necessary good thing... but self-deceived. And individuals get off the hook.

When a government substitutes itself as the source of provision through its programs it creates both an impersonal and unrewarding tithe on all taxpayers, and a self-limiting recipient dependency on government. God is man's provision - el Shaddai. Only He knows the right combination to draw and stretch each one to become what they were created to be - even through hardship. Individuals need encouraging help but not slavery to handouts. If I never fall, I never walk. If I never walk, I never fall.

In the same way, when a church tells its people that it is providing a "covering" to protect them from _____ they have stepped across the line. God is the covering of protection - Elyon. They have misconstrued authority and inserted themselves between man and God, creating a soulish dependency and a one-off relationship. Individuals need help removing the distance between themselves and Papa - not substituting for Him. God has no grandchildren.

Man's response to need is sometimes to create institutions to supposedly solve the problem. But they can create a more insidious problem of their own.

God's response is to pray for harvesters to bring men to Him, to call individual men to be His hands and feet one-on-one, face-to-face, life-to-life.

Day 120
Ready to Go

So...I used to think when old people said they were "ready to go" that they were mostly just tired and giving up.

No more.

Last week as I thought about heaven I suddenly got a glimpse of things and, oh my, got very excited, very envisioned by what might be, out of here and on to the next eternity. It felt very invigorating, very different, very... well, prescient rather than just present.

Paul felt it too, he did not know which to choose: "I am hard-pressed from both directions, having the desire to depart and be with Christ, for that is very much better" (Phil 1:22-23).

You see, my salvation is incomplete. And it cannot be completed until I leave this old body and get my new improved model: "we ourselves, having the first fruits of the Spirit, even we ourselves groan within ourselves, waiting eagerly for our adoption as sons, the redemption of our body" (Rom 8:23); until I see face to face and know as I am known.

I have heard someone was "too heavenly minded to be of any earthly good." But I think maybe NOT being tremendously heavenly minded may give me a warped perspective on right values and accurate valuation. It is much easier to lay a life down that I know is very temporary; to endure "momentary light affliction" in favor of an eternal weight of glory.

Jesus who "for the joy set before Him" endured even the cross. He was ready to go.

So... if some day you witness a very excited old man on his death bed it might be me.

Ready to go.

Day 121
Small Truths

So... today I reviewed a proposed "Integrity Management System" for a corporation. "What!?! We now have to manage truth to maximize profits? Are you kidding?" I was incredulous.

Then that immensely kind, wise and loving whisper... "You do that sometimes huh?"

"What!?! Are you kidding" I was more incredulous... for about two nanoseconds then...

It seems easy, even natural, to subtly managed truth to personal profit - insignificant omissions, minor exaggerations, little white lies of convenience.

What can they hurt? Plenty.

David says, *"Behold, You desire truth in the innermost being, and in that hidden part You will make me know wisdom"* (Ps 51:6).

God makes it clear that when we lie in small ways we are, in fact, liars - and He cannot entrust wisdom to such. The mixture is deadly - creating a wise liar. Lucifer was one... and we know how that turned out for everyone (Ez 28, Jn 8:44).

But if I choose truth every time - every time - then Papa will give me the wisdom to make that truth acceptable, attractive, compelling (Prov 15:2).

And I become credible, trusted, successful.

Fair enough?

Day 122
Not Just Me

So... what if it's not just me?

Sometimes my mind just goes into the ditch. I am suddenly humming "...but I shot a man in Memphis..." and think "What in the world?!" Sometimes it's worse. You?

It's not just me... or you.

In 2 Cor 2:11 Paul describes the "schemes" of the devil. That word means "thoughts" and implies "thought manipulation or suggestion". 2 Cor 3:14 and 4:4 talk about Satan dulling minds and blinding them. Same word.

Manipulated thinking leads to manipulated believing, acting, living... death.

In 2 Cor 11:3 Paul states he is afraid "lest as the serpent deceived Eve by his craftiness your minds should be led astray from simple and clean devotion to Christ." Same word.

The protection, the antidote to a mind being led down a crazy path to crazy harmful thinking and actions is NOT to stop thinking...but this:

"Be anxious for nothing, but in everything by prayer and supplication with thanksgiving let your requests be made known to God. And the peace of God, which surpasses all comprehension, will guard your hearts and your minds in Christ Jesus" (Phil 4:6-7).

Same word.

And replacement thinking like this:

"And whatever is true, whatever is honorable, whatever is right, whatever is pure, whatever is lovely, whatever is of good repute, if there is any excellence and if anything worthy of praise, DWELL on these things" (Phil 4:8).

Different word... "dwell" means to count up, do the math, memorize.

Word.

Day 123
Ownership

So... this came in the mail today.

I suddenly have a very keen interest in the political discussion about Federal benefits. Why? Because I have an earned stake in it - I OWN benefits.

Owners make the best employees - they will pick up trash in the parking lot, make sure it is right, work all night if need be. Why? They have an earned stake in it - they worked hard and OWN it.

God, in His wisdom, made us sons and daughters, not slaves or servants or employees: *"For you have not received a spirit of slavery but of adoptions... and if we are children, then we are also heirs of God along with Christ"* (Rom 8:15-17).

He made us owners. He knew that would be eternally best... unlike some other gods I know of.

I did not work for it, and did not earn it (Rom 4:5).

But make no mistake - I OWN benefits, I OWN the company. I OWN eternity and infinity and even divinity (and any other "itys" out there).

I Own it. I have a stake in the kingdom.

That changes everything.

Day 124
Choose Your Thoughts

So...choose carefully.

This morning someone said, "What if you HAD to say everything you thought?!" I said, "What if you had to THINK everything you thought?"

What? Here goes.

I once thought that if I only think something then no problem, as long as I don't say it. That is: choose your words carefully.

So wrong.

Thoughts we pay attention to go two directions - in and out. They CAN come out in words, but focused thoughts ALWAYS enter my heart like seeds planted or blown into my garden.

There some take root and produce fruit... or weeds... by themselves (Mk 4:26-29).

Thoughts, good and bad, neutral and vile, random and suggested, stream past my focus-er on the inside. I am NOT accountable for the stream (Even Jesus was tempted) - but only for that which I fetch out of the stream for focus.

My screen of focus is ALWAYS on - and the content can be my deliberate choice or supplied by "others".

The result of my choice of thoughts propels the course of my life and my speech (Prov 4:23, Lk 6:45).

So, I want to choose my words right.

But more importantly I must choose my thoughts.

Day 125
Hearing God in the Dance

"Is this the Lord or just me - I need to be sure!?"

She looked confused and a bit frightened. I think she wanted angelic visitation. "But, you're in luck", I said, "maybe it doesn't work like you think."

Hopeful frown of confusion.

Did you notice these verses in 1 Corinthians chapter 7 there is a lot of information about how Paul heard God? But its well hidden, disguised as marriage advice (which may also be mostly about hearing).

vs. 10 - To the married I give instructions, not I, but the Lord, that...
vs. 12 – But to the rest I say, not the Lord, that...
vs. 25 - I have no command of the Lord, but I give an opinion as one who by the mercy of the Lord is trustworthy.
vs. 40 - But in my opinion... and I think that I also have the Spirit of God.

Note the continuum of (un)certainty from "The Lord says" through "I think it is God", to "I, a trustworthy person, think" ending at "This is not written by God but..."

All four of those made it in the bible with God's stamp of approval I guess. He maybe says, "Paul, no problem man, you're good."

When we willingly become more and more conformed to His image, taking on His mind, transforming our thinking, an amazing thing happens: we become dance partners in life. He is always leading but usually unseen - preferring us, His bride, to shine. We twirl and pirouette along in seemingly choreographed steps - matched in the thoughts, words, and ways of our wonderful partner... who trusts us.

"Just me" is sometimes just fine.

Day 126
Sweet Dreams

So... near death experience.

I was crossing just upstream of 215 foot high Taughannock Falls (stupid college kid decision) when I lost my footing and was swept toward the precipice.

I panicked, clawing, scrambling, swimming - forty feet away. Just then my feet hit a large rock boulder and caught - I stood up, firm, shaking.

Shaken and trembling, I quietly thanked Papa. Then I just sat down to gather my thoughts – an Another's thoughts crept in.

I was reminded that David cried out, *"From the end of the earth I call to You, when my heart is overwhelmed; lead me to the rock that is higher than I"* (Ps 61:2).

We all sometimes feel swept along toward some inevitable bad end - maybe our own stupid decision. We seem unable to put our feet down and just stop the rush.

Peter said it too: *"Roll all your anxiety on Him, because He cares for you"* (1 Pet 5:7).

I tried it last night. I was anxious about a bi day coming up. I put my feet down on the rock higher than I was; named the anxiety; packaged it up and rolled it on to my Best Friend; took a deep breath and let it out slowly; and went to sleep.

Sweet dreams.

Day 127
Sign Language

So... sign language from God.

Somebody recently someone told me about "putting out a fleece" and looking for an "open door" from God.

I smiled and nodded supportively. Does God really need "sign language" to talk to us. Maybe sometimes but...

Let's talk fleeces.

Gideon (Judges chapter 6) already knew what God wanted him to do - he tried to not do it by putting god to a test he figured god would not pass. "Fleecing" God was a bad idea.

Didn't work.

It was an avoidance mechanism. "If it's really You God then jump through my hoop. When You don't then I am let off the hook guilt-free."

Let's talk doors.

Paul says of doors: *"I shall remain in Ephesus; for a wide door for effective service has opened to me, and there are many adversaries"* (1 Cor 16:8-9).

Like Gideon, Paul knew what God wanted of Him - that was the door, despite the circumstances. That is: "door" does not equal "circumstance". If it did then little that was hard would ever get done.

Bottom line is that every door, fleece, sign, word, and coincidence must enter our heart/spirit where we judge whether it is from God and what it means. No way around it, *"For all who are being led by the Spirit of God, these are sons of God"* (Rom 8:14). In the end I do all I can do then I trust God, not my discernment, take the risk and take the step. No looking back.

But before I set the standard too high – if my heart wants God's will then if all I know to do is flip a coin, then by all means flip away. God makes provision for me, and then works to grow up my discernment.

Day 128
Game Over

So…the trump card.

Somebody tried the trump card the other day. Didn't work. The game goes sort of like this: You are having a real-life discussion and then someone says "God told me that…" .

Game over…at that point they win.

Unless, of course, you are not playing.

- Solomon makes the point, *"It is a trap for a man to say rashly, 'It is holy!' (i.e. God told me) and afterward to make inquiry"* (Prov 20:25).
- Paul tells the charismatic Corinthians that it cannot possible be the Holy Spirit if you say "Jesus is accursed" so wise up.
- The most revealed to people making the most important decision of all time merely said, *"It seems good to the Holy Spirit and to us…"* (Acts 15:28).

So what about "God told me…"?

If I say, "God told me…" that by definition it IS prophecy and ALL prophecy is to be offered for judgment and proving by wise others (1 Cor 14:29). Every time and any time.

We are still in that time when we know in part, speak only partially right things. "God told me" might better be expressed as: "I felt like God might be saying" held with an open hand.

Our words are hard to eat; "God told me" ones particularly.

Unless of course you like the game.

Day 129
Balsamic Reduction and Lamb Chops

So… things of old were written for our instruction.

We apply Old Testament truth by boiling it down (like a balsamic reduction!) to its concentrated generic basis and then pour it over our own milieu salad.

In that light, Ez 34 talking about the shepherds of Israel, is a mirror and warning for all types of church leaders - shepherds. Here is my reduction:

"They feed themselves" - sermons are about me and my staff's interest, books and mp3s are strongly promoted, fads abound, it's a lot about talented superstars and social networking.

"They cloth themselves with wool and eat fat" - focus on giving to the ministry and supporting staff initiatives, the building, the programs, the events. Tithing to the church is a must.

"They slaughter the fat sheep" - potential rivals are marginalized, benched, or forced out, there is no power sharing, no leadership transfer, there is a strong sense of "professional-laity".

"The sick... diseased... broken" - the hurting and needy are marginalized, they take too much time away from the ministry, and in the end are quietly ushered out through neglect.

"The scattered... the lost are not sought" - those who walk or fall away are ignored as there was no real relationship to begin with. People can come and go with little follow up. We are not a body we are a religious corporation.

God says he Himself has a restoration plan – it seems to involve some hiring and firing at the top.

I'll leave the balsamic reduction of that one to you.

Day 130
More than Bell Ringing

"I consider that the chief dangers which confront the coming century will be religion without the Holy Ghost; Christianity without Christ; forgiveness without repentance; salvation without regeneration; politics without God; and Heaven without Hell."

William Booth cir. 1904
Founder of the Salvation Army.

Day 131
Planted Trees

So…some events define my faith. This is one.

Our four small children in car parked uphill, long steep driveway, street, then house across street downhill all the way. Forgot potluck dish, went to get with Susan. Child kicks parking brake and the car begins to roll, driver door open, picking up speed.

We drop everything and race after it - 25 mph for sure - Susan screams "Jesus!"

The car careens across the street and straight toward the house on the downhill side, gathering speed, into the front yard heading toward house. We cannot catch the car. Hopeless, I cry out to God, tripping and tearing my suit pants.

Then, as I watch from a prone position scrambling up, the car speeds past a small landscape tree, maybe three inches in diameter, that then wedges in door and slowly bends over under the weight and momentum of the car and children, perfectly slowing the car to a gentle stop inches from the house.

The owners run out of the house shaking their heads. We run up, shaking. We all cry. Kids fine. Bewildered.

She says to husband, "See, I told you to put the tree right there. He wanted it ten feet left. I told you Fred. I just knew it."

David and Job say *"My times are in Your hand; deliver me…"* (Ps 31:15); *"In whose hand is the life of every living thing, and the breath of all mankind"* (Job 12:10).

God has already made provision, planted trees, along my way.

I told you Fred.

Day 132
The Gate Agent

So... A Southwest gate attendant was facing a terminal full of tired storm delayed customers. Discouragement and grumbling all around.

I watched him as he got on the microphone and said how sorry he was, and that he loved us all. That we were all in this together. Synchronize.

He then said, "Here's what I do with my family when this kind of stuff happens." Offer an alternative.

He pulled out a guitar (go figure) and played and led the whole terminal in a rousing version of "don't worry be happy". Lead.

First incredulity, then a few earl adopters, then a spreading sense of fun, then everyone cheered and clapped, began talking to each other and laughing. Persist.

"Let no unwholesome word proceed from your mouth, but only such a word as is good for edification according to the need of the moment, so that it will give grace to those who hear. Do not grieve the Holy Spirit of God..." (Eph 4:29,30)

I don't know if he was consciously doing this verse. Bet not. Don't know if He was consciously not wanting to grieve the Holy Spirit by joining in the grumbling. Bet not. But I do know he loved his customers and stepped in to change the story of their take off.

I learned from him. You can too.

Encourage one another - gloom is mostly shallow water.

I'm off !!

Day 133
Only Child

So… enjoy, and smile knowingly, at the Facebook details about every new baby's first: smile, word, step, meal, cute outfit, and independent doo doo. I was that way about our four; like they are the only child in this seven billion person world.

Every child should have that, every parent should think that.

That need doesn't stop mattering as we reach adulthood - we are only better at pretending it doesn't.

So… I am amazed at David's Psalm 139. In it he seems to think he is the only one important to God in the whole wide world.

God pays minute attention to EVERYTHING about him - and to him that is a very good thing. Words, thoughts, actions, dreams, habits and ways. Protected on all sides.

Even when I try to run He stays with me - lest I run too far to find my way back. There is no back to find - there is only a "there".

I am assured I am made just right - wonderfully.

God somehow has the ability to make each one His only child - even while we enjoy our family.

It is like I am the only person that matters in this seven billion person world. "Such knowledge is too wonderful for me, it is too high for me to grasp."

You too - only child in a big family!

Day 134
Grace Chase

So... escape a fruitless conference luncheon, walk two blocks to outrun people selling me stuff. Lunch, upstairs balcony, back table, no one but me, empty.

Wonderful! Reading newspaper. Escape. Then...

"Andy!! Hey man imagine seeing you up here... was just talking about you. Meet Nancy and John who head up EPA's program on water." I jump up. These are VERY important people.

Nancy: "I heard of you, not sure where. Can you join us?" Me: "Ahhhh... sure."

Two hours of very interesting conversation, exchanged cards, "Call me any time" "Ahhhh... sure."

I then heard the smile (if you can hear smiles). Aha - I knew it!!

Long ago I had thought God pursued people to to punish, or make to obey... like Jonah. Sort of like parents coming to spank you, or a high speed police chase. But would have to work hard to earn and see His favor.

But I was wrong. Very wrong. It's the opposite.

Reflecting His character Papa says , *"All these blessings will come upon you and overtake you if you obey the Lord your God"* (Deut 28:2). God then lists about everything you ever heard of. God tracks me down to BLESS me, He causes His favor to come upon me, to chase and overtake me. He sends big shots to find me hidden away.

Irresistible grace.

You too.

A high speed grace chase. Want to be caught, expect to be caught.

Day 135
Length, Years and Peace

So... I was taught to give up my seat to older people.

On a NYC subway last week I realized that had become nearly impossible - I was the oldest... by quite a bit. I offered a couple times, then slowly sank back down, several smiles, and listened.

New York City - frenetic, frantic pace, crowds pushing, taxis racing, barked staccato phrases, going somewhere, getting somewhere... and everybody's got their game face on.

That was me at 23.

Back then I read this and did not really get it: *"My son, do not forget my teaching, but let your heart keep my commandments; for <u>length of days and years of life, and peace</u> they will add to you"* (Prov 3).

Strange. I realized that I mostly get it now.

I think older people slow down not because they have creaky joints and sore muscles... only... but because they begin to get it - to strive to enter rest (Heb 4:11).

Unhurried, un-harried days filled with plenty of time for all that is intended... and trust. Years stretching - enough of them to be life, enough to be called "full of years".

I think God says so often to "wait on the Lord" not because He is slow but because He Himself is waiting to see my impatience transformed slowly by slowly to peace.

Only then I will be a travel companion fit for eternity.

Day 136
The Devil's Disappointment

So... that old Jezebel spirit.

Had a conversation with a guy who just knew the "Jezebel spirit" was the reason for his long running marriage problems. He was told I could "access the Spirit" and free him from this high level spiritual assault.

Imagine his disappointment.

Jesus (the most important target of Satan ever) said, *"We'll talk later, the Devil is coming, but he has nothing in me"* (Jn 14:30).

John said, *"He who was born of God does not harbor sin, God keeps him, and the evil one does not touch him"* (1 Jn 5:18). Satan demanded to sift Peter due to his pride (Lk 22:31).

Most people I encounter who claim high level demonic attack should really be focusing on low level fleshy vulnerability.

When exposed to the light "deep spiritual battles" are often just simple and unattractive wrath, greed, sloth, pride, lust, envy, or gluttony - aided and abetted by darkness.

Not all. But most humans are just not that important.

Satan had nothing in Jesus, no handle to jerk. But in me, well, that's maybe another story. But when I purpose to let God sift me gently and remove that base vulnerability I become slippery, few places for a hook to nab.

The Devil is thwarted and his trade tools reduced to trials only. Look there first dear ones.

Imagine his disappointment.

Day 137
Change the World

So... I spent the day remembering key life transitions with two dear brothers - faithful to each other since 1974.

We recounted together how we have greatly influenced each other's' lives - in eternal ways: marriage, career, life. Small comments, actions, and kindnesses had made the difference.

They did not seem weighty at the time. But we changed each other's' world.

"You probably don't realize it but when you..." "Really, I never knew."

We all live life on a knife edge where a small nudge can push us to one side of the blade or the other and set us on a different path.

The decision to send a small band to rebuild the feeble wall in Jerusalem seemed a small thing.

But God saw things differently: *"For who has despised the day of small things? But the seven eyes of the LORD which range to and fro throughout the earth will be glad when they see the plumb line in the hand of Zerubbabel"* (Zech 4:10, 2 Ch 16:9).

God uses leverage - five loaves feed 5,000. A stone and a sling reset the course of a nation.

I never know when another is on the cusp of a "plumb line" event where a comment or action will tip the balance.

But God does.

When I sense that nudge to do or say a small thing, then I want to be faithful to go ahead... and change the world.

Day 138
You, the Comforter

So…Solomon had a bad day.

Ecclesiastes is Solomon's skeptical negation of skepticism (extra credit if you just followed that one).

In it he said: *"Then I looked again at all the acts of oppression which were being done under the sun. And behold I saw the tears of the oppressed and that they had no one to comfort them; and on the side of their oppressors was power, but they had no one to comfort them."* (4:1).

ALL men need someone to comfort them.

ALL men are disquieted about some part of their lives, unsure of decisions, beliefs, actions, stances.

ALL need assurance and encouragement, kindness, acceptance, inclusion.

Even the rich and powerful, the oppressors and the oppressed... all men. You needed comfort.

So God sent a Comforter (Jn 14:16). He speaks comfort to you. Listen. Be comforted. He also speaks from within you comfort to others (1 Cor 14:3 - same Greek word).

You ARE a comforter.

ALL men need what you have to give.

ALL. MEN. Need you.

Day 139
No Fairy Tale

"Tragic" and "tragedy" are two vastly different things - not to be confused.

I have a friend who lost his father rather abruptly. No chance to say "goodby". He said, "It is tragic, but it is not a tragedy."

He is not living in a fairy tale.

"Tragic" describes a transient event whose ending has not yet been writ, whose outcome can yet be triumphal, redemptive.

"Tragedy" carries the finality of a noun fully defined - hopeless, done, irredeemable. A trapeze artist who attempts a great feat and falls to his death is a tragedy, but one who falls to the safety net is only tragic... and that only from a limited perspective.

There is NOTHING on earth that can happen to me that is beyond being merely tragic.

Earth does not get to have the last word, does not possess the power of finality... of tragedy.

Paul says, *"If we have hoped in Christ in this life only, we are of all men most to be pitied. Be not uninformed, brethren, about those who are asleep, so that you will not grieve as do the rest who have no hope"* (1 Cor 15:14, 4:13).

However unfashionable, I am not ashamed to dream of heaven; not afraid to long for it. I know, "happily ever after" is my destiny.

And it is no fairy tale.

Day 140
The Ask

So... two stories happened this week.

Real God.

A PhD athiest is friends with a Christian for a year.

He finally asks, "Is this God stuff for real - I mean how do you know?"

Friend, "Why don't you go sit in your car and just ask Him?"

PhD, "Ok - really?"

Fifteen minutes later he comes running in, "This shits for real... for real!!"

A young man who left religion years ago - thought he maybe left God behind with it.

His girlfriend prays that God would be the center of their relationship - afraid to tell boyfriend. Next day he is driving.

He told me, "I suddenly heard God so strong I felt I needed to pull over. He said He wanted to be the center of our relationship. I said OK to Him. Tell me, how do I do that?"

Sometimes wisdom keep sit's mouth shut.

I said, "Looks like you and Papa got a great start. I would ask Him."

James says you do not have because you do not ask.

God says: "Ask of me"

Ask. Directly. Really.

Day 141
Peirasmos

So... the one bad word.

The Greek language is filled with multiple words for love, the three main ones are for spiritual selflesslove (*agape*), soulish love (philia), and physical attraction (eros)... and playful love, family love, etc.

But the Greek language seems to have but one for the three major things Satan tries to do to destroy us: *peirasmos*.

It means temptation (lure over the edge), trial (push over the edge) and test (throw yourself over the edge). "Over the edge" is the singular goal. Falling to death. But Satan is stuck in a dangerous game... to him.

1 Cor 10:13 defines the rules: *"No peirasmos has overtaken you but such as is common to man; and God is faithful, who will not allow you to be peirasmos-ed beyond what you are able, but with the peirasmos will provide the way of escape, so that you can endure it."*

Common things, faithful God, limited tests, a way out, endurance necessary. Every time. Every. Time.

Satan has but one chance - he exposes a weakness in me and, if I work with God, it is destroyed and replaced with strength and righteousness. It is God's plan to perfect me; Satan's to kill me.

Satan demanded to sift Peter and Judas - Peter passed, Judas died (Lk 22:3, 31). Same *peirasmos*. God, too has but one word - *sozo* - to save, heal and deliver, to perfect. Package deal.

When I feel dragged close to the precipice edge I remember His promises, His rules, His kind understanding grace and I find He causes me to fly like an eagle - right off the edge.

Falling upward. Every time. Every. Time.

Day 142
Words of Life

There are things in scripture that seem like tension-causing contradictions. For example these two:

"I buffet my body and make it my slave - lest after preaching to others I myself might be disqualified" (1 Cor 9:27).

"God has given us eternal life, and this life is in His Son. He who has the Son has eternal life" (1 Jn 5:11-12).

There are three sources of reaction to such seeming contradictions within our makeup. The flesh (*sarkikos*) nature may take proud offense and say, "See, this is all religious bunk - I thought so." The soul (*psychicos*) nature may want to study and exegete its way to a logical answer saying, "In ancient times... and in the Greek it says...".

But the spirit man (*pneumatikos*) will let the words wash over himself, feeling the gentle ebb and flow of wisdom, not in some empty, mindless religious way but knowing that there is a way of God that far outstrips both flesh and soul - and can offend both. When this happens most such tension-producing opposites transform to become like two tent lines pulling in opposite directions holding up the life within in balance, creating wisdom without words, peace without striving, life without death.

For these two verses for example, this can create an ability to both live in confidence in God's eternal love all the while vigilant for things that attempt to destroy it.

And rather than take offense we begin to get Jesus when He said, *"It is the Spirit who gives life; the flesh profits nothing; the words that I have spoken to you are spirit and are life"* (Jn 6:63) and say like Peter *"Where else shall we go, You have the words of life".*

Tension can be a good thing.

Day 143
Be a Nana

So... the Nanas have been outed.

Who!?

For over twenty years nine grannies saved their money and, upon overhearing a need, would secretly leave money and a freshly baked cake on the doorstep.

Can you imagine the faces and hearts of the ones who opened the door to that?!

Jesus was a Nana (Jn 13:29) who secretly gave from the money box. His Father founded the Nanas International: *"When you give to the poor, do it in secret; and your Father who sees what is done in secret will reward you."* (Mt 6:3)

Its an act in three plays: (1) give to meet a real need, (2) make it special, and (3) make it secret.

It's harder for the rich to join up - they have less association with the needy and many requests. Easy for you and I.

Maybe there is a way to use web-media to help find needs - Nana-technology (I couldn't resist!).

Did you catch the part where Papa has been secretly planning a reward for Nanas?

It: (1) meets a need we have and (2) is special - but sometimes He can't help himself and rewards openly - even embarrasses.

Such a lavish dad!

Be a Nana.

Day 144
Wealthy Nation

So…it is the glory of God to give anonymously.

It is the glory of man to figure that out. Its just not normally in our nature.

I live in the wealthiest nation of all time and am at the very top of my field. I know how I got there - and its not all about hard work. And I think I know much of how we all got there as a nation since before 1776. Ditto.

God said to the Jews *"My favor prospers you above your wicked neighbors so do not say 'my power and strength did this'. It is I who is giving you that power"* (Deut 7-9).

Paul said, *"For who regards you as superior? What do you have that you did not receive? And if you did receive it, why do you boast as if you had not received it?"* (1 Cor 4:7).

I think that is one of the most important things today for our nation is to remember in this time of critical decision making. We must surely guard against creeping arrogance - it is deadly poison.

And we must be wise stewards of all we have been given (1 Cor 4:1).

That wisdom must inform decisions in my personal life from my house and car, to the time and money I spend... and national life.

God is watching to see how we treat the poor, immigrants, sick, and even free loaders in this nation. God anticipates everyone who is able will work... and bear their fair load. Not all are wealthy and can afford the best of anything.

To some He entrusts extreme wealth - anonymously. Then He watches.

It is the glory of man to figure that out.

Day 145
Narrowing

So... I noticed that the long narrow land out back felt even narrower than my original work 15 years ago to clear it.

I checked old pictures and sure enough.

Its inconvenient to keep pushing back thorns when mowing. Giving way 3" a year over 15 years to avoid stickers... is, well, a lot of lost ground.

When Jacob was young he wrestled with God and prevailed (Gen 32:24). I think God wanted him to win. Even more impressive to me... now... is that he held the line over many years and when very old he "blessed his sons, and worshiped, leaning on his staff." (Heb 11:21). What a testimony, what a legacy!

When we are young we struggle to make godly life choices and changes - we are determined to hold the line. And we establish ground. Jabez called on God, *"Oh that You would bless me and enlarge my border..."* (1 Ch 4:10). David asked God to enlarge his heart (Ps 119:32).

God grants those kinds of requests. I want to be one who does not give ground little by little - thorns or no - to be hemmed and constrained by creeping vines of malaise. So today I enlarged the border (I always look for excuses to use the tractor!).

And I prayed like Jabez and David and asked God to search me and to push back thorns and thistles in my own narrow way. God grants those kinds of requests.

Enlarge dear ones, and hold the line.

God grants those kinds of requests.

Day 146
More Lord

So...Americans are known the world over as super consumers... "rabid" a German friend said.

We can always be craving more but rarely really enjoying what we own... having but never truly possessing.

In circles with which I am familiar we often cry out, "more Lord, more Lord".

Now I know its biblical (Phil 3:14); and not wanting "more of God" is anathema. But I sometimes wonder. I sometimes feel like I need to step beyond "normal" life to experience Holy Spirit - do something edgy and "different" this Sunday. Dance. Goosebumps. Shake. Swoon. Fire tunnel!!

Is that what I mean by "more Lord"? Do I truly possess the Holy Spirit I "own" right now.

Can "more Lord" look different?

Can I in the stillness of the night lie there and be flooded with thankfulness and joy? Can I sense His friendship and partnership on a sales call? Can a sudden "knowing" make my heart skip a beat? Can I stop and marvel at His goodness in saving and changing me? Can I read a book on doctrine and not fall asleep but be jolted awake by the immense truth of it all?

Can I just whisper... thank you Lord?

Day 147
Bee Government

So... imagine my surprise to learn that ultra conservative bees had taken over one bee hive, and extreme liberals the other.

The conservative drones set up honey exchanges making the worker bees bring all their honey to them for next to nothing, and working them overtime without compensation saying, "it's a free market, no one is making them work for me." No bee could deposit honey in the hive without their permission. Come winter the drones plan to sell the honey back to them at high prices. Each drone had more honey than they would ever need.

The liberal drones took control of the other hive for the good of the bees and set up a honey location and regulation program. All bees needed a license to collect honey and could only collect it at hive approved nectar sites. Because finding the sites was now the duty of inefficient and unmotivated government nectar-locator drones few sites were found and licensed and most worker bees were unemployed. The hive demanded ever increasing amounts of sugar water from me to feed them promising to repay me from future honey. They now owe gallons of honey.

But we urge you, bee-thren, to excel still more, and to make it your am-bee-tion to lead a quiet life and attend to your own bees-ness and work with your hands, just as we commanded you, so that you will bee-have properly toward outsiders and not bee in any need. (1 Th 4:10-12)

Based on this, the worker bees rebelled this week restoring the government to a benevolent matriarchy - one queen, under the care and control of the workers. The drones were driven out. Each worker bee uses its innate ability to find nectar and dance joyfully showing others where it is.

The hive is thriving - in the ways it was created to, with each bee endowed by its Creator with certain inalienable rights, among them the right to life, liberty and the pursuit of nectar... and the responsibility to work hard and honestly and to enjoy the fruit of its labor.

Day 148
My Favorite Roll

My favorite role, and the place all oldies like me enjoy is watching, smiling, knowing, guiding, sharing thoughts, helping, serving... not the focus.

In this picture I get the best seat in the house as a wonderful couple pledges love and service to each other.

I told them that Adam did not know Eve at all when they met ("So, tell me, what do you like to do after work? Where do you like to go to lunch?"). So he had to trust God; and that

we are all, in the end, in the same situation with our mates and our marriages. You never know enough not to need to trust.

Someone once told me that the four phases of men are squire-knight-prince and king.

She said I was a king. Maybe, but I think not. Who would want to be that - sitting on some throne distant, scary and remote?

God calls us kings reigning with Him and priests - and yet commands us to be much less in the eyes of the world (1 Pet 2:9, Eph 2:6, Mt 23:11).

I think "servant-of-all" is more what God has in mind.

Besides, the wrinkles and bald heads do not photograph well.

Day 149
The Riches of the Poor

Jesus and James on the poor: *"You will always have the poor with you; banquet with them; give freely hire fairly and obtain kingdom treasure; the poor are rich in faith"* (Mt 26:11, Lk 14:13, Mt 19:21, Jas 2:5).

Jesus on the rich: *"How hard it is for a greedy rich man to enter the kingdom of heaven, woe to you, you will be sent away empty"* (Mt 9:24, Lk 6:24, 1:53).

There will ALWAYS be poor... and rich by comparison.

I think that God's plan is that the "rich" and the "poor" live in a relational and mutual exchange of their unique riches.

The rich are to mingle with and hire the poor, giving them the benefit of their money-making know how. The poor give the rich labor - but so much more. They show them how to live rich in faith, how to trust God, how to be citizens of the kingdom, how to receive eternal treasure and, as world "happiness statistics" show, how to live in simple joy.

Some government programs on one hand, and the hording greed of the rich on the other, separate rich and poor, frustrate God's plan, and leave both much the poorer.

Both extremes, liberals and conservatives, can exhibit godless idolatry and arrogance. Both, in these partisan times, can cling to the shards of truth they possess and point fingers.

It should not be so among us. I want to make a difference, spread truth, step out myself. *"With people this is impossible, but with God all things are possible"* (Mt 19:23).

Day 150
Sexxxxx!

So... a young shy family friend accidentally texted me from her honeymoon.

No one you know. It just said, "Sexxxxx!!!"

Despite all the voices in my head suggesting clever responses I unaccountably demurred.

Go Song of Solomon!

God intends that EVERY relationship begins with God-led spirit-guided serving and giving (agape - serotonin). We may become friendly. With some it progresses to the deep trusting friendship of the soul (phileo - oxytocin). It will be accompanied by appropriate physical touch (friendly hugs, holy kisses – Rom 16:16, 1 Th 5:6); with the ultimate intimacy (sexxxxx - eros - dopamine) reserved for the one we have agaped, phileoed, and covenanted with in marriage.

My brokenness, ignorance or lack of self-mastery can short circuit this process leading me to avoid the time or pain of real intimacy while gaining a false sense of relational satisfaction (and the brain drug dopamine); I may lose control over my sexual behavior while trying to gain relief from relational pain.

It never works out well in the end. Anyone over 24 knows that.

Paul did: *"We ALL formerly lived in lust, indulging the craving of the flesh and the needs of the mind. But God being rich in mercy... "* (Eph 2).

Its NEVER to late to start over... to run the race ... to finish well.

Rich... in mercy.

Yesssss!

Day 151
Breaking the Law of Gravity

So…I once received three (yes three) traffic tickets in one day

One was for doing 21 in a 15 no less.

After the third one even I knew God was trying to tell me something… so I pulled over without even being asked this time.

God clearly said, "Son you think breaking my laws is like speeding; you rarely get caught. But breaking my laws is like violating gravity - you always get caught. You're living too close to the edge - pull over."

Gal 6:7 says *"Do not be deceived God is not mocked, whatever you sow you will reap."*

Do not let the time delay between sowing and reaping cloud the fact that it actually happens. I just reap it later – often so much later that I miss the connection and wonder why God, karma, luck, or (fill in the blank) hates me.

I reap what I sow, I reap more than I sow, and I reap the same thing I have sown.

Despite what I may have thought.

Day 152
Transformed

So…the big issues in our lives - the ones we seem to not get over, let's talk about those.

We can define two extremes. In the first I stuff the pain and confusion saying, "Oh, it's no big deal". This is called denial. Its unhealthy.

In the second I focus it into an overwhelming impossibility probably taking most of a lifetime to overcome. Let's call this false identity.

Brain science (especially in PTSD treatment) and God (especially in Phil 4) agree that there is an approach that is mostly not on this continuum.

In it we understand there is a difference between "true" and "real". The feelings are real - they are just not based on what is "true".

I can squarely face the feelings, name them, describe them. But I, being in charge, choose to assign them a status of far lesser importance, the event of far less consequence... especially compared to what is true.

I see to see (maybe with the help of others) what is true and mindfully focus on and picture that. God already recognizes me that way - coming as He does from our destiny not our history.

"This happened. I feel this way about it. I believed this untruth when that happened. But it does not actually define me, it is not greatly important to me today, and it's hold on me can be changed. I now know THIS is true. It is very important. It is who I am actually."

I focus on it. And I smile more, stress less. And I go do something physical in keeping with that truth; like Sing.

And I find this too is very, very true: *"Be ye transformed by the renewing of your mind so that..."* (Rom 12:2).

Day 153
The Heavens Tell

So…why did Herod not know about the "Star of Bethlehem"?

Same reason we will not recognize the signs of His second coming (Lk 21).

"Then God said, 'Let there be lights in the expanse of the heavens to separate the day from the night, and let them be for signs and for seasons and for days and years.'" (Gen 1:14)

God declared that the heavens tell His story not ours. The stars and planets are for signs (pointing to a greater reality) and epochs (transitions in the plans of God) (Gen 1:14).

He has and will use them to telegraph His major doings. Western astrology and science have conspired to corrupt the original intent of God.

Signs became horoscopes – rightly shunned by Jew and Christian alike. And the heavens were declared by science to be random works of impersonal physics – making God's foretelling appear laughably primitive. But that is not God's intent for the heavens.

"Lift up your eyes on high And see who has created these stars, The One who leads forth their host by number, He calls them all by name; Because of the greatness of His might and the strength of His power, Not one of them is missing." (Is 40:26)

The heavens are telling of the glory of God; and their expanse is declaring the work of His hands. Day to day pours forth speech, and night to night reveals knowledge. There is no speech, nor are there words; their voice is not heard. Their line has gone out through all the earth. (Ps 119:1-4)

He named them. They show His glory and tell His story.

He will have the last laugh (Ps 2:4).

Meanwhile… take back the sky!!

Day 154
He Does that Sort of Thing

So... several years ago I befriend a worker for my client - middle aged middle level... middle... attorney down on her luck, marriage, kids, health and job working for someone hard to work for.

She is sad and has lost her vision for herself and her life. We chat a lot, I encourage her, saying things I think Papa wants to say to her but she cannot hear. She credits me with heling with her turn around. I mostly just reflected Papa's love through a mirror dimly.

God uses people...even donkeys. He lets me take credit.

He does that sort of thing.

Last week I walk into a very large project interview in another town. Nervous, strangers, new area for me, sort of unprepared. Almost ready to start, head chair is empty. We wait a minute - then (drum roll)... then... then... YES you guessed it.

In she walks, chief attorney - beaming. We lock eyes, she screams, I jump up, we hug like separated siblings. She tears up. I do too. Yak yak yak while everyone smiles and waits.

No strangers in that room then, just family. Jokes and laughter for two hours - questions and talking about work too - she brings things up about how I helped her. Nice.

Today it was announced we won... with the board unanimously; with Papa anonymously; with Andy undeservedly... but you knew that part.

He does that sort of thing.

Day 155
Thanksgiving

So…why, oh why, did I say that?!?

Have you felt that way?

Oh that some of my words could have a kite string, to be hauled back in. But I find when I try to watch my words, especially when greased with emotion, their source is deeper... the come from my heart (Lk 6:45).

Transforming and tuning the overflow of my heart is the focus... not my tongue.

Tongue control alone makes me a poser. Heart healing makes me transparently real. But how?

Here is THE key: *"Be anxious for nothing, but in everything by prayer and supplication with thanksgiving..."* (Phil 4:6). *"Devote yourselves to prayer... with an attitude of thanksgiving..."* (Col 4:2). *"Nor should there be... but rather thanksgiving"* (Eph 5:4). *"Always giving thanks for all things..."* (Eph 5:20). *"Give thanks in all circumstances ..."* (1 Th 5:18). *"Whatever you do, in word or in deed, do all in the name of the Lord Jesus, giving thanks..."* (Col 3:17).

I can start every day, every sleep, every prayer, every relationship, every debate, every every with thanks.

I can stop every rampaging thought insisting on invasion and all beggarly worries demanding an emotional handout with thanksgiving.

It can revolutionize my prayer life, thought life, family life, work life... life life.

God shows me plenty to be thankful for when I ask Him.

Thanks Papa.

Day 156
Who Knew?

So... last night the refrigerator would only "luke-cool", dripping freezer.

Even the water dispenser stopped.

Head scratcher. I read that the slow accumulation of dust can choke the ability of the coils to do their one main job well - doesn't wreck it, just chokes its ability. Who would have noticed that!?

So I MacGyvered a small hose, duct tape, and vacuum and cleaned the coils, put a glass of water in the freezer and went to bed. Next morning I awoke to FROZEN water and a cold refrigerator. Yes !

Dust build up - really? Who knew?

And... then... I suddenly saw it, felt it, heard it, "Careful, the slow and unseen accumulation of dust is robbing you of your first love making you lukewarm. I miss you - come close. Clean it out!"

I dropped the tools on the floor and drove to the wildest worship I could find. Arms up, I felt the wind blowing dust out. Dust... who knew?

Papa did and wanted me close. You too.

We slip away from hot passion by unseen degrees - as streams run to rivers, and rivers to seas.

When I got back even the water dispenser was working again. Who knew?

Day 157
Plans

So... I asked the counselor, "what is your plan?"

She just smiled, "No plan... just a destination in mind. Trust me, walk with me, I know the way."

When God called Abraham He just said to go north. Only reluctantly did He answer Moses' many detailed questions about "the Exodus Plan". He warned Paul there would be suffering... but that's about it.

I think this is an important part of the nature of God. He does not give plans except for construction of temples and arcs. He shared little except if it was to be very, very scary.

I (and maybe you), on the other hand, love plans. I feel like I need to know where I am, when I will get there and what is involved.

Church programs and self-help books seem to excel in plans and steps: the ten steps to ..., five steps to a fulfilling..., eight week course in discipleship.

In my experience those things, abundant as they are, NEVER work like... well, like planned.

They are a bit katywompus with the ways of God.

I have a destination: with Him and like Him (Rom 8, Eph 1).

But, but, but... He only smiles when I demand to know much more... "trust Me, walk with Me, I know the way. If it were very, very scary I would tell you... it's not."

Day 158
Plans and Obedience

So…Peter, the fisherman, walked on water.

Wave-walking Peter, responding to the prompting of the Lord suddenly, in the moment, shifted focus from Jesus and His promise to come to Him, to considering the very real impossibilities of what he was certainly just now doing and was sunk.

Yet elsewhere Jesus says to "count the cost" when building or warring (Lk 14) - to think, plan, ponder, weigh, and to gain a wise strategy. Seems contradictory.

There is a moment-by-monent-ness (tactics) in the Lord AND a count-the-cost-ness (strategy) too. Understanding the difference makes the difference.

Solomon explains the dynamic in a sentence or two: *"The plans of the heart belong to man, but the answer of the tongue is from the LORD. In his heart a man plans his course, but the LORD determines his steps"* (Prov 16:1,9).

Don't pack up and go to China on a whimsical word saying "God will supply". Without fear, plan it through. But when a prepared heart meets an opportune (kairos) moment it is normally a good move to go on "auto Spirit" partnering with the One who prompts you what to say or do and see what happens (Lk 21:14).

Normally good stuff happens, God stuff, stuff you write down later thinking - "I thought I was sunk, I am not that smart!"

Walk on... water.

Day 159
Gourmet God

So... last night I experienced a meal like I have never had.

My son put on a gourmet showcase that had me almost in tears.

Oh my, course after course - each made of multiple ingredients exploding my taste buds. Too much, to extravagant?

Hmmm. I can guilt myself sometimes.

I laid down last night thinking of how proud I am of his self-taught skills... and I heard "Lavish is My middle name you know. I could use a man like that."

I suddenly recalled this long forgotten verse *"The LORD of hosts will prepare a lavish banquet for all peoples on this mountain; a banquet of aged wine, choice pieces with marrow, and refined, aged wine."* (Is 25:6).

Yesssssssssss! God is a foodie!!

He lavishes love on us (1 Jn 3:1), grace on us (Eph 1:8), and... food too.

He could use a man like that... well done son!!

Day 160
If You Love Me

My friend Scotty Smith wrote:

Jesus says to us, "If you love me, you'll obey my teaching",

not, "If you obey my teaching, I'll love you."

(John 14:23)

Day 161
Christ Like

So…you are what?

Friends of mine are suffering strong criticism for claiming to "hear or see God" in the midst of a prayer ministry session for somebody.

The critics say they want the ministry to be "biblical". I have to ask - what bible are they reading?

Let's put it this way. I want to be Christ like. Well, what was Christ like?

Here is what He said verbatim about how He operated: *"I tell you the truth, the Son can do nothing by Himself; He can do only what He sees his Father doing. For I did not speak of my own accord, but the Father who sent Me commanded Me what to say and how to say it. So whatever I say is just what the Father has told Me to say."* (Jn 5:19, 12:49).

And for me too: *"As the Father has sent Me, even so I am sending you. For as many as are led by the Holy spirit they are the sons of God."* (Jn 20:21, Rom 8:14)."

And am I afraid I will only hear Satan: *"Now suppose one of you fathers is asked by his son for a fish; he will not give him a snake instead of a fish, will he? Or if he is asked for an egg, he will not give him a scorpion, will he? If you then, being evil, know how to give good gifts to your children, how much more will your heavenly Father give the Holy Spirit to those who ask Him?"* (Lk 11:11-13)

Of course there are safeguards. Of course we hear in part and submit what we hear to the word and each other. If you say you talk to God you are considered holy. If you say He talks back you are thought a heretic. Are we crazy? Are we misled?

As a parent if a child avoids direct conversations with me it makes me kinda wonder... what are they afraid of?

What?

Day 162
Listen Up

So…afraid to come to America?

Last night I heard that some Muslims are afraid to come to the USA for fear of the crime and violence. Some of us think most of them are terrorists. And the non-citizen Obama IS Muslim, right?

We, of course, know the first is silly. Muslims think the second is. And a high schoolmate of Obama told me that he witnessed him make a very real profession of Christian faith.

Jesus said *"If anyone has ears to hear, let him hear. Take care what you listen to. By your standard of measure it will be measured to you; and more will be given you besides. For whoever has, to him more shall be given; and whoever does not have, even what he has shall be taken away from him"* (Mk 4:23-25).

Listen up!

In God's economy the rich in godly spiritual listening and God-led thought get richer still. Those who lust after ear-tickling foolishness become dimly discerning, and "merely human" (Jude).

Paying attention to gossip, myth, and suspicion make me think I know less than I NEED to know, but in reality they lead Me to know less than I OUGHT to.

Be constantly nourished on the words of the faith and of the sound doctrine which you have been following. But have nothing to do with worldly fables fit only for old women. On the other hand, discipline yourself for the purpose of godliness; godliness is profitable for all things, since it holds promise for the present life and also for the life to come. (1 Tim 4:6-8)

I have the mind of Christ - with it I will listen up… not down.

Day 163
One Spirit

So…Jesus prayed according to God's will and got His prayers answered right?

So then what happened to His most public prayer *"I would that they all be one even as You and I are one"* (Jn17)?

I was raised Catholic, my wife Church of Christ. She studied about me in her cults class (!).

Paul's standard of not being "one" was simple: *"You say I am of Paul, I am of Barnabus"* (1 Cor 3). He called it "merely human" in Jude. I have been a lot of places and now consider myself a very strict member of the First Apostolic Evangelmatic Cathyterian Bapticostal Church of Christ God Incarnate!

I think maybe God defines "one" a different way: *"But the one who joins himself to the Lord is one spirit with Him"* (1 Cor 6:17). *"For by one Spirit we were all baptized into one body, whether Jews or Greeks, whether slaves or free, and we were all made to drink of one Spirit"* (1 Cor 12:13). *"For through him we both have access to the Father by one Spirit"* (Eph 2;18).

One Spirit - in, through, above, among… one.

That "one" defining Spirit is a transcendent underground river flowing among children of God - non-doctrinal, non-hierarchical, non-geographic, non-exclusionary, apolitical, mutually dependent, and unselfish.

One.

Prayer answered.

Day 164
Hand Wringing

So…one more thing added to the long list of things to not wring my hands about.

NASA just doubled its estimated number of asteroids - 4,700 - potentially able to hit earth. They have spotted only 30% of them.

Revelation's third trumpet blast could even be an asteroid: *"The third angel sounded, and a great star fell from heaven, burning like a torch, and it fell on a third of the rivers and on the springs of waters"* (Rev 8:8).

When Mount St. Helens erupted hundreds of springs got muddy even thousands of miles away (including in Williamson County) and rivers ran with much more sediment shaken loose. When I-840 blasting was being done our well, two miles away, turned brown for three weeks. Not unscientific.

Jesus again and again in Matthew 6:25-34 asked this telling question, *"...and why do you worry about...?"* He then appealed to the reality of Papa's knowing love and sparrows and hairs (Mt 10:29,30). Even so.

Why do I worry about the times, as they affect me - MY times?

David lived this way: *"My times are in your hands oh Lord"* (Ps 31:15).

I will too.

It's all outside my sphere of control, outside my sphere of influence... outside my hand wringing.

If there is any hand wringing to be done I want to let God be the one doing it... though I think He too has better things to do.

Day 165
Crossing the Line

So... today I escalated.

After weeks of fencing, netting, scaring and warning I shot the four rabbits (out of a dozen around) constantly in my garden.

Uncivil? Inhumane? They stopped eating my vegetables.

I remember clearly the line that got crossed when spankings of children happened in our home - and it was very rare, very controlled, very humane... but certain. Archaic? Mean spirited? *"Those who spare the rod of discipline hate their children. Those who love their children care enough to discipline them"* (Prov 13:24).

ALL godly authority has a line and it is a certain fearful comfort to know that.

God says: *"If we deliberately keep on sinning after we have received the knowledge of the truth, no sacrifice for sins is left, but only a fearful expectation of judgment..."* (Heb 10:26ff).

When there is no line or it is delayed (think about our court system): *"Because the sentence against an evil deed is not executed quickly, therefore the hearts of the sons of men among them are given fully to do evil"* (Ecc 8:11).

Given over to evil because there is no line.

When I water down the "fear of the Lord" to mean simple respect, that is way too diluted. Sometimes it is...well... just plain fear. God is faithful and sure to discipline, to punish and to judge. Happy day.

Hebrews writer (and I will too) finishes that thought like this: *"Even though we speak like this, dear friends, we are confident of better things in your case—things that accompany salvation"* (Heb 6:9).

Day 166
Islam

So...I often hear how the Islamic church is SO different from the Christian church. An observation.

As I understand it in Islam there was a general schism into Sunni (original church) and Shia (let's call them protesters or even protestants) over arcane theological differences of lineage and authority.

Each has further split into many liberal and conservative regional and follower-of-famous-Imam-of-the-day flavors stressing sin, grace, obedience, rites, pilgrimage, jihad, freedom, dress, and all manner of side-bar beliefs.

Salafists (Saudis), seeing how complex things got, want to imitate the early church (let's call them "nondenominational") and are seen as intolerant and overzealous by others. Ismailis are laid back and about good works and justice but Shias think they are not "saved" because they ignore doctrinal "purity". Alevis are liberal and want sexual equality but are greatly distrusted by Sunnis. Sufis, ignoring all this mess, took a mystical, sort of "charismatic", turn - even dancing to worship spontaneously and are looked on with distrust by everyone. Ahrnaddiyas are revivalists (lets call the "river church people") but are persecuted by both sides as a "non-biblical" sect. Alawites (ruling Syria) have taken on some non-Islamic rites and beliefs and are seen as post-Islamic heretics (let's call them "Unitarians") by all.

Non-believers wonder at all this discrimination, laugh a bit at the inbreeding, could not tell them apart, think they are wasting time over unimportant religious trivia, and wonder what the ruckus is all about.

See...not so different after all.

Day 167
Real-Time God

So... I am not sure it is a good thing for an engineer to be on the evening news two nights in a row in real-time.

But last night standing in front of about 100 people including a mayor and council and three university professors I got grilled by a large watershed group and flood victims.

The mayor left a little early and a minute later a woman whined - "how can we get the help we need when the mayor leaves!!"

Panic!

Then with my other ear I heard - *"A gentle answer turns away wrath."* (Prov 15:1).

Then I knew.

So I took a chance and said, "Yes, but consider that he was here to listen as long as he could be. You were heard. You have no idea how rare that is."

Time stopped for a second. Then she smiled and others nodded. Staff beamed. And I thought, "I have such a Wonderful Counselor, my real-time God - thanks Holy Spirit."

You do too.

So trust the One who said, *"Do not worry about what to say or how to say it. At that time you will be given what to say"* (Mt 10:19).

Day 168
Conforming

So…I have been to a lot of churches.

I have noticed an interesting thing church to church.

In each one people are very much alike - clothing, spiritual manifestations (or non-manifestations), mannerisms, phrasing, and focus.

Seems we are conforming to each other somewhat… outward mimicry… go along to get along. Its human nature. It is also limiting, stifling, inbred.

My friend Roger said yesterday, "We are supposed to show each other Christ, not that we are Christians."

Paul said: "As a father to you be imitators of me as I also am of Christ (11Cor 11:1, 1 Cor 4:15ff)."

Susan said: "I think we are to encourage and imitate the 'following of Christ' in others not their outward behavior." Seems biblical: *"For those whom He foreknew, He also predestined to become conformed to the image of His Son, so that He would be the firstborn among many brethren."* (Rom 8:29)

Peter wrote: *"You have received a unique grace, employ it in serving one another as good stewards of the manifold grace of God."* (1 Pet 4:10)

"Manifold" means "many different colors."

I want to encourage uniqueness, variety, crazy colors… even paisley (you know who you are!).

And I want to follow hard with others after Christ, following the following of my spiritual fathers.

Day 169
Change

So…I found the old bearded man today at the farmer's market.

He is a bit famous, an expert in native plants and their many uses. Feathers in his cap. He told me, "The combination of ignorance and arrogance is deadly to the earth. We Americans, a minority in the earth, are at odds with God's ways in nature."

It has always been in vogue to be smarter than a boring old God. *"My people are fools; they do not know me. They are senseless children; they have no understanding."* (Jer 4:22).

It has always been fashionable to leave the old ways behind and to be a trend setter in new-think political correctness: *"Where is the wise man? Where is the scholar? Where is the philosopher of this age? Has not God made foolish the wisdom of the world?"* (1 Cor 1:20).

It has always been proud men's' ways to be the first to quickly push outside the old boundary: *"Although they claimed to be wise, they became fools."* (Rom 1:22).

"New, better, different" is not always superior to proven, organic, sustainable.

"Thus says the LORD, 'Stand by the ways and see and ask for the ancient paths, where the good way is, and walk in it; and you will find rest for your souls.'" (Jer 6:16)

I think I sometimes like being unfashionably late to the change-party.

Day 170
Happy Endings

"I have a saying. I believe that all things will end well. If it is not well... then it is not the end yet."

So says the proprietor of the Most Exotic Marigold Hotel (movie).

Love that line, but really now?!

But God said it too: *"And we know that in all things God works for the good of those who love Him, who have been called according to his purpose."* (Rom 8:28).

His eternal solid-gold hotel is the ultimate "making things right" end point.

But note that it is a very, very generous check - but not a blank check.

You still gotta check in I guess.

I love a happy ending - don't you?

Day 171
Father's Day

I believe in a God who is not some Scrooge weighing my actions in a balance ready to punish; not some nice but absent being busy somewhere else in the universe; not some lightening welding being only kept at bay by Jesus.

Nope.

That is not my experience at all.

Jesus says this one phrase many times... but I always missed it... for years: "the One who sent Me..." (Jn 7, 8, 12, 14). Sent me. Sent me.

Asked Jesus "Will you go help Me help them."

The story of Papa God, of Christianity, is the story of a loving Father in anguish that he lost all His children and, while we were still in ignorant rebellion, sent His only One after us, risking all to win us back.

Not counting our failures against us; not remaining aloof until we obtain some behavioral norm; not making us pay something back for running the earth into a ditch... but taking up residence with and in us - unalterable, unchangeable, undeniable love.

Happy Father's day Papa God... I love you.

Thanks for holding my hand.

Be home soon.

Day 172
All Growed Up

So... at a recent wedding as I looked at my kids old friends I kept hearing "all growed up."

I smiled.

I still thought of them as silly kids.

Today I met with the mayor of Huntsville. Sleepy little 80's town I thought. Nope - 190,000 population and a paneled skyscraper conference room. Again I heard "all growed up Andy."

What... Oh.

I (and maybe you too) have had this bad habit-of-mind of keeping people frozen in time, in development, in immaturity, in sin and silliness. I may have a sort of negative opinion of them, an attitude - and it stays and stays.

I think God wants me to give them the freedom He gives them - to get "all growed up" - to mature, change, and become the very thing I wished they would be... and more.

He wants me to believe all things about them, to hope all things... and, if proven wrong, to be genuinely surprised and sad and to endure all things (1 Cor 13).

Then maybe I can be all growed up too.

Day 173
Song of Solomon

It is good to remember

That the same God

Who slew the Egyptians

Wrote the Song of Solomon!

Day 174
Aggressively Righteous

So…my friend and mentor Don Finto writes:

From the days of John the Baptist until now, the kingdom of heaven has been forcefully advancing, and forceful men lay hold of it." (Mt 11:12)

I learned a long time ago that if I am not aggressively righteous, I become passively wicked. We can be "Christians" and still never taste life in the kingdom. Yes, He has taken our sins and given us His righteousness.

Yes, "He has made perfect forever those who are being made holy" (Hebrews 10:14). But it's that last part I'm talking about - the "being made holy."

If I intend to taste the holiness of God and live in the perfecting of who I am, If I am to come into the fullness of my destiny to become like Jesus, producing the fruit of the Spirit expressed in "love, joy, peace, patience, kindness, goodness, faithfulness, gentleness, and self-control" (Gal. 5:22), then I must continually press into Him or the world will begin to press into me and His nature in me will become dimmer and dimmer.

If I am not a worshiping man, then anxiety, fear and depression push into me. If I am not a man of prayer, I begin to be king of my own life. If I am not listening carefully for the voice and promptings of the Holy Spirit, my own voice and the voice of the enemy will control me. If the Word of God is not my daily diet, I cannot know the nature of God and will begin to shape Him in my own image.

Demon forces are waiting to invade an empty house (See Mt 12:43-45). I must stay full of Yeshua Himself and His Spirit. Only forceful Godly-aggressive men and women "lay hold of the kingdom!" I want to "take hold of that for which Messiah Yeshua took hold of me" (Phil. 3:12).

Day 175
Simple Enough

Prov 22:4 says, *"The reward of humility and the fear of the LORD are riches, honor and life."*

One simple statement and all that return on investment.

If that is true, and there it is in the bible (!), then there is little else I need to keep firmly in mind, keep tattooed somewhere I can see it.

So... I ask myself today, if that is so simple why do I seem to forget it so often?

Humility is about how I consider others above and before myself. Fear of the Lord is how I consider God above and before myself.

Growing old is as inevitable as gravity - and has the same effect. Growing wise? Not so much. I sometimes feel like I haven't had 40 years as a believer but 1 year with 39 do-overs!

When I look back on the things that went not so great this is what I see - one of those two things, humility or fear of the Lord, was missing in the situation.

But this is cool about that: you and I actually get do-overs. That is encouraging.

God knows I can eventually get it right - even normally and naturally (with a bit o' super help before that "naturally").

He is pulling for me.

Seems simple enough.

OK, Tomorrow.

Day 176
Choose Life

So...there are two ways to primarily live life...two only.

The first is to live on the basis of circumstance. "circum - stance" - the word means to stand vigilant looking around me - 365 24/7. I spend my life in an effort to control things around me to my benefit and in fearing...fearing circumstances beyond my control. If I am full of the wisdom of the world then I can become the master of most circumstances. I hedge all my bets when I can. Insurance was made just for me, retirement plans too, and gated communities - extracting from my workers, enslaving my enemies. I can become rich and powerful and seem wise to those around me. I win wars. Solomon was the best there ever was at gaining the world's wisdom to be able to control men and circumstance. Rich beyond measure he was given all the wisdom contained in the world...in the world. And he failed in the end... personally and politically.

The other way is based on principle...God-given, righteous, unchanging, eternally true. These principles derive from another kingdom, the heart of another king, that is superior to this one. Their ways are as high as the heavens are above the earth (Is 55:9). If I attempt to break them I only break myself upon them.

They can appear nonsensical. But they always cause me to prevail...always. When I seek first this kingdom and its way of right living all good things belonging to the first way come to me too. All circumstances work to my eventual good...all circumstances...all (Mt 6:33, Rom 8:28). David chose this way and was given peace on every side - 365 24/7...peace (2 Sam 7:1). I win hearts. Jesus was the best there ever will be at demonstrating a life lived based on God's immutable principles. He did not control men nor did He gain riches. He was killed for His trouble. Or so Jew and Gentile alike thought.

He conquered Rome. He conquered death. Transformed the world. His loving power is all that keeps the world from a hellish existence. All who follow it find peace. He will come again in the midst of the most intense world conflagration that ever will be... and give peace...not as the world gives it (Jn 14:27). Solomon should have asked to know God's heart, not His mind...like his father.

And you... look around you... then choose life.

Day 177
Walking in the Lord

So...I watched a baby learn to walk today.

Down, up, down, up, down, up.

All the while both the baby and the parents were encouraged - even the stumbles were learning, joyful experiences.

Learning to walk is a stumbling experience before it is a walking experience.

So too is walking rightly in life.

"For we all stumble in many ways. If anyone does not stumble... he is a perfect man." (Jas 3:2). Solomon: *"For a righteous man falls seven times, and rises again."* (Prov 24:16)

And just like the parents cheer the baby on our God stands before us, kind eyes, smiling, arms open saying "come to Me!"

"The steps of a man are established by the LORD, and He delights in his way. When he falls, he will not be hurled headlong, because the LORD is the One who holds his hand." (Ps 37:23)

We walk wobbly before we learn to walk worthy. A mistake is not a failure. Even repeated mistakes.

But giving up learning to walk... crawling through life... maybe that is failure. Grant each other grace.

So... *"be steadfast, unmovable, always abounding in the works of the Lord knowing my work in Him is NOT in vain."* (1 Cor 15:58).

Get back up beloved - you are cheered on! There is plenty of time to learn to walk. May even the stumbles be joy in the end.

Day 178
Hidden, Faithful

So...Paul we've heard of. Barnabas, not so much.

Wasn't he the guy who restored Paul?

And Andrew... wasn't he the brother who went and found Peter?

And Mordecai Ham. Who?

Ham was an eighth generation Baptist who tried business but couldn't not preach.

In 1934 in Charlotte he preached a sermon that changed a young man's life. Ham went on to obscurity in the world's eyes.

That young man he led to the Lord? He was named Billy Graham.

Graham has preached to 2.2 billion people, 3.2 million have responded to his sermons. I am one of them. Thank you Mr. Ham - I owe you.

There are many hidden notables, faithful men and women whose quiet witness, consistent lifestyle, ever present encouragement, obedience to prompting, and personal sacrifice have changed the world in ways unknowable... except to God.

I have observed that these are God's favorites. He chooses them, prefers them, watches them, shares His burdens and secrets with them. Most of them are mothers.

You might be one.

We owe you a debt incalculable. Be steadfast, be encouraged - your faithful seeds will yield a harvest.

Day 179
Tempting Temptation

So...temptations are tempting because there is something in me that can actually be tempted.

Seems logical huh?

I spoke last Bleat about the "big three temptation buckets": the lust of the flesh, the lust of the eyes and the boastful pride of life (1 Jn 2:16).

Jesus is talking to his guys and says this: "I will not speak much more with you, for the ruler of the world is coming, and he has nothing in Me." Jn 14:30.

Want him to have nothing in you too? I sure do.

Jesus told us exactly how to get the thing-able-to-be-tempted out before the temptation hits - to get demagnetized. He gave three matching things and told us exactly how to do them in Matthew 6: fasting, giving and praying.

When I make a practice of fasting I directly counter the lust of the flesh and the voice by which I say a resounding "NO!" to my food appetite teaches my flesh to also hear "NO!" to every other temptation and submit. I have better things to do.

When I make a practice of giving (especially directly to something specific) I break the back of the lust of the eyes. I give away the means to obtain that lust - and find I deeply enjoy the love and joy it yields... lasting and rich. I am made rich. Things seem so trifling.

When I make a practice of praying I speak directly against the the boastful pride of life by humbling myself before the One who has every right to boast but does not...He washes feet. And in so doing I realize my own insignificant-yet-lovedness and find true humility. I am so little yet He makes me feel so big in His eyes...He must be near sighted...He sees me when I am near. Pride seems so silly then.

And the "big three"?

Not so big after all.

Day 180
Vitamin Deficiency

So…Susan and I were talking and this is what I heard her say:

The various facets of God are all there to be discovered and absorbed by us; to become part of us.

Various traditions emphasize the part of God that first impressed them.

It may have gotten a bit stale for them, maybe not. But they are mostly proud of it and defend it as being God – "God is…"

We have emphasized certain facets in our circle for a long time. I had not appreciated that those other parts were, in fact, parts of God I knew little of. As if I could apprehend all of God in my few short years.

But not immersing myself in some of the other parts has felt like living with a vitamin deficiency. I am not thriving on a well-rounded God-experience without even knowing it. Like a child first discovering a love for salad, or steak.

I don't know what I don't know – that is the scariest kind of ignorance.

But if I push my puzzle pieces to the middle of the table and take my hands off of them and admit, "You know the sky pieces are just as nice as the green grass pieces, and that piece which has part of the person's face on it, now that cool." There are no "skyites" or "groundaterians" in the Lord.

If I do that, then a beautiful, full, and balanced picture emerges and we all, together, can look in greater awe at our amazing God.

Day 181
Self Portraits

So…such a lovely self-portrait.

I have an ability, shared by all men I suppose, to paint a rather complimentary picture of myself or my institution over time and then to look at it as if I think it is a mirror not a painted image - appreciating its loveliness.

God has a gentle habit of removing the painting to expose the real mirror - and the man (or institution) in the mirror.

Here is one.

We churched-people all share a loathing of the Scribes and Pharisees. So blind, so self-focused, so... awful.

Jesus pulled no punches: *"They make their phylacteries wide and the tassels on their garments long; they love the place of honor at banquets and the most important seats in the synagogues; they love to be greeted in the marketplaces and to have men call them 'Rabbi.'"* (Mt 23:5,6)

But wait! Robes, fancy suits, cool clothing - check.

Front row center in church - check.

Hundreds of likes for almost any Facebook post - check.

"Pastor, doctor or elder so and so" - check.

Symptoms of course. But of what?

Maybe a budding case of log-in-eye syndrome.

Day 182
History in the Heavens

So...want to see history?

On June 30, (2015) at sunset in the West, Venus and Jupiter will be in close conjunction almost exactly (within about 5 seconds of arc) the way they looked when the Magi were leaving Herod's fortress the Herodian and heading toward Bethlehem along a roadway that "just happened" to run right along the ecliptic toward the setting sun (that time of year) - the pathway of the planets through the sky.

They planned to trick Herod, to find the child, present the gifts, and then escape under cover of darkness. The Date was June 17, 2 BC. As they made their way along the road, about a two hour journey, out of the gathering dusk appeared a brilliant orb - actually the conjunction of the third and fourth brightest things in the sky - Venus and Jupiter appear near the king star of Leo - Regulus. It slowly settled into the horizon, hovering and pointing the exact way to go.

You can see it, feel it, experience it (if the sky is clear) - bottom picture. You can sense how, as scripture says, they rejoiced exceedingly with great joy when they saw the star in the setting - the exact thing they saw months earlier in the rising.

A rare near conjunction - which just happened to occur twice that year - and for us once in 2015, and not again for a long time.

Enjoy.

Day 183
Wise Man

OK - you know who you are and you asked for it!

Conjunctions between Venus and Jupiter are not rare. Given the complexities of their two orbits, the fact that only about half of them are visible to us (the rest are too close to or behind the sun), and only a fraction of those are close enough for us to go "oh wow" (maybe 1 in 18 of those) they still happen often enough for us (and the Magi) to be aware of them.

The intervals tend to work like this: 450 days, then 300 days, then 450 days for about 4.5 cycles. Then there are two less than 100 days apart, and then back to the longer cycles again for another 4.5 cycles. About a third of these are less than a half a degree separation where they appear to almost be one whopping big star.

The angle of separation of this one is about 24' (less than half a degree). There will be a one coming up October 26 with a 1°4'. But it will happen on the other side of the sun - at sunrise about the same angle from the sun (called elongation) as this one. The next close angle one is not till November 2017 and then none for a while.

So the things that triggered the Magi to take a chance and travel west were Daniel's prophecy of when Messiah would come (He was due and everyone knew it including the Jews and Romans), this conjunction in Leo portending a great king's birth, and the crowning of Regulus by Jupiter with the mother present over the next few months.

Icing on the cake was the amazing timing of the second conjunction placed right before their eyes the very day they headed to Bethlehem causing them to experience the "triple conjunction of joy" : "When they saw the star, they rejoiced exceedingly with great joy" (Mt 2:10). Meaning, of course, that they did not see the star when they began their walk and then they suddenly did as the sun set and the stars came out. You can watch that phenomena for the next few days looking west and be wise, man.

Day 184
Helpmate Suitable

So…Adam was the CEO of the whole world - everything was under his authority and would be for all eternity (or so the plan).

Everything that was created God said, "that's good," until he saw Adam's state… it is <u>not good</u> for a man to be alone I will make him a "helpmate suitable."

Adam, typical man, looks at her form and says loosely in Hebrew "OOOO la la." He doesn't know her from…well, from Adam. Yet his naïve trust is in the creator.

But God's plan is far more attractive. "Helpmate" is a name He gives himself when talking about the Holy Spirit (see next Bleat). Adam can now hear God in stereo - for encouragement when he is down, correction when he is wrong, and love all the time.

"Suitable" also means "opposite, against, before, across from." She is exactly the same as him and exactly opposite at the same time - like two matching bookends - filling in where there is a gap, each holding up its end or it all falls apart.

Each man and woman perfectly matched, and perfect opposites.

On that one God said "very good" (Gen 1:31)!

Marriage was God's idea. YOUR marriage was God's idea.

Day 185
...And So Much More

So... more about Eve

About women, I think we got it wrong guys... on two counts (at least).

God called Eve a "helper suitable" to Adam, interpreted by some as "Adam's little helper" - sort of demeaning and limiting. Can she only find her life's meaning with respect to Adam. Nope.

First, God calls Himself by the same name in helping men (Ps 54:4, Jn 14:26, Heb 13:6). It is Adam's lack and limitation, not hers, God is addressing.

In that role she is "god-like" to him.

Second, that role "helper" is just ONE of her skills (the one Adam most needed) not her all-inclusive title.

Her universe of potential is unlimited by God. We see a litany of some of her other possibilities: business executive, artist, entrepreneur, trader, designer, manufacturer, mother, philanthropist, city leader (Prov 31).

"Give her the reward she has earned, and let her works bring her praise at the city gate."

It is only God's mercy that she so loves and wants to help her man.

Had she been made first we might not even be around.

Day 186
Living on Credit

So...God wants us to live on credit.

Yup.

A friend told me that he felt God said to him, "Turn in your two weeks' notice." He explained that both he and God were tired of that sort of "gotcha" relationship where he kept working to please someone who, in his mind, always found something else that was not pleasing - trying to earn that acceptance.

Can't keep up the payments.

It's a strange conundrum in Christianity: *"Now to the one who works, his wage is not credited as a favor, but as what is due. But to the one who does not work, but believes in Him who justifies the ungodly, his faith is credited as righteousness."* (Rom 4:4).

Living on credit - given freely by God - stopping the low grade feverish feeling of unacceptability on the inside.

Am I feeling ungodly? Unattractive? Unworthy?

If so (and only if so) then I am qualified for this out-of-this-world credit plan - and... no payments... ever!

Day 187
Trinity Tree

So... I mowed around it.

About ten years ago I was mowing and, uncharacteristically, decided to mow around a small group of three twigs that had sprung up - about an inch high.

I marked them with a flag - not knowing what they were but feeling like they were worth it.

Not sure why. I'm not that sort who coddles uninvited growth. I mow it.

That was 15 years ago.

Now this trinity-tree of three joined trunks is a daily delight when I stand at the deck with morning coffee. It stands 35 feet high, perfectly formed – three trees in one.

Last night a friend told me how the interest and encouragement I spoken to someone served as a key for her to continue a seemingly floundering singing career - now, ten years later, she is a daily delight to thousands.

Thought maybe God said, *"I like it when you see what I see in a twig and do not mow it over. See what great thing a tiny mustard seed of life can become."*

I want to look around every day when mowing through life - and stop, flag, and nurture the twigs of promise He shows the observant.

It costs me little but an encouraging word. My planted delight in them can become a daily delight later.

"Therefore encourage one another and build up one another, just as you also are doing." (1 Th 5:11).

Day 188
Wisdom

So…the accumulation of knowledge.

When the soul is at work facts are learned and assembled to become information.

Information is organized to become knowledge.

Knowledge applied again and again becomes understanding.

That is the best the soul can do – gain understanding. God aids for sure – like helping a child learn math.

But the ability to apply understanding wisely – to know the time, place, approach – to suddenly "get" something, insight, to see a road map or a next step, to know inside – that has another source (Prov 2). It comes from the other side – far from the brain.

To say to God, "Help me be wise in this," is a very good thing. Solomon did it (1 Kg 3:9) and it made all the difference. James (1:5) says to pray that way and know for sure God will answer…for sure.

But I must watch out – when I pray like that I must mean it. I will get on the moving sidewalk… for sure. Build understanding, ask for wisdom.

When they meet enjoy the ride.

Day 189
Writers Block

So… feeling indecisive? Or are you not sure? ☺

Indecision, writers block, the "paralysis of analysis" masquerades as thoughtfulness but, in the end, is outed as either fear or as mixed desire.

Jam 1:5-8 deals with fear and doubt - being in two minds leads to instability in everything - a lifestyle of second guessing.

1Kg 18:21 is an example with mixed desires - wanting Baal and God - lukewarm incompatibility leading to failure at both.

Every decision involves risk and uncertainty - or there would be no decision.

On the inside I must grab my heart with both hands, look it in the eye, and say, "I am going to <u>choose</u> God and I am going to <u>trust</u> God."

I don't trust my choices, efforts and decisions, but I know the One who can make even a mistake turn out right.

Writers block? Life block?

I can always edit a bad page.

I can't edit a blank page.

Day 190
The Making of a Great President

So...What to look for in a president?

Harvard professor J. Rufus Fears, in recounting the lessons learned from history lists four things that mark the great world-changing statesmen of the ages and sets them apart from mere politicians:

- a life built on unchanging principles,
- a moral compass in decision making,
- a vision for what they are leading is "supposed" to become, and
- an ability to make peace and build consensus among rivals.

From earliest civilization to present he tells stories about those men and women.

It makes me yearn for a David, a Washington, an Alexander... none in sight.

That calls for prayer.

But most of all it makes me want to build those things ever more in my own life and that of others I influence.

Hoping its not to late - on both counts.

Day 191
Know My Limits

So...God calls us to life on the edge; content and discontent - resting and striving.

History and scripture both teach us that God sets boundaries or limits on nations, organizations and men.

God sets national boundaries in space and time (Deut 32:8). Rome stayed, Napoleon and Alexander strayed.

Jesus was called only to Jews and would not engage the Greeks (Mt 15), Paul was forbidden to preach in Asia (Acts 16).

When we, in ignorance or greedy hubris, stray outside our God-set boundaries we inevitably invite destruction. Equally when we, in fear or laziness, shrink back from the fullness of our inheritance we invite loss and displeasure (Heb 10:35ff).

I want to be humble enough to live righteously within my boundaries - fully content with career and calling.

I want to be confident enough to expand fully to their edge - living and growing fearlessly under God in my career, relationships, and sphere of influence.

Here is life: understanding my limits and believing without limit within them; saying like David, *"the boundary lines have fallen for me in pleasant places; surely I have a delightful inheritance."* (Ps 16:6)

Day 192
Honest Abe

So...Honest Abe

Lincoln, the back woods man with one year of education, who told bad jokes and was awkward socially encountered the erudite exegetical religious hierarchy in opposing slavery.

The convoluted scriptural logic supportive of slavery is logically irrefutable.

This was his exchange with his senatorial opponent:

"Sir are you a Christian?"

"Yes, of course"

"Sir you always want to obey the golden rule then?"

"Yes, of course (idiot!)"

"Then sir, would you want to become the slave of another?" [angry silence - crowd cheers].

That inescapable simple truth won him the presidency, his head on the penny and the eternal gratitude of millions... and cost him his life laid down.

Not by might, not by power, but by my Spirit says the Lord.

More Lord.

Day 193
The Relevant Gospel of Love

So… his t-shirt said "Big Pimp."

I thought, in what parallel universe is that cool?

In church a 17 year old boy stood with his friends and spoke about his desire to save his classmates.

Same question, I thought, would be asked.

Which is the "real" world? Do I live in it? Is it poor, nasty, and violent? Is it peaceful, nice, even cheesy?

I think yes... to both.

I want to be relevant in the real world, to make a difference but how - my street lingo is pretty limited (understatement of the day!).

Jesus made a bold claim: "I am the way, the truth, and the life" (Jn 14:6).

I have found on four continents that God can create relevancy through me in any situation because the common "lingua franca" is the cry of the human heart for love and understanding and the answer to that cry can come from God through me to street thugs, church boys, rural African natives, south American Indians, Yankees, Catholics, the old, kids, European intelligentsia, and even Charismatics!

Day 194
Being Prophetic

So…are you prophetic?

Someone sort of criticized a ministry I greatly respect for "spending too much time teaching people to be prophetic."

Actually, I they have not gone far enough. This is what I mean.

Jesus said in places in John, "I do nothing 'out of' myself but only that which I see the Father doing and her the Father saying."

All He said and did was at the initiative of the Father.

What is "prophecy" anyway but trying to do and say what you are presently hearing God say and do. Paul even defines it in 1 Cor 14 as exhorting people that they can make it when they are about to quit, speaking about being in relation and building up that persons connections, and speaking sweet comfort to one who is in need.

Who doesn't want that in their life, in their friends, in their mate?

All we have to do is get it out of the church where it is held in sterile captivity and onto the streets and in families where it belongs.

Maybe we should just call it "doing life together with Jesus" and teach others to do it…

> …when I learn it, I mean.

Day 195
The Cost of Choosing

So…what is the real cost of choosing?

In real terms it costs me $35 and two hours every time I commute to work; could be $9,000 and 520 hours a year - out of my pocket and out of my life.

I think twice - drive less.

God wants me to be good at counting… counting the cost of decisions - good and bad. He wants me, for example, to know the cost of following Him. (Lk 14:28). Decisions have consequential costs. Col 3:25 says *"He who does wrong will receive the consequences, and that without partiality."*

Proverbs 7 talks of the young man unknowingly paying with his life for pleasure. Moses struck the rock and paid with a loss of a ticket to the promised land where such actions would cost Israel their lives. Esau bought the gruel and sold his birthright, proving he was not qualified to be the chosen one carrying the promise.

Paul says: *He who is spiritual appraises all things, yet he himself is appraised by no one.* (1 Cor 2:15) As spiritual people we have an ability to appraise the true worth of things - physical, spiritual, here and hereafter - out of my pocket and out of my life; to assay the risk and reward.

James 1:5 says I can ask God's opinion, get His wisdom - He seems to appreciate that. I want to choose wisely, not have the choice made unknowingly for me… by me.

Think twice.

Choose once.

Day 196
Perceiving God

So...Phillip wants to see God.

The story is recounted in John 14. He says, *"Lord, show us the Father, and it is enough for us."* Jesus says, *"Have I been so long with you, and yet you have not come to know Me. He who has seen Me has seen the Father; how can you say, 'Show us the Father'?"*

How indeed?

There is a way of living life with God where I am not really with God - I am always looking forward to a self-described time when God does something to grab my attention, for something sparkly to manifest, to awe me, goose bumps.

I am creating my own expectation of what a God-encounter looks like that God probably does not intend to fulfill. Phillip-like I say, "Show up God." I am looking up looking for God in the sky when He is maybe walking right past me, even right with me, all the time.

But there is another way to live, without discounting the other, where I find I can stop and savor God right now, this instant, right here with me, in the now, slowly, now. That is where He Himself says He dwells.

He IS here, I just need to stop and see, sense, hear, feel Him on His terms, in His way...not mine.

Then mmmmm. Like sipping an amazing something with a burn and a sweetness that leaves me slightly lightheaded, happy, warm.

You have so long been with me Papa.

And it is enough for me.

Day 197
Suffering

So...I generally oppose suffering as contrary to God's will.

Certainly it is contrary to mine. Paul did too and was surprised when God did not deliver him (2 Cor 12).

But there is suffering that God allows because it is the only way for me to learn a far, far deeper truth about His grace, strength, and ability within us. Christ learned it too: *"although he was a son, he learned obedience from what he suffered."* (Heb 5:8)

There is only one way to know the amazing grace that bears up wonderfully in the midst of suffering instead of the grace that simply rescues (good as that is)... and that is to suffer: *"those who suffer according to God's will should commit themselves to their faithful Creator and continue to do good."* (1 Pet 4:19)

I find Him all-sufficient, more than enough, and get a taste of the power that caused the martyrs to laugh and praise in the midst of deadly torment.

He will limit the test (1 Cor 10:13) to His grace in me and *"after you have suffered a little while, He will Himself restore you and make you strong, firm and steadfast."* (1 Pet 5:10)

On the other side of suffering abounding grace is no longer just theory,

...and neither is my character.

Day 198
Save Your Own Life

So...what is this greater love?

Jesus said, "Greater love has no one than this, that he lay down his life for his friends. (Jn 15:13)"

When young I thought of this in terms of soldiers who threw themselves on live grenades. Heroic life-laid-down action.

Now I know more.

A life laid down is not so much taking a one-time action based on making a onetime decision - that's relatively easy.

I think a life laid down looks more like a faithful father going off to work, a great teacher staying in a poor school, a 20 something caring for their aging parent, someone abused refusing anger in favor of forgiveness, an unwed mother giving her years to her child.

It is the faithful, hard, maybe even torturous decision to day-after-day do the right thing, to give up your rights even in the face of another's wrongs.

To take up your cross daily and follow Christ means to end up where He is... and there it will be...

your life...

saved for you...

for eternity.

Day 199
Maybe Syndrome

So…have you noticed the spreading pandemic?

I call it "commitment deficit disorder" (CDD), or "maybe syndrome".

It is spreading everywhere, even among believers (maybe especially) and looks like: agreeing and then backing out, promising and then forgetting, always being late, avoiding commitment, keeping your options open, being "flexible".

In Mt 21:28 Jesus called it what it is: unfaithfulness.

He named it's source: *"Simply let your 'Yes' be 'Yes,' and your 'No,' 'No'; anything beyond this comes from the evil one."* (Mt 5:7)

Solomon got it too: "Many a man proclaims his own loyalty, but who can find a trustworthy man? (Prov 20:6)."

I want to be loyal... be faithful; to let my "Yes" mean something... be found by Him trustworthy and so...

…I will find myself trusted by Him.

Day 200
Work While You Wait

So…three teachers won the lottery - but stayed anonymous and kept working.

I love that.

One is exciting - the other is satisfying... and effort to be sure.

Sometimes what I might want to call "faith" or "waiting on God" in reality is maybe a lot more about fear and passivity - I am hoping to win the Christian-lottery of supernatural blessing.

But God's blessing predominantly works as a co-laboring (1 Cor 3:9, 2 Cor 6:1). He initiates, and then I partner in work, investment, and effort.

I experience the supernatural as "supering the natural". It is not wrong to go hard after something you sense He has promised. Every bible character did it that way - Jesus too.

That is how the Promised Land was conquered. God said, "I have given you the land... now YOU take it." (Deut 1:8).

That is how the land of promises is taken too.

Don't be shy - give Him something to bless.

Let your sandals touch the river's edge and watch Him part it (Josh 3:15).

Day 201
The Truck

So… it seems kind of silly.

14 years ago I saw a pickup truck and thought "that is the truck for me country boy."

Then, others needed cars - one after another, after another... I so enjoyed providing for them that like Jacob in Gen 29:20 the years seemed but a few days until I realized: what... 14 years!?!

I have come to realize there is a proper God-planned time for everything in life - sex, children, marriage, job promotion, possessions, moving on, and four-wheel drive trucks.

Giving that good desire into God's keeping and pursuing the kingdom and life rather than that thing is the only way to live in contentment and joy (that "seek ye first" thing - Mt 6:33).

Waiting for that "fulness of time" somehow is right.

He will either change your heart or change your circumstance... in His time.

Today I bought that truck and the forgotten hope deferred all came flooding back in a quiet joy.

A truck!?

I know, it's a guy thing.

Day 202
Friend Indeed

So...1989 Denver hotel...

Four speakers on stage to speak knowingly about on important EPA regulation - three Western leaders and lastly a 36 year-old youngish substitute...me...

1,000 engineers from all over the West were eager to hear the new impositions. Except the regulations are stuck in Office of Management and Budget unreleased. I told a Wash DC friend my predicament that morning.

We have nothing to say!! I especially have nothing to say. SO nervous. The first... then the second say nothing but say it smartly and sit down. Third is mumbling about being sorry but... everyone just knows they have wasted their time.

Suddenly a bellman sprints to the podium and hands me a fax. "Merry Christmas" the cover sheet says. It is the salient pages from the regulations from my friend – 18 minutes after being released from OMB...18 minutes.

I stand up to speak trembling, "I have the regulations here just out of OMB. I will simply read them to you and then the others can weight in. I will be glad to make copies at the front desk for anyone who desires."

Dead silence... then a single clap...then more...then cheers. I read them out loud, embarrassed in that good way a child is when praised in front of strangers by their dad.

Handshakes, back slaps, business cards all around. Consulting doors opened throughout the West from that day on.

And I knew, knew, knew "not from the east, nor from the west comes promotion, but God...". (Ps 75)

Friend in need - Friend indeed.

Day 203

Ssssssssssssssssso

Ssssssssssssssssssoooooooooooooo... let me think about these humans. Their master tries to make them look at the sky at night to see His supposed glory and to understand His silly story. What bunk. He says they will be able to know all that is important about Him if they will look up...long and deep. How can I put a sssssssssstop to that? Hmmmmmmmmmmssssssssss.

Sssssssssssssssssay! I know. Perfect... perfect.

First I will take advantage of their gullibility and make them think that the sky itself is god... that the stars influence, maybe for the most easily misled even control, their lives. Yes the sun god, the moon god. By Jupiter I've got it. Sure I know it is me they worship. Sssssssssssssssso good.

Next, for those not so gullible but full of pride I will take advantage of them by making them miss the obvious and believe everything is lifeless and "just happened". I can pull that off but how do I handle the obvious "beginning of all things" problem? Ssssssssssssssssssssscience can solve that one... with my help of course. If "no god exists" is the starting place these men can be led anywhere. Anywhere...logical step by logical step, theory by theory.

Finally for those troublesome sons and daughters of light... what to do? Ah, of course. I can ssssssssssssssssscare them away from the heavens by having the gullible ones declare the stars tell their own story not Elohim's. It will be so deliciously blasphemous that they will shut up the heavens their own selves rather than participate in such godless astrology. Perfect. Throw the truth out with the lies.

Perfect.

How do the sons of Adam say it now... oh yes... three ssssssssssssstrikes and you're out.

Perfect.

Now all I have to do is shut up the ones who know... they are trouble!

Day 204
That Day

So…I try to just imagine how it was.

You know.

You see a Guy tortured to death and buried.

He's dead man… dead.

You are huddled in fear. When will they come for me?

And then some ex-prostitute runs in screaming she has seen Him - alive!! What!?!

You are sitting around in wonder - of two minds both of them in extreme emotional states.

And then…then… there He is.

And He did NOT come in through the door.

No matter how many times He says "peace" your heart is still a staccato beat.

This changes everything… EVERYTHING!!!

Everything.

Still does.

Day 205
Stress Reducer

So…just one more way good science seems to be tracking God (who is a bit ahead I guess!).

Harvard Business School Prof Michael Norton did a detailed study of stress and the potential impact of doing something kind for someone.

He found a remarkable correlation between spending time, even extra time, devoted to someone else and a feeling of wellbeing, rest and of "having more time" in life.

Of course his "why this must be" was sort of oblique.

I think it might just be: *"Give and it shall be given unto you good measure, pressed down, shaken together and running over. For whoever wishes to save his life will lose it; but whoever loses his life for My sake will find it."* (Lk 6:38 , Mt 16:25)

Day 206
Caught in the Act

So... older flight attendant shrilly, "everyone just STOP, I told you we have no more room for luggage now turn around and leave it..."

Shock and silence, nervous twitters.

I am outraged, I want her name to report her. She tries to make a covering joke. Awkward. Worse.

She was horrible, caught, right in the act... right in...

Then Papa mentions something, "Did you notice how my other Son handled that?"

Then I did. The woman caught in adultery...right... compassion for her pain, her exposure, her shame (Jn 8:1-11).

Wise words. Put down the stone, and be redemptive and compassionate.

A few kind words was all I had time for... but I had two hours to repent and change my heart.

He who began a good work in me will complete it until the day of Christ (Phil 1:6).

Day 207
New Every Morning

So…I love many things about God…

…how He is described, how I experience Him.

Maybe this is my favorite.

Many biblical addresses say that God <u>never</u> changes... never changes.

And one thing about Him that never changes is this: *"The Lord's lovingkindnesses indeed never cease, for His compassions never fail. They are new every morning; great is Your faithfulness."* (Lam 3:23)

Now get this.

His expression of loving compassion is fresh, new, alive, different, unique, intriguing, provoking, stirring every morning... every... morning.

And that fresh and newness never changes.

His never changing habit of being new every morning.

Oh my!!

Day 208
Immense

The <u>nearest</u> star to us - the one we would borrow sugar from is 4.3 light years away.

At 100 miles per hour that would only take... 29 MILLION years to get there (!).

To the nearest star.

One of maybe 400 billion in one galaxy; one of 200 billion galaxies. Good grief the galaxy is big, the universe is immense beyond understanding.

Now get this.

"He determines the number of the stars and calls them each by name." (Ps 147:4)
Who is like the LORD our God, Who is enthroned on high, Who humbles Himself to behold The things that are in heaven and in the earth? (Ps 113:6)

God has to stoop down, and squint (not really) to see it, He looks down on the whole thing like a bug on the sidewalk. He calls each itty bitty star, all 8×10^{22} of them by a unique name. And I'm betting they are not like Fred and Tex and Betty. That's 10 trillion stars per person.

Such numbers make me silly giddy.

And he numbers my hairs.

It is sometimes good for me, like David, to press the reset button on my "God in a box" circuit and to shake my head and admit *"such knowledge is too wonderful for me, too lofty for me to attain."* (Ps 139:6)

Day 209
I Am

So...I want some things to be so in my life. Just like everybody.

I want to know where and how to go. How to do life. I'm not sure I know how – pretty sure I do not.

I want what's real. I don't want to waste my life on the false and empty and to find out too late. I want to experience real life.

I bet you do too.

Jesus said "I am the way, the truth and the life." It is way, way too easy to dismissively say "right, I've heard that before" and assign it to the old-familiar-verse-heap at the back of the closet.

But look again. So this verse suddenly changed right before my eyes this morning when I asked about all that.

Something scary revolutionary is in the wind here.

He is not talking about knowing His teaching, trying to emulate His lifestyle, or attempting to be holy.

He is talking about Himself here not His teaching or even His example.

He is saying, "In a real, living, actual, measurable way I myself will live inside of you. No really. Two spirits will share one body and I will live heart-in-heart with you and within you. If you want to...that is."

I think I do. You?

Way. Truth.

Life.

Day 210
Genesis of Estrangement

So…back in the garden, back in the beginning there was a seed planted.

God said this: "From any tree you may eat freely but from the tree of the knowledge of good and evil you shall not eat or you will die."

The woman said this: "From the trees we may eat but from the tree in the middle of the garden you shall not eat or touch it, or you will die."

Did you see it? It is subtle. Read that again.

Herein is birthed the genesis and prototype of all alienation of men from God. The snake hissed "hath God really said?" And then helped her to subvert and pervert His words and thus His essence.

Eve unwittingly obscured and constrained God's lavish provision ("freely") and added a straightjacket of stupid and oppressive legalism ("or touch it") loathsome to any free man.

And she began tacking in a direction subtly away from the real God and His real character and actual love toward us. So do we all.

Such are the misbegotten seeds of rebellion against a contrived god-caricature who only exists in the dark schemes of Satan and his misled minions be they Pharisees, popes

… or sometimes me.

Day 211
Ready to Go

So... he was 90 years old. Ninety.

He was there for ministry - inner healing - Mexican man old and gnarled.

He had a long history of failings, but not this day. This day he started from before any were born and confessed, and wept, and opened his heart and life and talked some more. Ninety years of stuff.

Then he was finished.

Quietly the ministry team began to tell him of the forgiveness found in his savior. It's not about sin. Never will be again. Don't get me wrong. Sin is not unimportant. It is so important God took care of it Himself.

He saw it. Saw it clearly even though nearly blind... He saw again.

And wept. The team waited.

Then hesitantly he told them of something he was planning to do, something wicked. But he gave it too to God. Willingly.

Then it happened. He closed his eyes and saw God on a horse with a sombrero... God himself tipped his hat to the man in honor.

He wept and said, "I am ready to go now - I am finally ready."

The team wept.

Day 212
Made in Heaven

So… marriages are made in heaven.

God Himself walks with Adam and STILL says it is not good for Adam to be alone.

Hmmmmm.

So He brings Eve, and even though Adam knows NOTHING about the girl (she has been alive for like 15 minutes) he is ecstatic.

Why? The answer is <u>the</u> key to marriage.

Adam believed that this woman was God's very best choice for him and everything, everything else was intended to play out with that in mind.

The good and the bad, easy and hard, joyful and sorrowful;

the "for better or worse-ness" of marriage, when cast against the backdrop of that certainty - this girl is made for me, and I am made for her - will bring joyful fullness to each if both hold on to that one truth and order all else in its light.

It is the foundation to which I can return after a misunderstanding, a sense of distance, differences over an issue. I can value whatever she says and does in light of this…and then I find I change in subtle ways, She does to.

And the sparks and light we bring each other hone us to the character ready for eternity. Fit for heaven.

I've tried it for over three decades.

Works. Good.

Day 213
The Heart for It

So... everybody complains about the weather but nobody does anything about it.

The weather - today, tomorrow, next week and next year is a product of the climate. Climates produce weather. The debate about the causes of climate change (as reflected in weather change) is raging but this fact is true - we men CAN influence the climate. If we have the heart for it.

Everybody talks about behavior but nobody does anything about it.

But behavior is like weather - it is an end product - it is the out-flowing of character. Character is like climate. Character produces behavior. And character, at its essence, lies in the heart of a man. That is why Solomon says: "Above all else, guard your heart, for everything you do flows from it" (Prov 4:23).

My heart is exactly like my garden. Today I weeded it, pruned it, pulled off bugs. I want good fruit (and vegetables). Proverbs says to "tend" our hearts - the same word God used with Adam and Eve and Eden. Jesus says that out of my heart my mouth speaks and my behavior erupts - can't help it - I am what my heart is (Mk 7).

How do I tend my garden, change my climate?

First of all, I can watch what goes in - junky input; junky heart; junky me. I can put a gate guard on my soul, my eyes, my ears, my time... my affections.

Secondly, I can watch how I water what is there. Thinking, pondering, preoccupation, meditation is like watering. I can put good things close at hand so in free moments that is what I think about, that is what runs through my head. Not some cheap lyric, not some violent movie, not some angry revenge.

I can bring about climate change - my own personal climate - I can change my heart.

If I have the heart for it.

Day 214
Thinking Like God

So...God's mysterious ways huh?

God: *"For My thoughts are not your thoughts, nor are your ways My ways. For as the heavens are higher than the earth, so are My ways higher than your ways and My thoughts than your thoughts."* (Is 55:8,9)

Yesterday I was sitting on a park bench downtown waiting for a meeting. Just day dreaming – the best time to be engaged by Papa.

Looking at a building and a tree I observe an example of God's ways versus man's ways worth meditation.

The building is square, ordered, planned, functional, climate controlled, plants on the desks - quickly built, immediate efficient bottom line results.

Yet dead.

The tree is wild, seemingly random, gnarled.

Yet ALIVE!

Each leaf, twig, root and branch carries life and plays a vital part helping to seek light and water, withstand the storm, make shade - extremely effective.

It produces and reproduces with seeming little effort, spreads, fills the open space.

There may be a sort of beauty in both but there is life in only one - except for the potted plants.

That is God's way – seeming wild and unpredictable. But only because I do not think like God...yet.

Day 215
Never Alone

So... night and I am in church men's room stall alone...

Then I hear giggles and steps, hide in stall looking down over top, as two 15-year old girls exploring furtively thinking they are alone.

Ooooo its delicious.

I watch silently, they laugh and joke. I whisper just audibly, "Hey you."

Suddenly one sees me and SHRIEKS, they scramble out.

I guffawed and about peed in my pants (lucky thing I was...) and Papa did too I think.

Then He says "You are never alone Andy - and that's a good thing"

Those two were naively innocent - curious. But some love darkness thinking their deeds are hidden. Some, on the other hand, want to be sure God is there with them.

"'Can a man hide himself in hiding places So I do not see him?' declares the LORD, 'Do I not fill the heavens and the earth?'" (Jer 23:24)

Neither is alone... and that's a good thing!

Day 216
Kurfur

So... Andy frustrated at the grocery store customer service counter: "Excuse me, I have looked everywhere and cannot find it...where is the kefir?"

Lady with deep south uneducated accent: "The what...kurfur?"
Andy a bit frustrated:"K-E-F-I-R, kefir - it's a yoghurt drink. Surely a place like this has that!"
Lady: "Well, I'll do my best to find it sir...let me call dairy."
Long talk with dairy about "kurfur" without luck. Andy frustrated.
Long talk with the manager about "keefeer" without luck. Andy incredulous.
Lady: "Seems to me something that healthy would be in nutrition...did you try there?"
Andy: "Look, I tried everywhere - stood staring in the nutrition area, it was not there. I'm going to get a prescription. YOU are customer service - how about serving me and finding someone who knows what they are doing ok?"

Andy goes to get prescription and comes back.

There is a bottle of kefir standing next to his shopping basket.

Andy: "You found it, where was it?"
Land: "In the nutrition department on the bottom shelf. We have four flavors you know."
Andy: "I must have been looking on the upper shelves I guess."

Pause

Lady: "Sir, I don't know but maybe you should spend more time looking down instead of up."

Andy stops dead...that... that was truth... real truth. Andy looks hard at her. She is smiling sweetly. God is smiling sweetly. They are having fun. Andy is squirming.

Andy: "I...I'm sorry. You're right. Thanks."

Lady: "That is what customer service is all about sir. enjoy the kurfur."

Day 217
Still Talks Like That

So...I wonder what would have happened if, instead of broken sorrow, the Prodigal son came waltzing back one day saying, "Hey pops, what's happening man? Yeah, love my new condo on the Dead Sea. Great walkable neighborhood. Spending a lot of time hanging out drinking single malt with my buds. Really into..."

Would there still have been a party?

In Ezekiel 14 some elders of Israel come to the prophet to "get a word" from God. Things are heating up internationally and they are getting a bit nervous. Time to hedge their bets.

God says three things about them to them: "You value many things but I am not one of them; you deserted Me for them. You indulge in things that make you stumble; they are in your face continuously. And last, you ask the prophet to get information from Me, as if I am just some planet orbiting around you in your solar system of self-focus."

He says they will be destroyed unless they make a U-turn; and that their destruction will turn some who see it back to God. His desire was to push them one way or another from their drifting lukewarm twaddling lives, and to set them on a path of society-changing goodness and purpose.

Psalm 50 says: *"These things you have done and I kept silence; You thought that I was just like you; I will reprove you and state the case in order before your eyes."*

There is a great danger in living a sort of self-satisfied life that slowly devolves into a focus on the accumulation of things, ideas, and experiences. And if I am not careful I begin to think maybe god is sort of like me...at least my god. And he or she or it fits well into my framework.

Siri...set an alarm for now. Wake up!! I have better things to do.

God tells Ezechiel, "Therefore say to the people of Israel, 'This is what the Sovereign Lord says: Repent! Turn from your idols and renounce all your detestable practices!'"

I think He still talks like that.

Day 218
Check In

So...moving quickly through the airport check in. In my own world, absorbed in my own thoughts.

But then I hear, "sorry miss, I can't get you to the front of the line..."

I look up to see a woman eyes reddened, desperate, hopeless long line snaking to the lobby.

I leave my world - catch her eye - motion for her to duck under here... hesitant, security watching me questioning - look directly at them and mouth - "come on, she's with me" - who cares whose fault it is - knowing smile - lifts the ribbon for her.

She ducks - we breeze down the platinum line - special entrance - *"excuse me this one is late gentlemen how about some chivalry?"* The black suit and jeans sea parts - she moves to the front and on through - eighteen minutes - perfect. She turns and waves and is gone.

I have an older brother who taught me this: *"Do not merely look out for your own personal interests, but also for the interests of others. Have this attitude in you like Christ Jesus. He left His own world and and entered ours that we might enter His own platinum-lane world. And Papa rewarded him for it."* (Phil 2)

Today - look around - leave your own world - enter another's - just for a minute or two.

Godlike sometimes looks servant-like... maybe most times.

Day 219
They Can't

So...at what point in things did Christians start hiding Jews ahead of Nazi aggression?

Was it just before they began illegally rounding them up for reasons of national safety and security? Or did they wait until the USA refused port landing to a ship filled with frightened and weary refugees?

At what point were we Americans collectively ashamed we placed Japanese Americans in concentration camps? When they began to give their lives to fight Japanese invaders?

This raft filled with women, children and men - 60 in a raft designed for 35 - made it.

They paid their life savings to shady operators to flee Syria after resisting both ISIS and Assad. 11 died in the next one when it sank. When they came ashore in Lesbos many wept, some collapsed, all shivered from the cold and wet.

Should they want to come to America they will face 18 months of criminal checks waiting in a camp.

Most want to go home and live in peace. They just can't.

How they love freedom.

Day 220
Street Person

So... I was talking to a street person the other day.

He had no job but supposedly drank a lot and partied. I don't know where he got his money though I hear He somehow cajoled some women into giving him some from time to time - who knows why, though he was a sweet talker - feeding everyone this line of BS. They probably felt sorry for him. He was obviously homeless and seemed to be part of some sort of gang.

They stole food from peoples gardens to eat.

He was insane I am sure, claimed to hear voices, said he came from a far off place and was very, very ancient though He did not look a day over thirty. Can you imagine - just like everybody else who claims to be God.

He would go around and cuss out church people a good bit and talk in a sort of mystical dreamy way about truth. A real story teller. They asked the government to do something about him to get him off the streets and put away.

Just crazy.

He went viral for a while - sort of a pop icon. Not sure why though some wild stories were told. Everyone wanted to see if they were true I suppose.

After a while he got in trouble with the law and everyone turned on him in favor of the next flavor of the month guy - Barabbas somebody. I'm not sure but I think he was eventually executed for something - good riddance.

Though I did hear a strange rumor... somebody said they saw him. He had cleaned up his act.

Maybe he went to prison and got rehabilitated.

Probably.

Day 221
The Foreigner

So...you don't know me. I'm a foreigner.

I was born in a land far away and, not totally voluntarily, went to a land where I was a stranger. A number of my fellow countrymen had arrived there ahead of me, and a few had caused trouble. A very few had committed murder, rape, and theft. That made all the papers.

Statistically our crime rates were higher and our pay lower. Many of my kind came as single men with all the problems that implied. Our culturally derived way of acting, of talking, of driving, of EVERYTHING was just...different. Unacceptable.

Our talk was louder and we seemed coarse and uncultured. We tended to live together apart from their society. Our neighborhoods were more trashy and our cars were dented and dirty - theirs were clean, new and kept spotless. We had our own stores and restaurants. They never went there. Never.

When I went out shopping, no matter how hard I tried, I did not fit in. I got the look. When at a restaurant the owner barely greeted me - perfunctory politeness. I spoke their language poorly...stupidly. My money was fine - just not me. At least that is how I felt. I could have been overly sensitive.

I dated one of their daughters a couple times. Her father was a rich executive. I was questioned and invited to "the dinner". Only after I beat the eldest son in chess was I seen as potentially acceptable. "Just don't marry her and take her away to your land."

They professed to be Christian and I know their Jesus said, "I was a stranger, and you did not invite Me in."

He was telling them that was wrong; that they would be questioned about it at some point...too late to make it up.

They forgot that part.

...continued

Some were very kind, of course. I loved those. One greeted me many days with a picnic table and two beers waiting. Come, sit, let's talk. I loved that man. He made all the difference for me. All. The. Difference.

Who am I? Syrian? Egyptian? Mexican?

No.

I am 2nd Lt Andrew J Reese US army, stationed in Germany in 1977 living in a small village.

I saw it.

Felt it.

Lived it.

This stranger in a strange land sense of disquiet, of discomfort, of disenfranchisement. My bones felt it.

Polite distaste.

And I have made a decision.

I have decided to keep this other command of that Jesus, *"Therefore, in all things, do unto others as you would have them do unto you. This is the summation of all law and the prophets."* (Mt 7:12)

Welcome to America...you who can become my friend.

Day 222
Counter-Terrorists

So...let's be counter-terrorists.

Once again we are faced with seemingly senseless acts of barbarism, brutality, terrorism, and inhumane religious insanity.

Among the many things I feel is this one overriding truth.

This world will be filled with evil and terror. Christians and non-Christians all experience it together. I can only imagine the craziness if only and all Christians were spared; the maneuvering, the false conversions, the loss of free will. It is only a short term fix but long term disaster.

God is wiser than men.

So what then?

Paul was facing the strong possibility of his own execution at the hands of the brutal anti-Christ terrorist Nero.

Beheading.

And in Philippians 1 we are let in on his thought process. He says: It is far better I go to be with the Lord.

Far. Better.

But it is far more useful to the kingdom of God, and comforting to you in these terror-able times, if I stay...far more useful. I am torn. Maybe I'll stay.

Maybe.

...*continued*

Then he says this: *"Only conduct yourselves in a manner worthy of the gospel of Christ. I want to hear that you are standing firm in one spirit, with one mind striving together for the faith of the gospel; in no way terror-ified by your opponents—which is an obvious and clear demonstration of ultimate and eternal destruction for them, but of God's witness of rescuing and ultimate saving and preservation for you...that strength you feel is from God."* (Phil 1:27-28).

We get to play both sides of eternity with God. Staying or going? Win-win.

And that knowing, that open secret, caused thousands of Christian men and women to gladly give their lives.

A few give it all at once in an act of martyrdom.

But we all have the choice to give our lives away little by little, over the days and years of choosing. I can lay it down for others in selfless serving and loving.

Choosing death.

Gaining life.

Like Paul, that calm knowing, that sure balancing of realities and truth, in which I face such acts makes me the ultimate counter-terrorist. Nero and his kingdom were disarmed and transformed by such brothers and sisters...such knowing.

And at the end and forever?

Far. Better.

Win. Win.

Let's go be counter-terrorists.

Day 223
Willing and Able

So... let me tell you a secret.

Each of us has issues that seem to track us, temptations that follow our steps, things we just cannot seem to muster up the strength, even the will power, to overcome. The prowling lion of darkness is on our trail keeping us on the run and failing. I may find I am at a stalemate or worse in my efforts to "resist the devil" and move on to become the person I was made to be, that one partially hidden inside of me. Here is the problem - I have skipped a step. I may think that I need to clean up my act and then I can go to God. He gave me His word and I will try to stand on that and behave. That is not possible. Hebrews 6 says this about God: "He who comes to God must believe that He <u>is</u> and that He <u>is a rewarder</u> of those who seek Him." God is both able and willing to reward me, to help me, to partner...He "is" and "is a rewarder."

Willing. Able. God.

So... how does that help me exactly? Like this: "Work out your salvation... FOR it is God who is at work in you, both to WILL and to WORK for His good pleasure." (Phil 2:13) God has this strange ability to make me BOTH willing and able too.

Willing. Able. God. Me.

I access this amazing dynamic by one simple three-step, one simple secret when I feel things coming on: "Submit therefore to God. Resist the devil and he will flee from you. Draw near to God and He will draw near to you." (Jas 4:7-8) Submit first. Then resist. Then draw near.

And I find the will and the ability seem to flow right from Him into me. It is not just Simba roaring...but the Lion King standing behind me makes the poser run in terror!

Willing. Able. God. Me. Victory.

Day 224
Changing Someone

So... if you want to change someone's mind . . . teach them. But it's a hard and unsure slog. The door guard of boredom often blocks your way.

If you want to change someone's behavior . . . model it. But it's an uncertain and long term commitment easiest when someone is your captive audience (i.e. child).

But if you want to change someone's heart . . . .

The best way, the best, is to grab the imagination; the place where the inner-life rules all things. The imagination is the deepest place within the soul before you begin to plumb the depths of the heart and spirit. It is the screen on which God premiers His best personal movies.

The language of the imagination is picture, imagery, sudden thoughts and story. It is parable and meditation. It is memory with commentary. It is both fleeting and sure, evanescent and lasting.

This is God's preferred means of communication.

"I will instruct you and teach you in the way which you should go; I will counsel you with My eye upon you. Do not be as the horse or as the mule which have no understanding, Whose trappings include bit and bridle to hold them in check, Otherwise they will not come near to you" (Ps 32:8-9).

"Jesus stood and cried out, saying, 'If anyone is thirsty, let him come to Me and drink. He who believes in Me, as the Scripture said: From his innermost being will flow rivers of living water.' But this He spoke of the Spirit, whom those who believed in Him were to receive" (Jn 7:37-38).

Out of our belly's, our spirits, will flow a river of life from God's Spirit who swells there - and if we give honored preference to that flow then that life will find expression within us as pictures, impressions, sudden thoughts, and memories.

I think this is the ultimate home entertainment center - Papa and me on my own inner screen watching and listening.

Make popcorn.

Day 225
Addiction

So... am I an addict? Are you?

There is a test commonly given to see if someone has "addiction" issues called the CAGE test. Its remarkable accurate.

Let's try it out on our social media and smart phone practices.

1. Have you ever felt you needed to Cut down on your smart phone time?
2. Have people Annoyed you by criticizing your looking at your phone when they are trying to talk with you?
3. Have you ever felt Guilty about spending so much time looking on your phone?
4. Have you ever felt you needed to look at your phone first thing in the morning (Eye-opener) to get yourself up for the day?

Yep... sorry.

But here is the key question: Are YOU an addict?

When I engage in an "addictive" practice what happens inside my physical brain is a sudden release of dopamine - the pleasure drug. I like that feeling, and when I continue to indulge, it causes a craving for this action and the associated dopamine in various parts of my brain. It feels good and is predictable... and, really, I can't help it right? Its just me.

That is a very common mistake - that of thinking I and my brain are one in the same.

I am NOT my brain... I have a brain. It is a pretty predictable brain chemistry machine. It is also a machine that I can learn to operate more effectively, to control and bring under my sway. I may have a social media addiction (you ARE reading this right?) but I am not an addict - it and me are not one in the same.

...continued

Paul puts it this way: *"All things are lawful for me, but not all things are profitable. All things are lawful for me, but I will not be mastered by anything. I run in such a way, as not without aim; I box in such a way, as not beating the air; but I discipline my body and make it my slave."* (1 Cor 6:12, 9:26-27)

"I HAVE a brain and an addiction - but I am NOT that brain nor an addict"

When I think this way about all sorts of similar "addictions" - it is not who I am but something I do - then I find I obtain leverage to actually do something about it. I step outside of its immediate grasp and can look critically at that behavior.

That one thought...that one...is nearly the whole basis of God's plan for making us like Him found in Romans chapters 7 and 8. From that leveraged place, and with the help of God ("If by the spirit...") I can find change, success, and freedom.

Turn off your phone.

Go read about it.

Set your brain to thinking about it.

Change it and your life.

Then post your results...

...woops.

Day 226
Bestseller

So...I may be a writer...or maybe mostly a manuscript.

I have been sitting with a group of wonderfully supportive...and honest... writers - Heartprint.

The honest part is good but is scary for almost everyone in the room... or maybe just for me. Sharing the things your heart has bubbled up seems awfully intimate.

But they want to help make it inviting, captivating, intriguing... perfect.

So...they do.

I'm seeing that in the beginning there are lots of things to cut out of a first draft, and they go fairly easily.

Fairly painlessly.

They were not that important, not precious.

Let it go.

It's those latter drafts, when you know it's not quite there that hurt; when someone says, "I know it's funny, but are you sure it fits? You like it I can see, but does it add something important?"

"But I LOVE that paragraph!"

I got to thinking. I am also a manuscript.

So are you.

We each come to early adulthood a rough draft of who we are meant to be. It's sort of written inside us. We *"show the work of the law written in our hearts, our conscience witnessing it."* (Rom 2:14)

...continued

As we mature we find that some of the things of youth are inappropriate for an adult. I know it's funny, but are you sure it fits? And if we listen, we find that there seems to be a writer working within us, imprinting our hearts...someone who is sure footed in walking, healing in speech, and gentle in touch.

But relentless. So relentless!

"I know you like it but does it add something important?"

He is a gifted author, He creates manuscripts that are captivating, attractive, rich and full... perfect. He is *"the author and perfecter of my faith, who for the joy set before Him endured the cross, despising the shame, and has sat down at the right hand of the throne of God."* (Heb 12:2)

He is not writing anything inside of me, in my heart, He did not experience Himself.

The later drafts are harder - this taking up my own cross - when the things that I am asked to let go of seem more precious than before... back when I was a rougher draft.

They feel familiar and comfortable.

They are not perfect though...not for me.

Let it go.

Till at last I give up my very life and, like my Author, sit down at the throne, perfect, complete, lacking nothing...

...a best seller...

...given away freely.

Day 227
Well Known

So...want to be well known?

I took an online webinar about building your readership base, your platform, your email list. It was frenetic and stuffed with information and infomercials - a polished and well done example of itself. Such a loud, noisy and discordant world...cacophonous. Seems everybody wants to be "liked", to be joined, to be followed and shared...to be known. Is that really an end game worthy of life and living? It made me a bit depressed. I may be sort of like that...just maybe.

Susan shared this with me this morning.

When Hagar was fleeing Sarai lonely, pregnant and rejected an angel intercepted her - giving her a promise and hope. "You are not alone, not unseen - I see you and have plans for both you and your son. I know you Hagar." Long before He was known as "Allah", the progenitor of all Arabs called Him "El-Roi" - The One who sees me and I see He sees me. And I live. (Gen 16)

She was well known. Well. Known. She knew it then forever.

David, alone with the sheep - overlooked by father and brothers - composed a song saying, "You see me, everything about me, all my ways and means, and I am precious to you." (Ps 139)

He too was well known. Well. Known. And knew it.

Paul says, *"For now we all see in a mirror dimly, but then face to face; now I know in part, but then I will know fully just as I also am fully known."* (1 Cor 13:12).

Relax, enjoy, share truth peacefully. Follow faithfully. Like what you do. You are already well known.

Well. Known.

Day 228
LOL Cats

So... I've got a new Bleat: "Six things that will blow you mind at what happens next when you see this one little trick that will change your life."

Perfect.

Well except for this one liner by Jesus: *"But I tell you that every 'idle' word that people speak, they will need to explain to Me later."* (Mt 12:36)

"Idle" is "a-ergon" meaning: without energy, lifeless, careless, idle, lazy, thoughtless, unprofitable, injurious, empty.

It may tickle the ear but always leaves the craving soul empty.

Everyone chats together.

Small talk is part of the lubricating commerce of friendship and life.

But if I find that my words and conversation rarely, if ever, bring life, change life, encourage, uplift, hit a heart target then I should hit "pause" on the pithy empty input button and "play" on the kind of input that will allow wisdom to seed, root and grow in me.

Solomon said: *"The beginning of wisdom is this: Get wisdom. Though it cost all you have, get understanding."* (Prov 4:7)

Maybe for the rest of Lent I should fast from intellectual junk food and soak in wisdom.

Maybe start at Prov 4:8 and keep going.

The LOL Cats can wait a month.

Day 229
The Scorekeeper

So... one thing I really, really like about God is how He seems to keep score.

Sure at the end of my life He and I will go over my "investments" and I suppose I will be asked, *"How much joy did you have my son - did you discover all I had laid away for you to find? Let's review your checkbook and calendar."*

But in the middle of life He is NOT about some game of "gotcha", He seems to look right through a lot of stuff I used to think would get me zapped - David and Bathsheba for instance.

He can do so because His valuation seems to be maybe 80% the intent of the heart, 20% on my attempt at obedience, and near zero on actual outcome.

He said to Samuel about David, *"Do not look at his appearance; for God sees not as man sees, for man looks at the outward appearance, but the LORD looks at the heart"* (1 Sam 16:7). Jesus said, *"You are the ones who justify yourselves in the eyes of others, but God knows your hearts. What people value highly is detestable in God's sight"* (Lk 16:15).

He knows my heart and that out of it will come my "ways" and then my actions. He knows that only He can finally bring about an outcome no matter my actions - God causes the growth.

If I focus ONLY on outcome, outward appearance, performance metrics, and rules then the thing most precious to Him - the knitting of our hearts together - will be lost.

The one thing God says about David after all his adventures and misadventures is this: *"He is a man after my own heart."* (Acts 13:22).

Everything else is mostly just rounding error.

Day 230
The Old Angel

So... 1994, driving Raleigh to Charlotte.

I pass a prim old black woman sitting along the freeway on a suitcase. She is wearing incongruous shiny white tennis shoes.

"Go back".

OK. Off-back-on...and chicken out and pass by.

"Go back".

OK OK. Off-back-on-stop

"Need a lift? I passed you the first time"

She: "Yes, twice - knew you would stop honey – I'm going to New Orleans to preach. Yesterday a preacher passed three times, then bought me shoes."

We talk - I cry the whole way - she is so noble, so old, so given to God, all she owns is with her.

"I knew you were the one," she says.

I buy her a bus ticket.

"Yes I am" I thought to myself, "thanks to you."

Some encounters change you permanently, eternally.

Angels unaware.

Day 231
Languages

So…if the king were French we would learn French

If he were a Martian we would find a way - if we call ourselves subjects of the king.

If he communicated in sign language or some mysterious quantum force we would figure it out… we would want to;

to honor him,
to communicate,
and for our own wellbeing.

Well, God is not human and His first language isn't English.

"God is spirit, and those who worship Him must worship in spirit and truth." (Jn 4:24)

The King's Son said that.

The good news is we have an Interpreter: *"Now we have received the Spirit who is from God, so that we may know the things freely given to us by God."*

"But a natural man does not accept the things of the Spirit of God, for they are foolishness to him; and he cannot understand them, because they are spiritually appraised." (1 Cor 2:12-14)

But to the mind man, the intellectual, the soul man who feels spiritual conversation with God is a bit too phenomenological.

To him…it's all Greek.

Day 232
B Bomb

So... thinking about the Millennial churched generation (born 1980 to 2000). I have at least six good reasons to do so and more coming I bet. One common characteristic often mentioned is they seem to hate it when someone says "the bible clearly says that..." (I might be a Millennial)

Dropping the "B-Bomb" shuts down the conversation and feels shallow and dismissive. It may be one of our churched generations' blind spots. We mean so well. What to do?

I think of it like this.

We are like two guitar players whose instruments are just a bit out of tune with each other. Now comes the problem. One of us could tune to the other and we could play. We could both adjust half way in a show of cooperation and we could play. But we are probably still both out of tune, even if we are in tune with each other. Consensus about the right tuning does not establish right tuning.

You cannot "crowd source" your way to the truth. There is only one way to be in tune with each other AND in tune... period. We need to get an independent and trustworthy source of the pitch. A is 440 Hz. I suppose there are many tuners out there. I have an old Korg CA-30 chromatic.

I have an old NASB too.

After 35 years I have found that bible, and SOMETIMES my interpretation of that bible, to be thoroughly trustworthy. It can produce giving cultures, selfless charities, and kind people... when we actually get God's intent in what is "clearly said" to our generation.

And because my understanding, especially for another generation, is often not as clear as God intends, I think the best is for both of us to fiddle together with the chromatic tuner and listen well, adjust carefully. When we enter into an open and honest discussion before God about what He might be saying, then the tuner would have done its job, met its intent, to bring us together in harmony with each other...

... listening to Him.

Day 233
Double Standard

So...God has a double standard!

In 1 Cor 5 He says NOT to judge those who are not in your local body - not to judge Obama, Pfizer, Afghan Islamists, environmentalists, abortion doctors, and criminals.

He will do that. I am not qualified.

No smug or supercilious Facebook potshots allowed!

But He also says to deal within our churches with strict accountability - deal boldly with the immoral, covetous, idolater, reviler, drunkard, and swindler.

Quietly, confidently, with restoration in view... and especially I am to spoil my brothers and sisters with favor (Gal 6:10).

Great mutual accountability. Hold me to a standard you want to be held to.

Great mutual love and support. Lay your life down for me.

Double standard?

Maybe double portion.

Day 234
Priests During the Week

So...I come in the name of someone.

Just read that I "have been chosen of God, holy and beloved, whatever I do in word or deed, do all in the name of the Lord Jesus..." (Col 3).

What if I thought of going to the store, or a business meeting, or washing dishes others left in the sink in the EXACT same way I think about a quiet time, small group study, or church meeting?

How would things be different if my quick office conversation were thought of like a prayer ministry session?

I think both would transform.

I think maybe that there are NO lay people in the church, and there are NO secular moments in life.

I am a priest and all is holy (1 Pet 2:9).

Day 235
The Rat Race

So…thinking ahead to next year.

Last night I lay and thought of the coming year, tougher competition, fighting and striving for everything or...

I was suddenly reminded of a strange dichotomy in God's economy

"Let us therefore strive to enter that rest..." (Heb 4:12)

Strive to rest, hmmmmm.

My first and most important struggle is not beating the competition or gaining a reputation it is just this - the struggle within myself to trust God.

"Cease striving and know that I am God"

…and the river that makes glad will overwhelm the roaring sea of anxiety (Ps 46).

God's plan is not to make me a winner in the rat race.

It is to take me out of it altogether.

Day 236
Man Cave

So... after many years, I am cleaning out the huge garage attic,

I am counting the boxes of precious junk hauled away - mixed joy and regret (I thought I NEEDED that!).

Now it's a cool man cave, ordered, mysterious, dusty in the right sort of way;

perfect for restful thinking and maybe a cigar.

I sit and muse on hard things and worries now in the corners of my life and hear,

"Count it ALL joy when you encounter various trials... produces endurance... so that you may be perfect and complete, lacking in nothing." (Jas 2:1-4).

And I smile.

Thanks.

It seems even hard things can be meaningful as Papa hauls away boxes of junk, even while I might be saying, "I needed that!."

Counting joys not worries.

Day 237
Ligaments

So…gifts and positions.

I thought and taught that Eph 4 was all about gifts and function in the church - I find my job and serve the organization - just like IBM or Ford.

And we'll grow.

Now I wonder about some of that.

I think maybe it says joints, not jobs, hold the body together - healthy relationships more than proper function.

As I am intentional about joining to those whom God brings my way the body holds together and grows. It's not disfellowshipping its dismembering.

My function has context mostly within relationships.

I am not joining an organization - I am bonding to people… real humans speaking the truth in love to each other.

Ligament relationships - flexible, hard to break, life giving...

…and laughing a lot.

Day 238
Baby Steps

So... I was watching a baby taking their first steps the other day. Seems like a whole crowd was watching and cheering. Dad was at one end with his arms out, mom at the other letting go. Each time the baby stumbled everyone, everyone, wanted to rush to help the baby get up and try again.

Everyone.

James says this, *"For we all stumble in many ways. If anyone does not stumble in what he says, he is a perfect, able to bridle the whole body as well."* (Jam 3:2)

Everyone stumbles when trying to figure out how to walk through life. Everyone.

We stumble in our words, our actions, our inaction. We step on toes and offend. We try to be a man or woman instead of a boy or girl but are not sure how sometimes. So we fall. We are all babies.

Sometimes it feels very hard to get up.

God tells us how to respond to each other when we stumble when learning how to walk: *"Above all, love each other deeply, because love covers over a multitude of sins"* (1 Pet 4:8); and *"Brethren, if someone is overtaken in a fault, you who know how to walk, pick up the one who stumbled in a spirit of gentleness"* (Gal 6:1).

Love deeply. Cover quickly. Restore gently.

Everyone. Everyone.

Day 239
Yes, You

So... you, you there...yes you

You are made for a good purpose that is meaningful to some special others.

Don't forget.

If your very hairs are numbered, and all your tears are gathered in a bottle...

...then how can it be that your very heart is not held tenderly by One who loves you dearly.

Day 240
Good Boy

Susan: "Why are you pulling out your phone?"

Andy: "You asked me if I knew the name of that star."

Susan: "When you are with a woman in the back of a pickup truck under the stars and she asks you a question she is wanting connection not information."

Andy: "I'll just set my phone on the truck cab roof ok?"

Susan: "Do you know the name of that star?"

Andy: "Aren't they beautiful, what do they make you feel?"

Susan: "Good boy."

The man said, *"The woman whom You gave to be with me, she…"* (Gen 3:12)

Day 241
Following Directions

So...at the risk of letting my left hand know what my right has done... this conversation:

Them: "We have completed all the changes for your web site Mr. Reese."

Mr. Reese: "Thanks I think that should wrap it up - nice work."

Them: "Right...we were not sure we would get there in time."

Mr. Reese (feeling nudged): "By the way, I want you to send me another invoice for such and such more to give to the programmer. We were so inefficient in providing him comments he had to do many things twice."

Them: "You...what!? Ummm... will you repeat that?"

Mr. Reese: "Our lateness and indecision caused your programmer to work longer than he should have - I hate that when a client does that to me. So..."

Them (male voice): "Mr. Reese, I'm the programmer - that has never happened. Thank you so much!"

Mr. Reese: "You deserve it - thank YOU so much. I want to be straight up with you."

Them (male voice): "Hey, I have an idea to make your site more efficient, mind if I just go ahead and do that? It's on me."

Mr. Reese: "Man that's great - thanks. OK we're good then? Bye?"

I may have a tendency not to follow instruction, to wing it. That is a bad move in relation to God: *"Now that you know these things, you will be blessed if you do them. Do not merely listen to the word, and so deceive yourselves. Do what it says."* (Jn 13:17, Jam 1:22)

When I neglect to actually DO what I read I end up living a life indistinguishable from the world - only maybe slightly nicer. But God preaches a pretty radical gospel. It will soften the hard world around us, soaking it with unusual displays of love. For me, today it looked like responding to God's whisper and remembering to do this: *"So in everything, do to others what you would have them do to you."* (Mt 7:12).

Pretty simple. Change the direction of your world through radical direction following.

Day 242
The Whole Truth

So... the slimy lawyer has been asking half-truth questions for five hours. I struggle to find a truthful answer that will not mislead the judge.

At the break I close my eyes and ask the King for help, complaining, "He gets to lie, I have to tell the whole truth, and nothing but the truth."

"Welcome to my world," I hear, "but truth will always win. He is his own counselor, and you, you get a Wonderful Counselor - relax and watch."

I believe truth did win my Mighty God, Everlasting Father (Is 9:6).

That was three years ago...

So... Today the Supreme Court in the State of Ohio vindicated us and our cause.

The director called to say "Your baby has been delivered".

"I'm just the midwife", I said and under my breath, "thanks Papa."

Day 243
So Spiritual

Andy: "So God I have been offered an all-expenses paid trip for two to keynote a conference in Vail. What should I do?"

Maybe God: "Susan and I have made plans to hike in the Rocky Mountains together those days. You are welcome to join us. Love to have you."

Andy: "I was seeking Your face and, You know, waiting on Your answer."

Probably God: "Very spiritual. Don't wait in Me when I'm waiting on you my son whom I love."

Andy: "Ahhhh, right. Calling the airline for two tickets right now."

Sometimes I can make being spiritual way harder than God makes it. I make up all sorts of things about God, all sorts of mysteries and strange observations and create all sorts of obstacles to knowing God and hoops to jump through to get close to Him.

That is contrary to God's new, post-cross, dispensation:

"For we do not have a high priest who cannot sympathize with our weaknesses, but One who has been tempted in all things as we are, yet without sin. Therefore let us draw near with confidence to the throne of grace, so that we may receive mercy and find grace to help in time of need." (Heb 4:11-12)

"This was in accordance with the eternal purpose which He carried out in Christ Jesus our Lord, in whom we have boldness and confident access through faith in Him." (Eph 3:11-12)

Sometimes when I keep asking God what His will is in some little thing He answers, "What do you want to do? We're friends. A true friend doesn't always need to get His way."

It's a narrow gate to get in. But I'm thinking once inside things can get a lot broader in many ways.

Day 244
Sure as Spring

So... I kind of like end times theories. I preached this idea on April 14th, 2014 – just for fun of course!

I don't like them because they would cause me to change much if I actually thought a particular one was true (God already tells us in three parables what to do about all that) but because they change the way I think about life today.

God has in the past, and will in the future, intersect this world in time and history. Most miss it each time He does. This next big one may have trumpets to make sure we do not. But when I keep that in mind it causes me to think about today - today - and how He might use me to intersect the life of someone, or how He might intersect my life if I will only walk with eyes wide open, ears tuned. Today.

But... here is my favorite.

So... IF the generation that will not pass away before all these things happen is the same one alive when Jerusalem is not trampled underfoot by gentiles any more (1967). And IF they are counted as 30 year olds then, and IF life expectancy for those born in 1937 is 80 years then 2017 is the year of something. And IF Rosh Hashanah is the date (September 21-22) , and IF Revelation 12 is all about the signs in Virgo about the first and second coming on Rosh Hashanah, and if the signs that seem amazingly like Revelation 12 are "it", and if Revelation 12 is mid-tribulation, and IF the rapture is pre-trib and three and one half years prior to that, and IF we use 360 day lunar years then...

...guess what? I don't have to pay taxes this year because the rapture is April 10th, 2014.

Whoa.

I think I will pay taxes anyway, just in case.

But still... I want to live expectantly, for today, for some day.

Slow as Christmas, sure as spring.

Day 245
You are a God

So...I might be a god.

At least so said a couple of mid-level engineers last week after a speech I gave: "You're like the stormwater god Andy."

I thought for a minute...hero worship makes me nervous, the high expectations sort of drive me crazy, and signing copies of my engineering textbook is so cheesy.

That night in my hotel I got thinking about my top five clients.

They are all cities you have heard of. They all have greatness within them. I think about them a lot - wanting them to do great things, to succeed. They are all trying to make big changes. All want to have beautiful parks and trails, rain gardens and safe streets, little flooding and clean water.

For one of those cities my advice seems to fall on deaf ears and some senior staffer comes along and changes everything. I am afraid they will fail - publicly.
For another they really believe in what I am telling them and seem excited. But after I leave they get hit by financial woes and quickly forget what we agreed to - and get nothing done. We will miss the deadline.
For the third the ideas we share to really change things permanently seem to get choked out by flooding and screaming citizens and little is accomplished.

They all make my heart heavy. I know how great they could be if only...

But there is one. What a place!

I recommended hiring a leader for stormwater and by that afternoon they had the ad written. My list of key changes and how to get there is on the wall in the CFO's office.

...continued

I have been down this road over 75 times before - I know the way, the truth and the...wait...wait just a minute.

"Hear then the parable of the sower. When anyone hears the word of the kingdom and does not understand it, the evil one comes and snatches away what has been sown in his heart. This is the one on whom seed was sown beside the road. The one on whom seed was sown on the rocky places, this is the man who hears the word and..." (Mt 13:18ff).

Maybe I am the stormwater god...sort of.

And maybe being like God is not so much about worship and power and majesty. Maybe it is much more about longing and heaviness and seeing potential and urging someone to be what they could be.

Because I can see it in them even when they can't.

It is lying awake at night dreaming of ways to help them help themselves because I cannot MAKE them be great, be successful, be examples.

I actually love them.

That is being godlike.

Jesus replied, *"It is written in your own Scriptures that God said to certain leaders of the people, 'I say, you are gods!'"* (Jn 10:34)

I can only show the way, tell the truth, and walk with them to the end...

...or until they fire me.

Day 246
What if You're Wrong?

So...what if you're wrong?

That is what someone asked me. They were commenting on my sort of "all in" lifestyle when it comes to God (or "god" to them).

What if what you claim to believe is totally the invention of weak people who feel they need something meaningful to live for? What if there is no god, no heaven, no miracles, none of that?

Well... if I am wrong then my delusion has still produced some very good things including:

a very strong sense that I am not walking this life in purposeless loneliness but with a wonderful loving counselor with a great sense of humor;
a sense of peace and joyful confidence throughout my life;
guidance on how to live life to the betterment of myself and those around me;
relationships that are life giving and love bringing; and some very good answers to the problems in this world;
and tons more I can't think of now.

And I bet, if there is something greater out there, Someone greater, then they would seem to be mostly good and my attitude to try to know, sync with, and rightly relate to this something will be appreciated.

It's a win.

If I am mostly right then the end of this earthly life is the beginning of something beyond words wonderful; I am rightly related to the cause and carrier of all that is and ever will be; and I am eternally in great shape.

It's a win.

...*continued*

If you are right, on the other hand, then I wonder how you create arbitrary meaning out of nothing; love out of brain chemistry; and purpose out of primordial soup. It seems impossibly hard and self-delusional.

Seems like a lose.

If you are wrong then...

...my hope is that this something (or Someone) would also look at your heart and desire to help mankind and be merciful to you just as I hope for mercy myself and count on it.

Seems like higher risk.

Seems like it takes a lot more faith and effort to hold your position than mine.

And I am basically lazy.

Day 247
First Things First

So...a rare sight below the surface.

I was walking in Vail today and, seeing this, had a conversation I want to share.

The thing that makes the tree strong, stable, and healthy is different from the thing that makes it beautiful, prized, and admired.

While the blossoms, leaves, and shady limbs attract us to a tree, none of those things are possible without the root system - especially the tap root that goes deeper and deeper until it finds a constant source of water, or nurture...constant.

Let the wind blow, let it even strip all the leaves from the tree, breaking limbs. The roots can restore the tree. But let the roots be weak or cut and the tree will wither regardless of the sunshine of appreciation.

David said this in his first song: *"Blessed is the one who does not walk in step with the wicked or stand in the way that sinners take or sit in the company of mockers, but whose delight is in the law of the Lord, and who meditates on his law day and night. That person is like a tree planted by streams of water, which yields its fruit in season and whose leaf does not wither— whatever they do prospers"* (Ps 1).

The primary feature of the tree - its basis, is that it has pushed deep roots downward until it has found a constant source of water. Unseen, unappreciated, secret.

...continued

First things first.

Jesus said it too: *"Everyone who comes to Me and hears My words and acts on them is like a man building a house, who dug deep and laid a foundation on the rock; and when the flooding torrent burst against that house it could not shake it, because it had been well built"* (Lk 6:47ff).

The thing that makes the house strong, stable, and solid is different from the thing that makes it beautiful, prized, and admired. The primary feature of the house that is its strength is its foundation - underground, solid, set in stone. Unseen, unappreciated, secret.

First things first.

Who I am when I am alone; what I do when no one is around; where I invest my time and energy when no one can see and appreciate it - that is who I am.

Who I really am.

And when the inevitable storms hit I will be strong, stable, and able to be held on to for dear life, and to shelter others.

My foundation, my tap root - that is my life.

First things first.

Day 248
Canadians

So...I have come to the conclusion that every American should be required to send their children to be raised until age 18 in Canada.

I am late for a meeting and doing (I know I know) McDonald's drive through. And this conversation happens:

Me: "Can I just get something quick - maybe a burger."
She: "Sure, no problem - I'll make it happen fast for you."
Me: "Great, no onions OK?"
She: "Got it"

At window

She: "I put a few extra napkins in there for you sir, I figured you'd be eating in the car and noticed you were dressed nice eh? Want some water?"
Me: "Wow thanks so much - you are amazing."
She: "No, just doing what I need to do to help you. Oh by the way, I put a card from a child at the Ronald McDonald house thanking us for helping them. Figured it would cheer up your day since it is your money we send to them."
Me: "Are you all this nice?"
She: "All who?"
Me: "Canadians."
She smiles - I think that means "Yes, but I would never say that."

See what I mean?

Maybe send church members there too!

Day 249
Hakuna Matata

So...hakuna matata

I confess I was a little let down when I found that the life changing words spoken to the young Lion-King-in-waiting meant "no worries". No. Worries. Come on. Not exactly something to build your life on.

There are four things that I seem to hear myself say to myself and the atmosphere again and again, all the time, in the midst of all sorts of situations. Last week in front of an angry dysfunctional county commission and TV cameras; two weeks ago with a suicidal young man; three weeks ago when my friend found herself with Parkinson; and yesterday when asked to babysit my granddaughter for a few hours

"I trust you Papa"
"I am so very loved"
"I have an unstoppable purpose"
"I am OK even if I mess up"

Those four...those four...are like the points on my life compass, steering, guiding, calming...true even when everything else seems to say they lie.

I can give you a detailed biblical exegesis and life experience examples of why, for me, these four statements of unalterable truth are like the four legs on the table that serve up a feast for all of life and living.

Simple. Honest. True.

But it will be better for you if you find your own reasons - your own words of life - your own unalterable truth.

Just make sure that the One saying them is Himself true, unalterable, and the source of life.

Otherwise you might just come up with hakuna matata.

Day 250
Half Truths

So...time to take off my red or blue tinted glasses.

Recently I have read posts from friends that: disingenuously blasted:

the woman in Kentucky for using her position to break the law she is sworn to uphold while ignoring the five or six times others in her position also broke the law allowing gays to marry;
decry Palestinian resistance to West Bank settlements while ignoring the fact that those settlements might be illegal in the first place;
belittle white Christian nations for not taking all the refugees while ignoring that fact that some wealthy Arab countries have taken almost no refugees (at least in terms of eventual immigration) despite the fact their faith also commands them to do so.

It is endless.

This sort of blind one-sided shouting drama has a name... no, not that name... this gentler one: Confirmation Bias.

Confirmation bias happens when I search for, interpret, favor, and recall information in a way that confirms my beliefs while giving little or no attention to information that contradicts it. It is false reasoning. It is false.

It is selective data gathering, and truth bending. It interprets ambiguous information to show some group or person in a poor light. It demeans and devalues some while giving others preferential treatment.

It makes me look smarter. It makes me feel safe from being seen as wrong, misinformed, or non-conforming in the eyes of my self-identified group. It gets me followers and blog readers and speaking invitations. Huffington likes it. My friends like me.

...*continued*

It is lazy and disingenuous. It is based on fear and insecurity... and insensitivity. It demonizes another, creates an absurd caricature masquerading as truth allowing me to then take easy pot shots at them - all to the cheers of those I want to impress.

I have joined the shouting polarizing dramatic insanity. I am no better than reality TV, trumping truth with arrogance.

Telling half the truth is just that...a half truth.

I always find myself thinking, "Oh my friend, you're better than that, I know it. This is not the one I know and love."

This was Paul's prayer: *"We have not ceased to pray that you may be filled with the knowledge of His will in all spiritual wisdom and understanding, so that you will walk in a manner worthy of the Lord, to please Him in all respects, bearing fruit in every good work and increasing in the knowledge of God"* (Col 1).

And that is mine for those I love... be filled with wisdom and understanding, walk worthy, speak love and truth, bear good fruit, increase.

Please One.

Blessed are the peacemakers - they are called God's children.

I want to tell the truth, the whole truth and nothing but the truth.

So...help me God.

Day 251
Conspiracy Theory

So...got your end times conspiracy theory hat on...good.

The poor, and especially immigrants, are being abused by the financial system. It is not just. Not. Just.

Bank fees can bankrupt them. Payday loans carry a 322% interest rate. The earned income tax credit comes once a year and is needed monthly - bad mismatch. Welfare cards have strict limits and high fees. They often only work at one non-neighborhood bank. Inflation rates are three times higher on the things the poor buy.

For the burgeoning billions of immigrants sending remittances home to their family things can be even worse. It costs almost 8% on average to send money to another country. The total of all remittances is more than twice the total of all US Aid - over $440 billion. It is what keeps many neighborhoods afloat...at both ends of the chain.

Not. Just.

There are three problems:

(1) The greed of those preying on the poor;
(2) identity theft throughout the whole system; and,
(3) transferring money across international lines is not easy - regulations designed to protect against drug money laundering catch the small legitimate breadwinner almost every time.

Not. Just.

What can be done? The Economist Magazine over the last year has reported on pieces of these ideas. Technology to the rescue.

...*continued*

First we can create an international cashless money system that makes such transfers easy. No exchange fees, no hassle. Like moving money between your own accounts. Cubit technology used in Bitcoin has made it possible to create such a system that cannot be used fraudulently. Just.

Next, as India has shown in food distribution fraud, we can solve the identity theft crisis at the delivery end through the use of biometrics. A simple chip injected in the hand or forehead and all identity problems (well, most of them) go away. It is undeniable identification. Just.

Then we can control access to such a system only to those who have been positively identified and...

Who would oppose such a solution?

Are you crazy? It is so just, so right, so modern, so able to be controlled.

Who? thieves, robbers, hackers, identity thieves, conservative wingnuts, bigots, and the those who are suspicious of immigrants.

That's who.

Oh...and those who believe this old archaic writing. Anti-progress, anti-truth religious nots.

And... *"the beast who looks like a lamb but talks like a dragon causes all, the small and the great, and the rich and the poor, and the free and the slaves, to be given an impressed sign on their right hand or on their forehead, and he provides that no one will be able to buy or to sell within the economic system, except the one who has the impress..."* (Rev 13).

Just... thinking out loud.

Day 252
God's Big Ideas

So...one of the greatest injustices on earth is how the public school systems in many poor countries are corrupt, inept, and militant against change - leading to uneducated children probably doomed to poverty and ignorance.

17% of Pakistan's state schools are faked to keep the revenue coming to non-teachers. Sierra Leon found 20% of its teachers were "ghosts". In India 60% of 14-year-olds from state run schools cannot read beyond second grade levels. Across Africa teacher absenteeism is 15-25%.

In the face of this thousands of private schools are stepping to fill the need - often at risk of violence or persecution from the state, unions and even some NGOs.

Nairobi's biggest slum now has 120 private schools. 400 nursery and primary schools are now functioning in shipping containers in Kenya - funded, among others, by Mark Zuckerberg and Bill Gates.

And the cost?

The average is $1 per week per student. $1 per week.

Are these schools perfect? Would they match Western education? Nope. But they outperform the matching public schools by 0.32 standard deviations or better in reading and maths; the can make it on their own without Western aid; and the students thrive.

When Jesus found the 5,000 without food He took what was available and multiplied it to feed them. And they were fed.

Sometimes a good deed looks like a good deed. Sometimes it looks like changing society.

Let God give you a big idea... or a big heart to support someone with that idea.

Day 253
Wise Investments

So...this email exchange

Admin Person: "Here is the information you needed."

Me: "Thanks Mary, you are wonderful to work with – want to be president of the company? ☺"

Admin Person: "We do not always get pleasant emails from employees, we tend to get angry ones, so thank you. You made my day. President, maybe not. ☺☺"

Hmmm.

Now let me see. It took me 10 seconds to type that to her.

It made her whole day.

I'd say that was a sound investment.

"Like apples of gold in settings of silver is a right word spoken at the right time." (Prov 25:11)

Invest wisely...and often.

Day 254
Faster Than Light

So... millennia ago the oceans were a barrier to the growth of men who, by traveling overland knew of distant shores. Then ocean going ships were developed. Centuries ago the skies were a limit to reaching distant lands with great speed until airships, propeller then jet, were developed. Decades ago reaching the distant moon was thought to be impossible... until spaceships were developed.

Today the limits imposed by the seeming impossibility of faster than light (FTL) travel would seem to keep the stars ever out of our grasp... well... until a few years ago.

Theoretical physicist Miguel Alcubierre postulated a way to contract space-time just ahead of a space-time machine creating a sort of downhill slope through space-time allowing travel at near infinite speed.

Wish I were a ten year old to live to see this.

Einstein said: "We can't solve problems by using the same kind of thinking we used when we created them." Every limitation is just an invitation to innovation and change and growth... in disguise.

This is true for individuals too. Things out of grasp were solved by learning to crawl, to walk, to climb. Need were solved by pointing and crying and then by learning to talk, to read, to write, to work and do math and... to text I suppose.

Limitations set before us, as a race and as individuals force us to understand that there is a great difference between the idea of "I can't do this this way" and "I can't do this - period". A barrier that keeps me from doing a certain thing a certain way does NOT keep me from doing it and along the way changing in ways never imagined using the old methods.

I can do all things through Christ who strengthens me... who inspires me... who helps me to have strength, courage, and tenacity. (Phil 4:13).

What is limiting me today?

Every limitation is just an invitation in disguise.

Day 255
Worship Style

So...I heard this about worship in a diverse church from a wise old leader

I feel 'deference' not 'preference' is key.

A consumer mentality has no place among us - as if we shop churches like used cars.

Disciples are producers, not consumers. As a disciple I want to defer to others' preferences in worship style and song selection in honor of God, whom we all worship.

And when I do, I find that the unity we feel can carry both us and our hearts into the Presence almost no matter the song.

Behold, how good and how pleasant it is
For brothers to dwell together in unity!

It is like the precious oil upon the head,
Coming down upon the beard,
Even Aaron's beard,
Coming down upon the edge of his robes.

It is like the dew of Hermon
Coming down upon the mountains of Zion;
For there the LORD commanded the blessing—life forever

Ps 133

Day 256
The Marriage Feast

So...after 34 years I have learned a thing or two...or four about marriage.

Here they are - my four legged table on which all other aspects of marriage stand. You need all four. Declare and believe them. Trust me.

First, "Divorce is not an option for either of us." That decision implies a whole lot of other things, a whole way of thinking, of considering actions and thoughts and decisions. There is no back door, no escape clause, I am all in. No chips left. Some complex things get simple then. There is no nuclear option. None.

Second, "I believe that my mate is God's gift to me." When I know that then every action, argument, misunderstanding and difference of opinion takes on a whole new meaning. God may be in this. I better listen and learn. I may not be right. I need to press higher and further in. And I find that I die some more to self, live more to God, and my character and my mate's are perfected. Marriage is doing its work in me.

Third, "My job is to lay my life down for my mate." This is scripture. I am not my own, I belong to another and I will give up anything, stop anything, and do anything to serve and please my mate. When both agree and act on this truth peace, love, and mutual humility begin to take hold. Kindness reigns. Engagement with each other is the hallmark of your time together. This one gives the first two a playing field.

Finally, and this one is also key, "I fear God. "This may seem like it does not fit. But when the other three seem shaky it is the fact that I know that God is the avenger of someone who cheats on their mate, who abuses them, who abandons them that keeps me on the straight and narrow. It is like with children. When nothing else works the sure knowledge that if I do this I will get spanked will keep me straight. I have seen enough to know this is true.

With these four legs, the table of life gets decorated in linen and lace, set with fine china and silver and loaded down with all manner of wondrous food and drink; and the company around the table is a feast that nothing else will ever match. Trust me.

Day 257
Harvest Time

So...it's almost harvest time in the South.

Have you noticed that the ripening crops have quite a number of weeds growing among them? You only really see it when it gets close to harvest time. Then the real differences - the heads of wheat - stand out.

They were all watered, fertilized, and all protected from pests. All treated the same. Weeds and wheat treated well. God has a field too. It is His. It is explained this way:

"The kingdom of heaven may be compared to a man who sowed good seed in his field. But his enemy came and sowed weeds among the wheat. When the wheat sprouted and bore grain, then the weeds became evident also. The workers said to him, 'Sir, did you not sow good seed in your field? How then does it have weeds?' And he said to them, 'An enemy has done this! Do not by chance harm the wheat. Allow both to grow together until the harvest; and in the time of the harvest first gather up the weeds to burn them up; but gather the wheat into my barn.'" (Mt 13:24-30)

His church is His field. We expect weeds in the woods...not in the field. But here they are...just as spoken. In the church are weeds and wheat. The weeds ruin the reputation and work of the church, making it into a country club, creating division and rules and hierarchies. They grow fast and tall and green...but they never produce anything worth eating... feeding egos not the hungry.

I think they grow together partly because Papa God hopes to the last minute things will change.

It is not over till it's over.

Ask the thief on the cross.

Its almost harvest time in the South.

Day 258
Two Old Soldiers

So...37 years ago two young second lieutenants faced some serious stuff... in the Army in Germany.

It was dark and deadly.

I asked my friend if he would pray together for authority and breakthrough. That day the he gave his heart into the trust of God Almighty.

And the next week everything changed...everything.

Light came, and freedom and an eternal relationship.

Last night we met again after all that time.

And it is true, in the Lord a thousand years is like a day...37 like a couple of hours, only.

And he said, "You changed my life back then, and I am still thankful."

And I said, "You just changed my life now - reminding me of what is eternally true, eternally life giving, eternally timeless...

...my brother."

Day 259
Habituation

So...my first Coke in 28 years. It's the real thing all right. I felt flushed, sick, dizzy, and it took me about 2 hours to feel right again. And I thought, "People drink Coke all the time and it doesn't seem to bother them. Why is that?"

Humans have this capacity to get used to almost anything - it's called "habituation". We develop a tolerance for things that once made us sick or shocked us. So to impress us, to move us, to get our attention takes ever more edgy things. Well, maybe not Coke exactly (you knew this was not about Coke) but the emotional and spiritual equivalent - pornography, violence, dishonesty, reality TV, theft, alcohol, unfaithfulness, sloth. Pick your poison.

Here is truth: "I rejoice because of you; and I want you to be wise about what is good, and innocent about what is evil" and "I am sending you out like sheep among wolves. Therefore be as shrewd as snakes and as innocent as doves" (Rom 16:19 Mt 10:16). This is the battle for my soul. Right here.

It is not a good thing to be able to tolerate higher and higher levels of unrighteousness, to be "wise and experienced" in the ways of the world, of darkness. It is not something to brag about. Alternately, God has this way of making me world wise without having to become worldly, shrewd about the ways of evil but innocent in the personal experience of it.

Evil is SUPPOSED to make me sick, flushed, angry. Sweet smiling Jesus, in a tornado of raging fury, turned over the tables of the temple money changers...twice. Nobody dared get in His way, such was His fearsome authority. "Too late for me" I might think? Nope. God made Mary Magdalene pure again, Paul the murderer kind and true - He can make me sick at the "coke" in my life too. *"Create in me a clean heart; renew a steadfastly spirit within me"* (Ps 51:10). Let Him.

Unless you become like a child you cannot enter the kingdom of God - this is part of what that means.

Day 260
One Way Road

So... the straight and narrow way has a ditch on each side.

I have crashed into both in my life. So let me save you some grief and towing charges.

I was recently told by a well-known very conservative bible professor that I was too "phenomenological" in my spiritual life and not thoroughly bible-based. I think that means he felt I put too much weight on the real-time experience of a living God in my daily life - in an "unsafe" way.

Recently I was also lightly chastised by a Charismatic leader for turning away from the things of the Spirit toward the "things of man-made religion" and works-based Christianity. I was apparently not paying enough attention to the big three of Charismatic circles: prophecy, miracles, and deliverance.

So I think I'm within the lines now (smile). Here are the two ditches as defined by Jesus:

"You search the Scriptures because you think that in them you have eternal life; it is these that testify about Me; and you are unwilling to come experience Me so that you may have life". (Jn 5:39-40) and... *"Many will say to Me on that day, 'Lord, Lord, did we not prophesy in Your name, and in Your name cast out demons, and in Your name perform many miracles?' And then I will declare to them, 'I never even knew you; Depart from me you workers of lawlessness'"*. (Mt 7:22-23)

Here is the center line:

"Then the King will say to those on His right, 'Come, you who are blessed of My Father, inherit the kingdom prepared for you from the foundation of the world. For I was hungry, and you gave Me something to eat; I was thirsty, and you gave Me something to drink; I was a stranger, and you invited Me in; naked, and you clothed Me; I was sick, and you visited Me; I was in prison, and you came to Me.'

...*continued*

Then the righteous will answer Him, 'Lord, when did we see You hungry, and feed You, or thirsty, and give You something to drink?

And when did we see You a stranger, and invite You in, or naked, and clothe You? When did we see You sick, or in prison, and come to You?' The King will answer and say to them, 'Truly I say to you, to the extent that you did it to one of these brothers of Mine, even the least of them, you did it to Me.'" (Mt 25:34-40).

Both ditches have vital, rich and powerful truth.

Neither IS the truth.

If I go off-road into either ditch I find my walk begins to become mostly about conformity without much actual life (note I did not say there was no excitement or satisfaction - just not much kingdom as Jesus describes it).

It is the tail-chasing circle described by Paul: *"For we are not bold to class or compare ourselves with some of those who commend themselves; but when they measure themselves by themselves and compare themselves with themselves, they are without understanding."* (2 Cor 10:12)

And, as Jesus describes,

I will be sort of disappointed when I get to the end of the road.

Drive down the center line...

...it's a one way road after all.

Day 261
The Actual Issue

So…the bible clearly defines what bible believers believe.

Unfortunately that is not the real debate.

The real issue is all about how I live in a non-Christian world with a Christian world view and make a difference.

Here is some guidance from a couple of folks who did it right:

"Let your light shine before men in such a way that they may see your good works, and glorify your Father who is in heaven." (Mt 5:16)

"Live such good lives among the pagans that, though they accuse you of doing wrong, they may see your good deeds and glorify God on the day he visits us." (1 Pet 2:12)

I note here that the emphasis seems to be on example, on goodness, and on giving kindness; not on always preaching, judging, asserting our rights or demanding some sort of treatment or recognition.

Why is that?

Here is one reason. That way, if you are accused of anything it is about what you believe not about who you are and the way you live.

I have noted that God tends to be a pretty effective defender of that approach.

Day 262
Unconditional Love

So...you have to love me unconditionally right? What does that even mean?

I have been involved in a number of instances lately where somebody pulled out the "unconditional love" trump card. It sounds like this, "I am trying to find myself and, in so doing, if I hurt people and violate vows so what - you must love me" or alternately "Even if I don't love you in a way that allows you to grow, you must put up with my dysfunction without challenging it".

We confuse "true love" with "no consequences of my irresponsible or selfish behavior". Love creates inter-dependencies. I lead people to lean on me, and me on them. I birth children, I make solemn marriage vows, I begin a relationship with communication and honesty, I lead another to believe I will be there for them and they build their lives on that basis.

It is a limiting and harmful mistake to not keep myself healthy and strong through appropriate self-focused healthy habits - and not to help one I love to do that. Just as it is a blind and vicious mistake to unilaterally and selfishly abandon the promised interconnections I have developed - and in so doing greatly harm another. In so doing I forget this unalterable truth: *"Whoever tries to keep their life will lose it, and whoever loses their life will preserve it. Greater love has no one than this, that one lay down his life for his friends."* (Lk 17:33, Jn 15:33)

I lay down my life for you...and you for me. And in so doing we both find our lives, and we find that love is a plural word, it is inclusive, it is a shared thing. When I wrap it up in a cloak of self-focus it rots and petrifies. When I seek to control another for my well being or stop pouring life into that love it hardens and breaks.

That is the biggest mistake. And in my 62 years I have seen many come to deep sobbing regret at making it. Please do not.

Let Papa God love you. Get help...together.

Day 263
Dark Side of the Moon

So…the moon has no dark side…Pink Floyd was wrong.

I grew up thinking it did.

The side I cannot see from where I sit, that side I am suspicious of. I think it must be dark. Perhaps there are aliens there…secret space stations… something evil.

From where I sit it is easy to imagine the worst about what I cannot see.

Picture Courtesy of NASA

In reality the side of the moon we never see is a lot like the side we can see.

It's only dark and foreboding in my mind, in my ignorance.

Now deep into the political silly season (yes I just watched the Republican debate) it seems that our "dark side of the moon" prejudices get stirred up.

Life becomes more like a reality TV show.

I don't really know Republicans, Jews, Muslims, the French, Fox News broadcasters, the administration, Russians, immigrants, liberal college professors and suspicious bloggers (pick your very own dark side dweller), but I have my suspicions and opinions and prejudices.

They look dark from where I sit.

I want certainty, clear lines drawn, safety. There is a great tendency to assign people black or white hats; to see society as a battle against dark and light – and of course, I am on the side of light.

...continued

That is called judging. It's pretty dangerous (Mt 7:1).

Should I oppose clear injustice? YES. Should I take an unshakable stand against wrong? Absolutely.

But the dark side I see in another may be as much a product of my ignorant prejudice as their misbehavior.

Like my view of the moon, for most of those I want to demonize there is no huge "dark side"...no hidden demonic agenda, no secret desire to enslave the world.

Darkness and light both play across their features.

They are probably not as dark as I think, nor as light. Either am I. We are all, in some ways, shades of grey. *"There is none righteous, no not one. All we like sheep have gone astray, each one has turned to his own way"* (Rom 3:10, Is 53:6).

If I am truly a follower of Jesus then judging is not my job. *"How can you say to your brother, 'Let me take the speck out of your eye,' and behold, the log is in your own eye? Remove your log and then you will see clearly to help another"* (Mt 7:4).

I find that if I take a seat next to the source of light, like in this NASA picture, and take time to look quietly with a goal toward understanding, then I get a chance to see every side bathed in light.

Clear... nothing hidden.

Discerning has no judgement in it.

I like that.

I think I'll try to find that seat and see if I can get a season ticket.

Day 264
The Active Word

So...you should have seen what my bible was doing yesterday. Huh?

This may sound churchy, but trust me on this one. I am an Ivy League engineer. And in over 35 years of almost daily bible reading and testing I have found something strange. I have stopped asking, "What does the bible say?" or even "What does it mean?" but always ask "What is it doing?" Huh again?

A good book can evoke emotion in me, make me cry or laugh or stay up all night reading it. But it is me doing something in response to words well written. But the word of God is very different from that.

Here is what God says about it: *"I am watching over My word to perform it. It itself is active and sharp - separating within you your spirit, soul and body and illuminating your thoughts and intentions. It, by itself, is alive and working in you - in every person who is willing. It accomplishes in the world what I intend for it - for every person who is believing. The person who regards it so will prosper in whatever they do."* (Jer 1:, Heb 4:12, 1 Thes 2:13, Is 55:10-11, Ps 1).

You see, the bible is not just SAYING something. It is DOING something when I read it. Sometimes that something is to change me... to give me wisdom, provide an answer, build my strength, make me love, help me understand, and comfort me. It does not simply tell me something, but it makes me something...new. I am transformed.

But sometimes when I read it something around me changes. From it I suddenly see with clarity, pray with understanding, and speak with faith and things happen. He is watching to perform His word spoken to me. It is suddenly not simply written but seems spoken - loud and clear - and something is created, changed, empowered, or broken. Something in the world is transformed.

Go ahead. Join Solomon in saying: *"Every word of God is flawless; He is a shield to those who take refuge in Him"* (Prov 30:5). Go ahead.

Day 265
Opium of the People

So...the opium of the people then?

Someone told me last week, "You know Marx said that religion is the "opium of the people." And I thought about it. Well...

Science tells us *("The Spiritual Brain"* by Dr. Andrew Newberg) that when we dwell on joyful thoughts, or on deep relaxing peace, our very brain waves change and there is a release of joy establishing chemicals in the brain. It shows that doing so habitually can even "rewire" the brain. Brain scans of nuns singing, monks chanting, and someone speaking in tongues (!) show this pattern. Deep joy is a hallmark of those who worship regularly.

We are told how to go about living the internal day-to-day life in several places in scripture: "Let the peace of Christ referee your hearts; and be thankful. Let the word of Christ richly dwell within you... with psalms and hymns and spiritual songs, singing with thankfulness in your hearts to God" (Col 3:15-16); and "Be anxious for nothing, bring things to God with thanksgiving and whatever is true, whatever is honorable, whatever is right, whatever is pure, whatever is lovely, whatever is of good repute, if there is any excellence and if anything worthy of praise, direct your mind to dwell on these things" (Phil 4:6-8).

My practice of my religion seems to do wonders for my brain, for my chemical balance - and it can do wonders for an oppressed people.

The full quote from Karl Marx actually translates as: "Religion is the sigh of the oppressed creature, the heart of a heartless world, and the soul of soulless conditions. It is the opium of the people".

He may be spot on right...well, except...

I think religion maybe is the serotonin of the people!

Day 266
A God Like Me

So...do I look like God? Does he look like me?

About five different people once first said: "God made man in His image and man returned the favor." I am fond of a god that is just as I want him to be: all accepting, all smiles, all giving, non-condemning of anyone. He sits well within the boundaries of logic I have set for him.

"How could a good God condemn someone to an eternity in hell for what he did in 85 years of life?" How indeed?

In this time in United States church history we are fond of our really, really nice God. Really. Really. Nice. And I find I can parse out scripture to prove it. Like when He told the woman caught in adultery (where was the man anyway?) "I don't condemn you, go and sin no more" I might think on the inside that she was probably OK with carrying on with the relationship. After all, God just proved He did not condemn anyone...right?

I suspect my god is sort of made up when I find he shares all my opinions.

Perhaps it is the one thing I know from experience is really, really true about Him that throws me off...He is slow to anger. He says: "These things you have done and I kept long silence; So...you thought that I was just like you; I will reprove you and state the case in order before your eyes" (Ps 50:21).

Big mistake...this using my human logic to define God. I bet the sound we will hear in heaven most often is that of someone hitting their forehead and saying, "OH, IT WORKS LIKE THAT !?!"

And it will make total sense. And we will find when we know as we have been known, we have way underestimated His love, His long suffering, His patience, His multiple-chance-giving-nature.

But also that we will have misunderstood the meaning of justice.

Day 267
Anxiety

So...babies can catch it in the womb...it can be a lifetime affliction...it's called anxiety. It has a cure. The two questions even pre-borns ask are: "Is the world safe?" and "Am I OK?" What I believe about the answers to those two questions makes all the difference in my life. Even as adults when anxiety seems to rise and rage inside, to eat away at all that seems secure and joyful it is because the answer to those two questions is uncertain. I feel insecure and I feel inadequate.

God answers both questions clearly and unequivocally. His answers are both realistic and true. To the first one He says: *"In the world you have tribulation, but be encouraged; I have taken care of the world. Do not fear those who kill the body but are unable to kill the soul."* (Jn 16:33, Mt 10:28) And to the second He says: *"See how great a love the Father has bestowed on us, that we would be called children of God; and such we are. So do not be afraid, little flock, for your Father has chosen gladly to give you the kingdom."* (1 Jn 3:1, Lk 12:32).

I'll face tension, testing, trials - because I am alive. But He promises a deep and abiding peace right in the midst of it. Right. There. Why? Because I know that I know that I know that my best Friend who already beat this thing holds me, loves me, and will never leave me. Even in death (of which we all will partake) He will be my comfort and my soul will smile...finally, home at last!! Knowing those two answers I can be unafraid and vulnerable even if I make mistakes...so what? I am so loved! I can be kind even when I feel mistreated or overlooked. What can men do that God has not already made provision for, not already overruled? It will never be about my performance again...never about my shaking hands and quivering heart...I belong to Him and it's good...so very good!

So anxiety can dry up. I have no time for it. I can ask with thanksgiving... whatsoever I need (Phil 4:6-7); and be assured of His grace that is deeper than any possible pain, whatsoever I face (1 Cor 10:13) - He is faithful to me to infinity and beyond.

Take the cure. Love wins.

Day 268
The Big Questions

So...it may have been the pain meds that got me thinking binary thought in the night...but there are two kinds of people in the world.

Not really, but play along OK?

When you look at the edges of the vast mass of humanity just trying to live you find there are those who think there is a "god" and those who think there is not one.

That god comes in all flavors but should lead us to consider the Big Questions (BQs) of "Where did everything come from?" and "What is the point of everything?".

The "I think there is not a god" folks tend, as a group, to think more critically about society and science here and now and conclude that thinking there is a god is a crutch that is unnecessary and a hindrance to human progress.

The best of these feel that helping mankind evolve into their highest and best expression of themselves is a great way to invest a life. While it avoids or waves hands at the BQs at the two ends of time, it directly addresses the immediate questions of pain, justice, service and self-actualization.

But if honest, they have to admit that science blows itself up when trying to answer the "where did everything come from?" question and gives a very unsatisfying answer to the "purpose" question.

Am I really just the result of a billion quintillion dominoes falling over? Am I simply a more complex set of responses to some initial stimulus - but no more significant than a rock?
Are free will, sentience, love, hate, and insight, no more than chemical reactions - just amoeba on steroids?
Avoidance of the BQs has to be a way of life.

...continued

The "I think there is a god" folks have answers for the BQs - though they might differ a bit. But they historically have tended to blunder awkwardly when they try to overrule science in the middle of those two BQs. A flat earth at the center of everything are two cases in point.

Avoidance of these questions seems to be a way of life too for many.

Christians, and most believers in god, are directed by those beliefs or that god toward working selflessly on questions of pain, justice, service, and less publicly, self-actualization.

The BQs will take care of themselves but provide both meaning for life and expectation for the future. And science tells us that those two things are vital for societal health.

Amazingly the Christian God makes great accommodation for both types: *"For when no-god people, without believing the written evidence and instruction do instinctively the things it says, these fare well without it in that they show it's work written on their hearts. Their conscience will accuse or defend them at the end when God shows us all our inner secrets."* (Rom 2:14-15)

I would love them to have the peace I feel, and they would love for me to stop being so foolish.

But we CAN agree together on what is important in the big middle, and work together for things that matter...

...and quit expending precious time and resources on things that don't.

Day 269
OK Its Jealousy

So... 169,000 views. That's what an old friend got. He gets mobbed.

I felt a twinge of...well...what was it?

Jealousy? GOD FORBID...not me. Why, I'm a mature Christian and... I want their piece of the pie...it's bigger!

It is so easy to look around and to see another who seems to have what I might desire. Or seems to be something I feel I am not. And invariably I will always lose when playing that bigger-pie-piece game. Why?

When I play that game several things happen.

First of all I take something in me that is simply normal and compare it to something in someone else that is their premiere gifting, their greatest strength. Of course I come up short... as does about everyone on earth. That is THEIR strength not mine.

They got a bigger pie piece...waa waa!

Second, I assume I know the price they paid (probably nothing, right?) and the pain they now experience bearing that thing (it's all glory for them, right?), and their own struggles with comparison (they HAVE no struggles, right?). And think things are unfair. let me say this. God is just, I simply do not have the capacity to measure His justice every time.

They got the pie for free... waa waa!

Third, I mistakenly suppose that God's kingdom is a zero sum game. If another gets then I get less. God's kingdom's greatness and expansion knows no end (Is 9:7). Lots of pie. When I imagine competition I invent division.

...continued

Paul too struggled with this and said: *"We do not classify or compare ourselves with another. When we do so it means we have no understanding of how things really work. I will simply tell what is happening with me, without comparing, staying within the measure I have been given by God. Not piggy backing on the glory of someone else as if it were my own. But I will boast about God's greatness and goodness. It is not the one who commends himself that is approved, but the one the Lord boasts about."* (2 Cor 10:12 ff).

I think he ended up writing half the New Testament epistles.

The disciples struggled too (doesn't everyone?) causing Jesus to wash their feet as an object lesson. Even to the end Peter did not quite get it (and John tells on him!). Jesus tells Peter about his own future martyrdom and Peter asks, *"What about John then?"* Jesus says it all in response: *"If I want him to remain until I come, what is that to you? You follow Me!."* (Jn 21:23)

I think the keys to the church were given to him.

And last, as my wise wife Susan said, "I think the things that cause that twinge in someone are things that would be death for them if they actually got them. They would hate it. It would not be healthy for them."

Would I actually LIKE their pie piece. Could I even eat it?

She was actually talking to me...but you knew that.

So we blessed them, prayed protection for them, expressed appreciation to God for them.

And meant it.

And the pie got bigger.

Day 270
The Street Person

So...entering Panera Bread I was dirty, stained, unshaven, smelly and sweaty... but I was NOT a "street person".

Not.

I had a large hand full of change and wanted a bagel. So I approached the counter and got "the look". The guy asked if I wanted fat free cream cheese (what?) "Nope". I counted out my money dime by dime, quarter by penny. Got the sigh. He washed his hands.

Then another woman stepped in...she had kindly eyes, "Do you want honey walnut - it's so yummy." "Uh...sure...thanks". She busies herself on my order. I look around - eyes avert.

She hands me my bag with a big smile- "God bless you sir." "Uh...you too." I walk to my truck ready to continue my dirty-job day.

Inside are three bagels and extra cream cheese.

It took maybe 20 minutes for me to get it. Maybe another 20 to really get it.

I am not a "street person" - though that is what they thought.

Then I heard that whisper I love, "Andy, neither is anyone else."

Day 271
Every Word is Tested

So...about to let my left hand know what my right hand is doing... for a good reason.

Trying to get time with Philly's director of water. Not an easy thing to pull off. Thought I had maybe 15 minutes late morning. At my favorite, the Reading Terminal Market, for breakfast, served by a young black woman with a summer vacation child hanging on her leg. She was an amazing waitress - getting me water, asking if I want ice, cheerful to all the patrons; no wasted motion; no wasted words, but so friendly and competent.

As I left I wanted to tip her on the $6.50 meal. All I had was 2 $1's and $20's so I started to shuffle away when a whisper stopped me; "Isn't my daughter extraordinary?" I stopped. Oh...right. I placed a $20 next to the plate too and started away when a shout stopped me, "Hey...hey." She held up the $20 waving me back. I smiled and waved back. She stared...then mouthed "Thank you" and I moved off.

The director greeted me like an old friend - we did know each other for many years but...still. After ten minutes he told me he had to be rude and take a call to appoint some director of a non-profit. I sat...he looked at me...looked at the phone and said, "Hey, you do the appointing I've got another appointment."

An hour later I knew all of the water director's retirement plans, we compared university teaching notes, laughed at stories, shared ideas. "Please come see me again." "I will, thank you". Beyond what I imagined.

Sitting on the plane I read my next Proverb's verse for that day, "He who is generous will certainly prosper. He who waters will himself be watered in turn" (Pr 11:25).

I laughed out loud, "waters", I get it, and mouthed "thank you."

Try Him, try His word. It is tested and true.

Day 272
The Behavior

"Righteousness exalts a nation, But sin is a disgrace to any people." (Pr 14:34)

I believe promiscuous sexual behavior disgraces a people.

Disgraces a nation.

Disgrace looks and feels like failure…

…inferiority

…shame

… and defeat.

No matter who does it. No matter who they are – race, income, sexual preference, conservative or liberal, and favorite sports team.

It is the behavior…

…in anyone…

… and without prejudice, that is disgraceful to our nation.

Don't make it about anything else.

The behavior.

Day 273
Four Dimensional Me

So…let's get meta-physical. It's good for our brains.

Imagine a 2-dimensional world in your tabletop.

You are a 3-D being.

You see all but are unseen, unimagined, mystical. By simply touching anywhere on the table you create a "visitation" and a miracle. A shrine would be built. The 2-D Einstein's postulate your 3-D world. 2-D priests sermonize about you.

Well, I am a 3-D being but there is at least a 4-D world (or a 13-D one).

Time may, or may not, be another dimension but it is a thing.

God says, *"As the heavens are higher than the earth, so are My ways higher than your ways and My thoughts than your thoughts. For I am God, and there is no other; I am God, and there is no one like Me, declaring the end from the beginning, and from ancient times things which have not been done."* (Is 55:9, Is 46:10)

That means more than He is smarter or different or deeper - He is multiple dimensions higher than us, multiple. He sees all time at once - like the table top.

4-D beings seem supernatural to me; they appear and disappear at will. The finger of God does wonders (Lk 11:20). We might even call that 4D thing the "spiritual world" if we like.

He invites me to be more like Him - part of me IS like Him... and all things are possible (Mk 9:23). My spirit can intuit what my mind cannot grasp.

So he says, "Why do you yet live like mere humans?" (Jude 1:10)

Good question.

Day 274
The Officiant

So... tomorrow I am honored to officiate the wedding of two wonderful young people whom Susan and I have come to love.

They will stand before God and men and vow things they fully mean though I know they have only a theoretical concept of that which they pledge.

And God will watch and will take them seriously, and will ally to defend their words with His name.

And they will remember to say "I really love you" and "You are God's gift to me - you are so precious" and "I am so sorry I hurt you, can you forgive me, I want to be your best friend and biggest fan all your life."

And they will say "I do."

And God will say to them, "I do too." This was my idea.

And with those things they will somehow grow old, and wise, and more in love each day - holding wrinkled hands as they hobble, stooped and gray, to the garden to look at spring's promise.

Day 275
Be Prophetic

So...you should be prophetic...no really...you. It's time to shatter another stained glass stereotype. If you care at all, and you should, you probably think of being "prophetic" as either some Old Testament lightening-caller-downer or as some stylized Charismatic "thus saith the Lord" type declaring from the front of a church meeting and putting everyone else off, "if this is what prophecy is I can never do it, and am not sure I would even want to."

So it has died a quiet death in most of the Christian world. So I love this. This kid anonymously posts encouraging things about each of his classmates on Instagram. By all accounts they were spot on and very insightful. They built up, encouraged and consoled. When he was "outed" during his speech many stood up and acknowledged him with great gratitude. THAT is prophecy.

Scripture says that speaking the truth in love is what causes each of us to grow up and grow healthy, not just grow old. And it says that God will help us say, not just nice things, but ultimately meaningful, insightful, and life changing things to each other. It is God's trick shot. He bounces something encouraging off of us on to another. If only we will listen and, in gentle love, speak what we feel we hear. We won't get it perfect - that is where vulnerable love and honest friendship comes in.

Prophecy is always and everywhere this: *"But one who prophesies speaks to men for edification and exhortation and consolation."* (1 Cor 14:3) Those words have deep meaning in the Greek language: "edification" - *"oikodomen"* - to build up the family house together, the edifice; "exhortation" - *"paraklesin"* - to run alongside the exhausted runner, stride for stride calling encouragement (the Holy Spirit is called the Paraklete); "consolation" - *"paramythian"* - to whisper sweet comfort in the ear, to hold another up when they cannot stand.

OK now do you want to be prophetic? Don't you wish the whole church... the whole world was? That is why Paul said he wished all would do it (1 Cor 14:1). Be like Konner Sauve - speak life, speak love...prophesy!

Day 276
Demagnetized

So...Magnets have this seemingly magical ability to attract or repel each other and to also to be able to latch on to certain kinds of metals (those with unpaired electrons - but you knew that!).

Sort of like that idea Satan has an ability to control people through either magnetic attraction or repulsion. He either tempts or tries me - pulling or pushing me toward the cliff edge of destruction. Temptation seems attractive - and my base lust is inflamed - and I thoughtlessly follow after it...to destruction. Trials ultimately lead to fear - fear of failure, loss, pain...myriads of fears. But the sum of all fears, the consummation, is death and destruction...the ultimate fear.

Satan's tools are not as powerful as you might expect - he uses my own strong will against me through deception and accusation. And I become magnetized - able to be jerked around and compelled. God's way is to demagnetize me to the temptations and trials of the world - not to take me out of it. He says about temptation: "Do not love the world or anything in the world. If anyone loves the world, love for the Father is not in them" (1 Jn 2:15); and about fear "Jesus came that He might free those who through fear of death were subject to slavery all their lives" (Heb 2:15).

Jesus was not magnetically influenced; Satan had nothing in Him (Jn 14:30). His way, for example, was to not be either attracted or repelled by a prostitute - but to be moved by love and compassion to see her as a human deserving respect, love and restoration. His way was not to be either attracted or repelled by a sinner, such as a woman caught in adultery or a tax gatherer - but to speak life and truth and forgiveness to them and then to invite them into relationship.

He was mobbed by the world. He had an attractive character, and an engaging way about Him...a magnetic personality even (!).

All the while helping others around Him to be demagnetized too.

Day 277
No Limits

So...Mrs. Bauer was a mother of three young boys and a mathematics teacher at an all-girls school who, in 1980, saw something called a computer. She knew she needed this for her girls and, when asked how girls were going to learn computer said, "I will teach them" and went to night school to learn. She paid her own way.

She encouraged her girls that they could be and do anything...even this. No limits. A small thing I suppose, invisible to most...

One girl who believed her, whose passion was stoked by her words and her example, went on to enroll in computer science in college - the only girl. She was one of the first women every employed at a new fledgling company called Microsoft.

Mrs. Bauer's sacrificial kindness was stamped in her psyche. No limits.

Today, she and her husband give away billions through the Bill and Melinda Gates Foundation. Its purpose is to remove barriers to opportunity for every child - no matter where, no matter what...no limits. Warren Buffet has joined them with his billions as have several other billionaires.

She credits Mrs. Bauer for giving her the vision and drive. That simple, small, nearly invisible sacrifice exploded into the world. There is no small kindness, no insignificant sacrifice for another. None.

When Jerusalem was about to be built and the first small step was taken God said, *"Do not despise the day of small beginnings. Even if it is only the plumb line in the builders hand. For the eyes of God see it."* (Zec 4:10)

Like the mustard seed, small but with immense potential, each act of kindness and self-sacrifice done for and with the Lord contains within it enough life to change the world.

Today...this day, be the one who plants the seed in another. No limits.

Day 278
Massage

So...parked by the side of the road near the Cincy airport after driving since 5 am and working all day there - heading to Denver. Such a long day.

I am on the receiving end of a tirade from a city manager about on my team's "mistakes that caused her personal embarrassment" in front of the media. I listen patiently getting more tired, more frustrated. She has only a very small point and is greatly mistaken about what we supposedly did but... "Yes, I am so sorry..."

I do my best to be kind and stuff it. Really.

I trudge into the airport exhausted, thinking of the 3 hour wait and the four hour flight, and glance at one of those massage chairs.

It turns on. Really it does. It starts moving.

I look around. Stare at it. It looks inviting... why not?

I sit in it lean back and just relax and enjoy...mmmmmm.

Maybe 25 minutes later I find myself really relaxed but still thinking: "Why do I have to put up with that beating - I wasn't the one responsible? Oh. Right. I almost forgot. The top person always takes the hit... right. So unfair God."

And I hear, "I know how you feel. Better now?"

And I smile out loud. I'm in good company.

Who for the massage chair set before him endured the cross...

Right. I AM in good company.

Day 279
Rains of Mercy

So...wet basement. Water seeping in the wall under the window well.

Wet carpet, destroyed padding, messed up room for the 7 young men staying with us. Pain in the... but...I am a stormwater engineer so... I can solve this, clearly.

I disconnect the three downspouts from the yard drains - semi clogged but not the problem. Maybe they fill when it rains too fast. Run the hose...might be it. But probably not. Getting more frustrated.

Then...it starts to rain. GREAT! Now I have to try to figure this out in the rain...grrrrrrr!! Cr&%$

I am standing in the garage looking out at the rain and hear a strange sound. I look up. Water is overflowing the clogged gutter 25 feet up - above all trees.

How in the world? It is running right into the window well.

If it had not rained just then I would never have seen the problem so clearly.

Just then I hear so clearly, *"Because of my mercy I send the rain on the just and on the unjust."* (Mt 5:45).

Which am I just now?

Clearly.... I have some work to do.

Day 280
In Our Family

So...in our family...

I was with someone the other day and we spoke about how we were raised and how that influences our perception of God the Father - mostly in ways we don't recognize.

I think many of us see God the Father as a sort of traffic judge (at best) or a fire-breathing angry drill sergeant (at worst). We feel controlled by the fear of facing him when we know we have done something "wrong". After a while, normally in our twenties, we tire of the pressure, decide the whole thing is bogus and become a cultural deist or sort of agnostic with a moral streak.

We see the Christian life as having some good but loaded with lots of dos and don'ts. somebody outside of me is doing a lot of decreeing and enforcing. Score one for the dark side. What if that way of thinking was totally wrong?

What if I saw things the way the have actually been established: *"God deals with you as sons; for what son is there whom his father does not discipline? If you are without discipline then you are illegitimate children and not sons. We had earthly fathers who disciplined us, and we respected them; shall we not much rather be subject to the Father of spirits and live fully? God our Father disciplines us for our good so that we can share His holy nature. All discipline seems hard in the moment but afterward yields the peaceful fruit of right living."* (Heb 12)

It actually works like this. God's desire is that we, as members of His family think to ourselves, "In OUR family we fogive. In our family we don't lie or steal. In our family we live and give generously. In our family..."

Its all about identity not behavior. I want to act this way not because I am told, but because of who I know I am. Im a member of a royal family and in our family...

In OUR family.

Day 281
Doubt and Unbelief

So... Peter walked on water. Peter sank. Then Peter walked on water again.

Doubt and unbelief are two very different things. Faith drew Peter onto the waves at the beckoning call of Jesus. Doubt caused him to sink - not the wind, not the waves...just doubt. Plain and simple. Jesus came quickly to help him. But unbelief (or maybe "common sense") kept the rest in the boat. They saw what Peter saw but quickly made up their minds that walking on water was impossible - the example of Jesus and even Peter notwithstanding.

Unbelief is wrong. Wrongheaded, wrong living, wrong outcome...no outcome at all. Unbelief starts with a closed mind already made up. It is a blind alley. Doubt, on the other hand, is honest. It remains open yet uncertain... testing... exploring... wondering...and even failing. God calls to doubt, "Come to Me and see." God comes to doubt, "Let Me help you to stand on the water even though it might seem impossible. Let Me pull you up to try again. Let's walk together back to the boat."

Here is what one of my very favorites says on this:

"What has happened to create this doubt is that a problem (such as a deep conflict or a bad experience) has been allowed to usurp God's place and become the controlling principle of life. Instead of viewing the problem from the vantage point of faith, the doubter views faith from the vantage point of the problem. Instead of faith sizing up the problem, the situation ends with the problem scaling down faith. The world of faith is upside down, and in the topsy-turvy reality of doubt, a problem has become god and God has become a problem. "The question the doubter does not ask is whether faith was really useless or simply not used. What would you think of a boy who gave up learning to ride a bicycle, complaining that he hurt himself because his bicycle stopped moving so he had no choice but to fall off? If he wanted to sit comfortably while remaining stationary, he should not have chosen a bicycle but a chair. Similarly faith must be put to use, or it will become useless." — Os Guinness

Get out of the boat.

Day 282
My Enemy

So...Islam and Muslims are my enemy.

Right?

I have heard it preached, and seen it demonstrated by some church leaders that we must be suspicious of every Muslim, keep distance, perhaps justifiably harbor anger and resentment. They are, categorically and by definition within their faith, my enemy.

So...I am struck by what Jesus says about those who dwell in His kingdom, His sons, *"You have heard that it was said, 'You shall love your neighbor and hate your enemy.' But I say to you, love your enemies and pray for those who persecute you, so that you may be sons of your Father who is in heaven."* (Mt 5:43-45).

Want to be a son?

Then it actually does not matter if every Muslim IS my enemy.

What matters is that I, as an individual, love them. LOVE them.

My enemy.

I understand that nations and governments are given authority to defend themselves against enemies and wrongdoers (Rom 13:4). I am 100% in support of counter-terrorist activities and proved it when I worked against East German spies in the '70s.

But we may have it backwards.

While nations have that authority in the kingdom of God, individuals do not.

Only in the world's kingdom can I harbor such a heart. I did not hate East Germans.

...continue

For me to individually take up hatred against Muslims is to put myself squarely in the wrong kingdom...on the wrong side of the equation.

It is to invite God's resistance...even to become His enemy.

Of course its unfair!

Of course it seems counter intuitive. *"Love you enemy and do good to them?"*

God's ways are not ours. But He has omniscience on His side, and omnipotence, and other "omnis" too.

Wonder why He says that? Don't you?

I think I should make it a point to try His way, and to resist those who would make every Muslim my enemy.

I bet if I do I will find that I am a son of the Most High. And I will find that maybe my enemy has nothing to do with another human...maybe.

And I might even find a radically changed perspective; that the vast majority of Muslims are worthy and seeking sons and daughters of Abraham ashamed of their brutal brothers; recipients of the first-ever angelically delivered promise of God given to a cast out woman and her son who was named by her, *"The God who sees me."*

He still sees them.

Watch and see what He does.

And I will find almost all of them warm and loving, great cooks, a little fearful of me, but laughing friends, lovers of the God they are seeking, and not...my enemy.

Just humans who are unsure too.

Day 283
Angel Talk

So... Angel #1, "How did your charge crack his rib? I thought you would protect him and..."

Angel #2: "Well, he tried to turn in spray cans of paint at the BPOE recycle place and they would not take them saying he should spray them empty, puncture them, and then they would be metal to recycle."

Angel #1: "And..."

Angel #2: "He got impatient and mad and hung around a dumpster till no one was watching and surreptitiously dropped them into the opening. Thought no one saw him. No human anyway."

Angel #1: "What !?! I bet his conscious was screaming not to do it..."

Angel #2: "Right, SO screaming but he ignored it. He even said something like, 'will you stop that!' Then he drove home. Sat typing and his conscious just murmured and whining. I think God also said a few things."

Angel #1: "And?"

Angel #2: "He finally shouted. 'Really!? Really !!!?' and, still mad, got in his truck to go fetch the paint cans."

Angel #1 laughing: "That must have tickled you."

Angel #2: "Oh just wait. So...he couldn't reach them so he leaned way in, picked up his feet resting his ribs on the metal ledge and...CRACK! But, so strange, he didn't even curse. He laughed."

Angel #1: "Laughed?"

...continued

Angel #2: "Yes and this is what he and God were talking about as he was trying not to laugh it hurt so: 'When I knowingly violate my conscious I stop being able to hear God. I am pretending I cannot hear when I really can and soon, if I keep it up, I will NOT be able to hear when I need to. But I WILL still be able to hear the temptation and it will draw me ever futher into a hardhearted place. So many people live in constant violation of their conscious in what they watch, do and think and then wonder why God is far away. He is close...but their ears are filled with cotton. Thanks Papa for saving me from that.'"

Angel #1; "So fun these humans. Didn't somebody say something like that in the writings...'Keeping faith and a clear conscious which some have rejected and suffered cracked ribs...' (1 Tim 1:9)."

Angel #2: "Cracked ribs...cracked ribs, it says that?"

Angel #1: "We angels have bad senses of humor huh? Can we ever learn to be more funny?"

Angel #2: "That's why we get to watch people."

Angel #1: "Oh"

Day 284
Puppet Strings

So...Jesus is having one of "those" conversations with the Pharisees.

You know the kind. Where you are feeling pretty smug until you get what He is actually saying, and then wonder if you are maybe also on the wrong side of that conversation.

He has been saying that they are master scripture-searchers but honestly, He is what they are searching for, but they love to impress each other more. Then He says this: *"I do not receive glory from men; but I know you, that you do not have the love of God in yourselves."* (Jn 5:42).

At first glance those two statements do not seem all that related. And you move on.

But wait. Let's rephrase that:

If I had the love of God firmly in myself, knew it, felt it, experienced it on a regular basis then I would not find that I am so attached, so jerked around, so dependent on what I think others think of me.

The puppet strings are cut.

I will be free to be myself, to do what I feel is right, to spend my time the best ways, to be different, to hang fashion and just dress nicely, to not be up on the latest dance step (or to be totally up on it), to...be...free.

Attractive to God, attracted to Him.

Demagnetized toward the world.

Abundant life.

Free.

Day 285
Steps Down, Steps Back

So…in Romans 1:18-32 God describes the downward spiral of a rebellious society - their acts and His response. It's a bit scary.

Step 1 is to refuse to recognize God in creation and to speculate foolishly about nature and evolution. God's response is to take a step back…He does not control or demand…He allows free will its course if it demands it.

Step 2 is the beginning of sexual impurity and the exaltation of a mechanistic universe – one apart from a God. God's response is to take a another step back.

Step 3 is for a growing movement in society to endorse and approve of homosexual and general immorality (sexual freedom) - with resultant disease. God's response is to take a another step back.

Step 4 is a general societal depravity and *"unrighteousness, wickedness, greed, evil; full of envy, murder, strife, deceit, malice; they are gossips, slanderers, haters of God, insolent, arrogant, boastful, inventors of evil, disobedient to parents, without understanding, untrustworthy, unloving, unmerciful; and although they know the ordinance of God, that those who practice such things are worthy of death, they not only do the same, but also give hearty approval to those who practice them."*

Recognize anything?

Might be time for our society to take a step back.

Day 286
Secrets

So... bison sentinel... bicentennial. Coincidence?

I don't think so. Nope, it's a hidden code!

A guy once told me so earnestly, "You do know that God spelled backwards is dog?" Changed my life. There is no end to interesting numerology, coincidences that might seem to be more than coincidence, patterns and hidden meanings, and Da Vinci codes.

Historical artifacts point to...well, to what exactly?! Bunk huh? And it is bunk until it isn't.

God Himself seems to use symbol, numbers, codes, and pictures for all kinds of reasons. Hmmmm?

How do I tell the difference? How do I keep from getting duped and being gullible?

The wrong answer is to just walk away from it - Ditch #1. When I do I am saying, "I don't care if God does choose to speak this way...I'm not listening."

Or to believe it all - Ditch #2. "Not saying its God, but it is something supernatural and..."

...*continued*

David, who knew a thing of two about all this said: *"The secret of the LORD is for those who fear Him"* (Ps 25:14). God has secrets.

Daniel too knew a few things about secrets: *"He gives wisdom to wise men, and knowledge to men of understanding. It is He who reveals the profound and hidden things; He knows what is in the darkness, and the light dwells with Him"* (Dan 2:21ff).

Solomon too spoke of it in Proverbs.

I have come to see that God speaks in a way that imparts deep insight and sometimes to know what you can't know by natural means.

But He is not human and His first language is not English.

But if I lean my ear His way, treasuring His communications above all else, with a heart that wants to hear clearly and obey fully (That is what "fearing the Lord" is all about).

My inner sensor gets keener and keener, things just "have sauce on them".

Then He becomes as much friend as mystery.

He shares secrets with friends.

Day 287
A Woman Who Fears the Lord

So... it suddenly occurred to me that I was missing something...at dinner with my honey tonight...something important God said:

"A woman who fears the Lord is to be praised. Honor her for all that her hands have done." (Prov 31)

She spoke so excitedly about caring for her granddaughter, about helping her mother, and especially about the school she set up for immigrant women to meet volunteers, to laugh together and to learn English. New friends. She wept about reading old, old letters from her grandmother to her grandfather when they had to be separated, and about missing her dad. She wanted to give to this one and that cause. Time sharing her heart...reserved for me.

She is so delightfully worthy of praise - beautiful and kind, truthful and generous. She loves people well and has given her life for her children... and for me.

Her insightful feelings about people and events is unmatched. Years ago a popular national prophetic voice visiting our church told me she was the most prophetic person he had met...but few would ever know. She would never stand before a crowd her gifting on display. It is hidden, used for prayer and gentle counsel... reserved for close friends...and for me.

She finds her life in quietly creating events and places where others can come together to experience life and beauty, to grow in some important way. Our home is one of her palettes. She is behind the scenes, quietly considering truth...meditating... helping me see.

That is what makes her tick. I love her so much.

I am pretty sure she is what make me tick.

Day 288
The Plan

So...I am honored to officiate today at the wedding of two dear friends who are the picture of God's redemptive work. And this picture on the right is our plan for the ceremony. Not saying who, but one of the two forgot to plan the ceremony while the other planned the honeymoon!

Funny that none of us are nervous...at least about the plan. I think it is because we have a pretty sound idea that God, who chose these two to be married (it's a set up), also has a plan. And it's pretty simple. Say real stuff before God and people that changes everything. Kiss the girl. Celebrate with friends.

Not saying that a detailed life plan (or wedding plan) is not a good thing...just not the most necessary thing. Knowing and trusting in His ability to communicate His direction in His way and in His time is far more important. He said to Abraham, "go north" to Moses "go to Egypt" to David "OK you're king" and Mary "You're going to be pregnant with God, hope that's OK?".

Sometimes in our lives we seem to know things well ahead of time. But, at least in my experience, most often He is sort of a "nick 'o time" God. Its not an intelligence test. It is a trust test. Sort of like when a dad says, "close your eyes" on Christmas morning and then leads a child into the garage to see their new bike. If I had a detailed plan handed to me I'd try to go off and do it. What fun is that?

His most fun is doing things with us. Ours too.

So this is our plan.

Day 289
Life

So...someone once said that your life passes before your eyes just before you die. That's true - it's called life.

In the 60's life seemed to stretch to an infinite horizon. Now in MY 60's it all seemed to pass like a watch in the night. My college buddies (now in our 8th every 5-year reunion) all look like fat wrinkled old men. There is something I learned in the middle of my life that I wished I had learned much earlier...its purpose.

Jesus summed things up for Himself like this: *"I glorified You on the earth, having accomplished the work which You have given Me to do."* (Jn 17:4)
Paul like this: *"I have fought the good fight, I have finished the course set for me, I have kept the faith."* (2 Tim 4:7) David says, *"Teach us to number our days, That we may present to You a heart of wisdom. Make me to know my end and what is the extent of my days; let me know how transient I am. Surely every man at his best is a mere breath."* (Ps 39:4,5, 90:12)

Paul says that our work, our investment in time and trouble, will be tested. That which is wood, hay and stubble will burn. But the gold and gems will glisten and shine (1 Cor 3:11-13). Wood is better than hay, and hay better than stubble; but are not in the same league as the gold and gems. He says I am God's workmanship prepared to do certain things, and those things are prepared for me...JUST for me (Eph 2:10). So I CAN find them fairly easily. Those things, that "course" the "work you have given me to do" are all that matters. Are all that will make me happy, those around me joyous, and the world a better place. They will sustain me, fund me, and fill me. They will bring me in and out of different phases, places, and relationships. They will lead me surely to my mate if I am to have and be one. Surely.

And I will be satisfied. Satisfied with life. Satisfied with the bonfire afterlife. Satisfied with the glisten and the smile and the eyes of fire and the words, "Well done good and faithful one... so very well done."

Day 290
Changes Everything

So...cheerio!

He was dead...certifiably dead, stabbed through the side dead. Buried temporarily. All His friends wisely fled and hid. Peter cowered before a slave girl. And all the plans, dreams and words were dead too. What kingdom? What power? What happened!?! "What do we do, go back fishing...guess so - if they will even have me back. What fools we were - what naive children." It all...all...came to nothing. N O T H I N G.

Then...suddenly in the upper room where they were hiding He is suddenly standing there and He says...He says... the first word from the risen King is.... "Hey y'all" That is the translation of *"chairete"*. "Greetings", "How ya doin'", "What's up?", "Cheerio". (Mt 28:9). Calm, every day, lets chat and then get to work - I'm heading to Galilee...see you there.

And in that instant - that very split second everything, changed. Everything became newly defined. Really. Everything. Reality, life, truth, God, purpose, destiny, nature, spirit, science... all different. All seen with new eyes. There was a ragtag fearful group. Then POOF!! A church.

Cowards began to proclaim boldly one story without wavering. Not through torture, not through privation, not through the years. The harshest cross examination imagined. Not one recanted, no cowards, no backpedaling. Bribery of the grave site guards could not change the truth. False stories could not. False theories could not. Based on the five tests of testimony forensic scientists would call that a factual story. It would stand up in court every time.

And you and I? We cannot change the story either. I tried my hardest before I began to believe. But now I have met the risen One and found it all to be true.

And it changes everything. He is risen. Cheerio indeed.

Day 291
Dramatic Pause

So... Chicago. I was standing in front of a thousand leaders in my field about to give a keynote address, being introduced. I have been practicing for over 35 years; given a hundred speeches. But at that moment I suddenly looked out on all the faces, heard the windy words I knew were more than the truth, and a wave of self-awareness and self-doubt washed over me... and I froze. Right. Then.

I lost all thought of what I wanted to say; forgot my jokes even. I was sunk. Frozen. But...

Peter, the seasoned floater on water, asked the Lord if he could walk on it. "Jesus said, 'Sure, come on!' And Peter got out of the boat, and walked on the water. Walked on water. But seeing the wind, he became suddenly self-aware, self-doubting, and beginning to sink, he cried out, 'Lord, save me!' Immediately Jesus stretched out His hand and took hold of him, and said to him, 'You of little faith, why did you doubt?'" (Mt 14)

I closed my eyes and whispered "help me Papa", and paused. I do not know how long, but when I looked up I knew for certain what I had wanted to say... and so much more. Walking on water again.

Each of us, each one, is called to live more and more conscious of the command to walk, even on water, than the slow walk of self-focus and self-doubt...the merely natural. Some part of our lives is to be super-natural, inspired, strengthened, beyond natural. Sure there is wind and waves... always is... so... you are walking on water!!

Jude chides those who walk as "mere men" (1:19). So does Paul (1 Cor 3:4); and David (Ps 56). Peter had the good sense to reach for Jesus when he began to sink... not the boat. When I do I can say like David, "The LORD my God illumines my darkness. For by You I can run upon a troop; And by You I can leap over a wall." (Ps 18:28-29).

Someone told me, "I loved your dramatic pause before you began... loved it."

Me too.

Day 292
Choose Life

So... is smoking "wrong"?

You might say something like," Well, hmmm, 'wrong' is not the word I would have chosen." Much of life is like this.

There are opposites that we often use to describe human choice and behavior: right-wrong, legal-illegal, good-bad, smart-dumb. Each of these has its place and application I suppose. Using these terms can often cause an angry reaction because they may seem to try to take away the hearer's freedom of choice, and to impose judgment or a false sense of arrogant authority (e.g. "It is no one's business whether I choose to smoke or not"). I react against the person, not the actual truth of the situation.

Have you noticed that God almost never uses these opposites? Throughout scripture in various settings God says this, *"I have laid out for you two paths, two choices. One leads to death. The other leads to life. I love you and urge you to choose 'life'. But the choice is yours as are the consequences"* (Gen 2:17, Pr 12:28, 11:19, Deut 11:26, 30:15, Jer 21:8). Life and death.

When someone who knows says to me, "This path you are on will harm you. It will look and feel like this. Trust me, I love you," something different and extraordinary can happen. The speaker gets out of the way and I am now confronted with the truth or consequences of my own action. My own. I own. Sure this is a box of fine tobacco. But my friend (the Canadian government in this case) has placed a true picture in front of the misleading and tempting one. I now see both sides clearly.

Rather than taking away my freedom with the "bad, dumb, illegal, or wrong" statement, they have given me true freedom. They have shown me both sides and told me I am free to choose - now with knowledge. That is what God does for us. His words and ways provide true freedom because they define the reality in which I am making a choice.

True freedom. My own. I own. Choose life.

Day 293
Warts and All

So...what do I want said about me when I'm gone? You? It is very tempting when someone passes away to make grand statements about how saintly they were, talented, nice, thoughtful, etc. And we are all trying to be both kind and comforting. But there is also something about that sort of canonizing approach that seems a bit empty, a bit misleading. Like we are all in denial but not sure what to do about it. No one is so perfect. Yet I pretend.

I sort of appreciate the Irish wake. It seems everyone gets just drunk enough to tell funny and real stories about the deceased - calling them names even, yet laughing and drinking toasts to them...warts and all. It brings about a loving catharsis so necessary to place the real person honestly and truly in the memory of those who loved them. You might notice that scripture is pretty honest too when it tells stories of our long dead heroes of the faith. David was an adulterer and murderer, Abraham a liar and a coward, Moses reluctant and a murderer, Sara a doubter before Thomas, the disciples jealous and petty, Peter a coward, Paul... well goes without saying.

Yet somehow it is that honest depiction of their flaws and warts that seems most attractive, most human, even most funny. And especially it is the amazing grace of the redemptive work of God in and through them that is the real story, the one that could get recounted again and again...with a warm smile. They let God do all that for them - they are amazing.

It is, despite their flaws...or maybe because of them, that the grace of God, His transforming kindness is put on display and this person who we love, warts and all, was both the recipient and channel of that grace into the lives around them. I could weep for joy for such a one, identify with them, smile and talk about them recounting fun, hard and lovely stories and call them a true saint without any sense of holding back.

That's what I want you to do for me when I am gone. OK? Warts and all...with a smile.

Day 294
The Man

So... when it comes to stormwater I'm the MAN!

I have set up stormwater programs for some of the largest cities in the US. Wrote the book. So when I was asked to speak to a group of seven small towns all from north Nashville I was sort of uninterested.

I'm the man after all. No one would ask Dylan to play a local coffee house would they? He's the man.

So I agree anyway and stand up to talk at lunch. City engineers everyone.

Then one young guy interrupts, "Hey lets pray first."

Right, of course. You know, bless the food and all. This is the South you know.

He proceeds to cry out to God for wisdom in administering the cities, stating that he and his friends around the table are young, barely men and women scant years out of college, saying they need His insight, His grace, His plan for their cities to be what they were destined to be for His glory. He got specific. Amens all around. Heads bowed.

And I remembered the Man said this: "You call Me Teacher and Lord (the Man); and you are right, for so I am. If I then, the Lord and the Teacher, washed your feet, you also ought to wash one another's feet. If you know these things, you are blessed if you do them" (Jn 13).

So... I sat down... the man (small m) and asked humbly; "How can I serve you, how can I help you do this thing you prayed?"

We talked for two hours. Servants all around.

The men.

Day 295
Raising Cain

So...think about Cain if you are able.

He is one of the most recognized names on earth and probably the only one so called...

...except in reference to being a "marked man", and "raising Cain".

It's in Genesis 4 and I have heard all kinds of explanations about "blood sacrifice verses crops" etc. and it all sounds very ethereal and smart and makes God out to be arbitrary and capricious.

Not very satisfying.

But how about this?

Cain and Abel come to God with their work. But God "looks past" or "looks around" Cain's sacrifice.

Why?

Because He is looking at Cain himself, and He sees something growing there that needs healing, needs fixing - He sees a flaw in His beautiful craftsmanship and sets about to change that.

But first the unaware Cain must see it... must experience it himself.

Now is the time.

So...Cain is provoked by his sense of God's unfairness.

What is in him, what is hiding there charges to the surface, incensed, like a dark prowling beast suddenly in the light - EXACTLY like a prowling lion seeking someone to devour (1 Pet 5:8) - it is exposed for Cain to see.

...*continued*

To insure he doesn't miss it God even clearly explains exactly what is going on, what is at stake: *"Why are you angry? And why has your countenance fallen? If you do well, will not your countenance be lifted up? And if you do not do well, sin is crouching at the door; and its desire is for you, but you must master it."* (Gen 4:7-8)

God explains the whole situation, lays out the alternate outcomes - both being possible - encourages him to "choose life" and not death. His destiny is in his hands...always has been.

He chooses death...and murder.

God STILL does not punish him but makes him a "marked man" not as exposure to ridicule but as protection: "Do not kill this man with My mark on him. I love him."

God preserved his life giving him another chance.

Cain's destiny was still in his hands. His recovery still in play. God was making sure he had time to repent and change, to master the thing that had mastered him.

Oh the injustice of God!

He is patient and long suffering, disciplining us for our good. And when we have turned, when we who have the power over our own lives have chosen life?

Then we find destiny. And more...

...we find this God whose ways are above our understanding has worked to perfect us, partnered with us, believed in us, walked with us, never giving up.

Day 296
Going Postal

So...an innocent trip to the small rural post office in my area and...

Me: "Can you tell me the postage cost to send this book by media mail?"

Guy: "Sure...interesting. Are you this guy...this Andy Reese?"

Me: "Uh... yes I am."

Guy: "What's it about?"

Me: "It's about how ill equipped we are as pastors, leaders and just friends in being effective first responders in the emotional lives of those around us, our loved ones, our flock, even strangers. And it shows in simple ways how we can be effective - in partnership with Jesus."

Guy flipping through it: "Really!? Oh wow. Where was this ten years ago? I'm an ex-pastor. I finally retired - I did not know how to help people and they all came to me... I was 'the pastor' you know but I felt just helpless."

Me: "I'm sorry. I sort of know how you felt - being just an elder but still."

Guy: "Man, this is so encouraging. I like this."

Me: "Can I give you this copy?"

Guy: "Well, great. Oh, and postage is $2.69 anywhere in the US. I guess that is why you came in."

Me: "That is why I thought I came in. But that is not why I came in."

Guy smiles.

Talk about going postal.

Day 297
Prodigal

So... he is an influential Jewish financial adviser to big cities. We were discussing money... huge sums of money... over a fine meal. All business.

Then he said, "I Googled you. What is this God thing you do. I need to ask you something."

He is a good man who made a bad decision. It ruined his marriage. He had not seen his beloved daughters for over ten years. Changed their names. He wrote a letter asking forgiveness each quarter. No response. He was in deep pain, deep regret, deep sorrow.

Normally I might have thought, *"Well, sowing and reaping... getting what he deserves. Have nothing to do with him. He is the oppressor and his family was the oppressed."* Throw the first stone.

But now. Sitting across the table, seeing his despair and distress, all I could do was to gently tell him about a God who loves and who will show him what to do, what to become, how to live, how to be comforted; giving permission and pathway to approach this Yahweh not as a sinner filled with self-hate, not as an avoider of pain... but as one who knows they are deeply flawed yet somehow loved to wholeness. A miracle.

Solomon saw this too: *"Then I looked again at all the acts of oppression which were being done under the sun. And behold I saw the tears of the oppressed and that they had no one to comfort them; and on the side of their oppressors was power, but they had no one to comfort them."* (Ecc 4:1)

Every tyrant, every perpetrator of injustice, every hypocrite and every arrogant tycoon needs what I need... understanding and a deep comforter.

Some come to know it.

That is the time.

Ask the father of the Prodigal son.

Day 298
That Disney

So...Disney got it right.

There is a statue of Cinderella in Disney World and to anyone over about five feet tall she looks like a peasant girl. Seeing only what eyes can see. But to children looking up into her eyes they will see a princess crown hovering above her head hidden in the background - and it makes them shout and point - seeing what only revelatory-heart-kindled imagination can see.

That Disney!

One of the coolest things about Jesus is that children flocked to Him even when not told to. When the disciples tried to keep the children from mobbing Jesus He said a strange and radical thing: *"Truly I say to you, unless you are changed and turn and become like children, you will not enter the kingdom of heaven. Whoever then humbles himself as this child, he is the greatest in the kingdom of heaven. Let the children alone, and do not hinder them from coming to Me; for the kingdom of heaven belongs to such as these"* (Mt 18:4,5, 19:14).

That Jesus!

In 2 Sam 6 David is dancing and leaping foolishly (in Saul's daughter Michal's eyes) but joyfully and wild in his own at the Arc finally coming to Jerusalem. David was ecstatic... Michal was embarrassed at her husband's childish exuberance and scolded him: "Don't be a child". The next verse about her is: *"Michal the daughter of Saul had no child to the day of her death"*.

There is something about the naive but trusting, playful and expectant way in children that attracts God's heart. There is something in having a vulnerable belief in the goodness and faithfulness of someone that does not even make room for questions, analysis, and doubt that is precious to God. Something in not holding back tears or shouts or dance.

Something in telling your brain to chill and making room for some princess fun.

Day 299
God Repeats Himself

So... when God repeats Himself I should pay attention.

In (of all places) Leviticus 25 and Deuteronomy 15 God is talking about the Jubilee where He tells His people to do unusually generous things for the poor and indebted, someone setting another free from slavery and crushing debt through their own personal anti-capitalistic sacrifice. Giving away my rights to possess people and make them pay what they owe, to keep their homes and evict them, to keep them in slavery, enslaved to...to... well, to me. And His explanation? *"For you were once slaves in Egypt."*

Why so?

Sabbath rest, Jubilee giving freely, treating immigrants as citizens - all these things of radical obedience to something that seems nonsensical and overly trusting in an invisible God were designed to make the Israelites a certain kind of people...free people.

After He has gotten His people out of Egypt His desire was to get the Egypt out of His people, to get the sense of limit and lack out of their psyche so that they could live in free trust of a generous Father thus becoming free themselves with regard to fear and greed. Why? They had attached their hearts in trust to God.

And us?

"But thanks be to God that though you were slaves of sin, you became obedient from the heart to that form of teaching to which you were committed, and having been freed from sin, you became bondmen of righteousness." (rom 6:17)

You and I have been rescued from slavery, from being trafficked... in slavery to all forms of sin. Now free I can practice generous living, free giving, sacrificial service and watch the Egypt come out of myself too.

Watch it melt away in the spring sunshine.

Day 300
Two Kinds of Authority

So…There are two kinds of authority in the world. Only one is earned.

Kind 1 is the authority derived from position. It can be inherited from, elected to, or promoted into. It can be usurped. It is hierarchical, organizational, and geographic. Qualifications are often optional.

Kind 2 is the authority that may often find its beginning in beauty or strength, in talent or intelligence. It is tribal in nature with voluntary followers. It only matures into actual authority over time through exercise of selfless service and strong character. Without these it burns out in "ten minutes of fame"… influence for a minute… mostly bad.

Bono expresses authority. Mick Jagger does not. Mother Teresa could preach the gospel to Harvard, Billy Graham could give a Ted Talk on Jesus …standing ovations. Kind 2 authority.

At 12 Jesus could have been recognized and set on course to be a Kind 1 superstar. God and his mother saved Him until age 33 when he was ready to be Kind 2. And it was said of Him, "He taught as one who had authority, and not as their teachers of the law." And He said:

And it is He who said, *"The scribes and the Pharisees have seated themselves in the chair of Moses; therefore all that they tell you, do and observe, but do not do according to their deeds; for they say things and do not do them."* (Mt 23:2)
"You know that the rulers of the Gentiles lord it over them, and their great men exercise authority over them. It is not to be so among you, one wishing to become great shall be your servant, and the first among you shall be your slave." (Mt 20)

with only Kind 1 people suffer, organizations rot, society weakens, and relationships deteriorate. And among God's people? It is not to be so among you… not to be so… not… no. You have a good chance of being in one of those situations right now. Be faithful… grow to be Kind 2 anyway.

So say we all.

Day 301
Becoming What I Behold

So... let's take a new selfie. In recent prayer and counseling sessions I have noticed how so many of us seem, over the years, to have developed a sort of mental selfie. And most of them are not all that complimentary. I find that I am so aware of my failings, my flaws, and my fears that I somehow think that these are what others see in me as well; these are what are projected as I enter a room, talk on the phone, am at work, and talk with friends.

When I look in what I suppose is the self-mirror what I see is not the real me but a painted caricature, constructed unknowingly over the years, made up of the pieces of my life, many of which I am not proud of and not happy with. But it looks sort of like me and, well, it IS looking back at me so... It is made out of the past, it is not real...and it is not helpful. God has a different approach to all this. He calls Saul to be Paul even in the midst of his persecution of Christians. He calls Gideon a warrior while he is hiding in the threshing floor. He sees David, still a shepherd boy, as a great king.

And me? God has this amazing habit of coming to us from our destiny not our history and calling us by names we have yet to manifest - Abraham, Sarah, Peter. Papa God is in the process of taking down that false painting and putting up a mirror. But there is something special about this mirror - it IS real and it reflects who we have been made to be, and who we really are on the inside. He knows this because He made us. He says I am predestined to become that image (Rom 8:29), and that in essence it will look a lot like Him and His Son - a family resemblance. *"And we all, who with unveiled faces contemplate the Lord's glory, are being transformed into his image with ever-increasing glory, which comes from the Lord, who is the Spirit."* (2 Cor 3:18). I realize He is standing with me, I have a Friend and partner, and that He will do the heavy lifting (Phil 1:6).

Time to trade in the bad selfie, and to look in the mirror with uncovered faces and watch the transformation. Besides, I have better things to be about anyway. We become what we behold.

Day 302
Capisce

So... let's try out a thought experiment.

Say you are part of a tribe that lives on an island called Capisce. A great chief who lives far away says to you, "Look out for men who will arrive in wooden boats. They are not to be trusted. Make no agreement with them." Sometime later such men arrive with many goods and freeing and new ideas. They say, "That chief is not to be trusted. He just wants to continue to rule over you. Join us." So... we listen to these men and sign an agreement with them. Unknown to us the agreement allows us to trade and profit with them, but it also has clauses and practices that eventually make us their indentured slaves. When we cannot pay many of our sons and daughters are taken away to slavery. We are in big trouble... legal big trouble... we signed a contract.

The great chief sees what is happening and unaccountably pays off the past debt himself and also finds a legal way to cancel the clauses that require slavery of anyone who so chooses to opt out. Many do, but also many love the trade goods and the wooden boat man's society and feel they can control the bad aspects.

They are wrong.

But each is given a free choice. No pressure. The great chief asks each tribal member to appear before him to tell him of their decision so he can make arrangements for them. Those that choose to side with the chief go with him forever. The others go with the wooden boat men. It seems fine for a short time but they eventually find they are entrapped and become slaves forever. Many on the island scream at the great chief, "Why are you sending us into slavery with the wooden boat men? We should be able to have all these goods and that society and NOT have to go into slavery."

They are wrong.

They are wrong in two ways. The great chief is not the one sending them to slavery - they are already slaves. They cannot have the goods and wooden boat man society and not be slaves.

Capisce?

Day 303
Good Investment

So…he is the son of an Ivy League New York Jew who found Jesus and a wise Minnesota beauty. But that is not why he is a good investment.

At ten he developed a lawn mowing business that made thousands. But that's not it either. He is a handsome high school senior, polite, well spoken, with super grades and many college opportunities – pursuing business. Nope. Not that either. He is a superb skier who made it in the top six to compete in the state championships. Getting warm.

Abraham was asked to sacrifice a precious possession to God… to give his seed Isaac to Him. He had already left his home not knowing his destination, given the best land to Lot, and a tenth of all his spoils to Melchizedek. But this was much more than that. This was unrecoverable.

Scripture says he got up early in the morning to do so – not knowing what would happen but knowing Who was the guarantee of grace (Gen 22:3, Heb 11:19). And because this was the kind of man Abraham found he was – the kind who would give up something precious at God's asking – God said to Him, "I will bless and multiply your seed like the stars and like the sand and you will possess the gates of your enemy, and become a father to many – watch and see" (Gen 22:17).

We will each encounter moments of decision like this; maybe not so big, but huge to us. Something will be asked of us that will make us question God and whether we might be too radical; to doubt and want to shy away. "Is this really God anyway?" we lie to ourselves. God does not lay out the reward at the beginning – that would be a trade – only the ask - not because God does not know our hearts, but because we do not.

This young man heard that another student, who had just missed qualifying for the skiing championships, had a father who had only weeks to live, dying of cancer. Without fanfare or permission, he gave that young man his position so that his father could see him ski one last time. Beyond that, he volunteered to carry the team's parkas up the hill to keep them warm until the last minute – humbly serving them.

That is why I would invest in him. That is why God will invest in him. Watch and see.

Day 304
Unchained

So... I was talking with some youngsters (anyone under 40 these days) who were bemoaning their boring jobs, chained to a desk. They were ready to go on some mission trip to a far off land; anywhere but here. Ready to do God's work... to travel like Paul roaming the world.

Really? Like Paul you say?

In Philippians we find a letter from Paul who also finds himself chained to his job... well, ACTUALLY chained... between two guards, rotting in prison, in Rome, for months. That is one view of it.

In those days the guards, in order to stay sharp, rotated every week or so throughout all Caesar's personal household and governmental domain. Each guard lived with Paul... chained to him for a week.

Oh the hidden ways and plans of God!

Paul writes: *"Now I want you to know, brothers and sisters, that what has happened to me has actually served to advance the gospel. As a result, it has become clear throughout the whole palace guard and to everyone else that I am in chains for Christ."* (Phil 1:12-13).

Do not overlook the fact that God always places His best where faithfulness becomes fruitfulness. Where the day-to-day-ness lived together can become a conflagration of life... if only I realize I carry something that is contagious.

Paul ends his letter with this delicious tidbit: *"All the saints greet you, especially those of Caesar's household."* (Phil 4:22)

Each. Guard. Caesar's. Household.

Rome. The known world.

Paul was not chained. That is impossible. But each guard was chained to Paul, onto life, unto eternity.

Day 305
Check It Out

So... I am not a control freak. Really I'm not. But I was always taught: "be prepared", "plan ahead", "stock up". I rehearse in my head what I should say in such and such a situation. I plan ahead the details of a trip or a client presentation. I set aside money for the future.

It is prudent. It is wise. Because why? Check it out. So I am struck with this: *"When you go do not take a lot of money in your belts, or a bag for your journey, or even two coats, or sandals, or a staff."* (Mt 10:9). *"When they bring you before the synagogues and the rulers and the authorities, do not worry about how or what you are to speak in your defense, or what you are to say."* (Lk 12:11,12). *"Do not store up for yourselves treasures on earth, where moth and rust destroy, and where thieves break in and steal."* (Mt 6:20).

I realize much of this is taken within the context of the disciples being sent out. But that is sort of what I am huh? Some of my preparation and planning is wise - remembering James 4:15. But some of it is based on this thought: "I am on my own and it depends on me." The basis of it is fear... fear plain and simple. I am afraid I am on my own. So my life gets complex as I watch all the perimeters of it 365-360-24/7. Alert. The end of each of these verses - not written above - is this: *"You are worthy of a wage from Me; I will give you what to say at that very minute; I will take care of you so store up heavenly treasure."* Check it out.

Each verse speaks to some part of my life - when I speak in the moment, when I am out in life pursuing career and relationships, when I think of my future the answer is the same: "I will take care of you because I care for you. I will give you what you need. Do not fear."

He says: *"Seek first my kingdom (the most important life changing, world changing things) and righteousness (my inner world, my heart) and all those other things... all those I will watch over for you."* (Mt 6:33). When I begin, however haltingly and ineptly, to trust Him and to shift my focus on His concerns then I find that He handles mine - He is ever present behind the scenes (sometimes not too well hidden either!) bringing about career progress, supply and prosperity, connections, sure direction and inspiration on what to say in that very minute. He is in me. Strange! And I am not alone. Not on my own. It's not all up to me... I have given it up to Him. Check it out.

Day 306
Love is Helpful

There is a lot of buzz about the Koran's teaching and I suppose if all surahs were taken literally by Muslims then maybe so. But, for example there are 4 million Muslims in Germany, the western nation with the tightest security in the world after Israel. Of that number 200 are deemed to be active jihadists and 2,000 possibly dangerous. And the other 3,998,000? Bad Muslims I guess.

Criticize when you have cut off your hand or plucked your eye out because it contributed to sin in your life (Mt 18:8,9).

The Muslims I know live in quiet fear at the growing animosity expressed toward them on the streets and in the stores of our Christian nation.

"Because lawlessness is increased, most people's love will grow cold." (Mt 24:12)

Don't be like most people.

Do what is helpful.

Love is helpful.

Day 307
Coincidences

So... a "coincidence" is two or more "incidences" happening in a coordinated way. "Coordinated" means to be ordained or decreed together in an unalterable way.

Today we have redefined this term to mean the random chance happening of things that we just notice are somehow related. That makes sense and it would be crazy not to think that is true. But... Thursday...

I am supposed to market Houston. I knew no one... NO. ONE. Then at an Opryland Hotel conference I am on a small panel. The guy next to me? He is THE GUY I needed to get to know from Houston. Totally connected, totally willing, totally the right time. Three hour lunch. New friend. Came to me.

Then a manager comes to my house to complete repairs on a tractor his mechanics messed up. He is just THE GUY who I wanted to talk to to ask to give a young man I love another chance at his new job. He came to me.

My son in law is in Beirut trying to impress some visiting NGO dignitaries about his local expertise. Just then, THE GUY, a well-dressed lost person wanders in asking in Arabic, "do you know where... is". Obscure organization... well except for the fact my daughter was volunteering with them last week. Dan explains the directions in flawless Arabic. The man gushes thanks. The crowd nods and smiles. He came to Dan.

The other thing about coincidences... the original thing... is that they are God's pseudonym, His ghost writer, His way of remaining anonymous.

He loves to give when no one is looking, even when few notice. He rarely lets the right hand know that the left is doing. It is His humble way.

But He has this amazing habit of having that needle in the haystack find me... and you.

Day 308
Rational Irrationality

So... there seems to be a lot of questioning about "god" going on about now; a lot of walking away from that old time religion.

Not always a bad thing.

Many young people seem to be slipping sideways into rationality based beliefs... a sort of functional deism and therapeutic moralism.

It sort of goes like: something greater, some prime mover, some initiator of it all started things off, but we are mostly on our own dealing with the universal laws and general providence. Let's call this force, or place, or idea "god" if we like. But the leap from that to anything else... too big a leap for rational minds.

It seems to make its entrance about every 50 years or so.

Susan and I sat long over coffee this morning talking about that and asking, "Well, what DO we believe after all these years? What are our non-negotiables; the things that, over the years, our hearts have landed on and have proven trustworthy and true?"

Here they are, poorly and incompletely stated for sure. But for me, each has been tested again and again and I have found I can put weight down on them. Could be wrong of course. I tried really, really hard not to believe the stuff I am about to share for quite a while. I failed pretty badly!

Here goes.

God is loving, is a personality, and is beyond all I can imagine or imagine I can imagine. He is also intimate in a way that warms places in me I cannot explain.

Jesus is divine in ways I cannot understand and ways I can, and said things about my own nature and reality I cannot grasp with my brain. People who knew Him personally died rather than deny this about Him... knew Him well. He somehow changed me and made me very grateful.

...continued

There is another plane, another kingdom and it's basis and reality is not easily sensed or reasoned into existence - yet it is perceived with eyes that can see what eyes cannot see. It is all around yet just out of sight; not shadowy but light filled. I have accessed it often, and it has accessed me just as often.

There is this set of writings whose origin and history, whose internal consistency and proven ability to transform men and cultures, has proven to be a reliable guide on how to live life even if some parts are confusing.

There is a sense of God within me, in my innermost part, that is constant presence, guidance, friendship, and freeing - I know I am not alone even when I seem to be. Thoughts and knowings come unbidden that have life and imagination and flow, pictures, fully formed or snippets. Coincidences beyond coincidence happen often, some foretold. And humor - gentle, warm, very funny.

And, I seem to have a heart that beats with hope for the future, with a smile, that all these things that seem to linger just outside the borders of my senses, of which I catch even daily glimpses, will make total sense someday and I will realize they had to be this way, and that wisdom and love kissed each other when this plan came about.

I know I did not say it as well as I feel it.

But these things sustain...

...not seeing yet believing the evidence within and without

...I suspect all through life

...and to infinity and beyond!

Day 309
Doers

So…I am a follower of Jesus and try to do and be what he commands however imperfectly. He tells me to love my neighbor. He tells me to love my enemy. I can say to a Muslim (and to my next door neighbor), "You are not my enemy, but even if you were I would still love you."

He tells me to hate what is evil. Fine. That is an attitude.

But look out. Attitudes without corresponding action morph into a charicature of Christ.

Hating evil MUST be followed up with this: He tells me to overcome evil with good.

"Good" looks like something I can see, touch, experience. It looks like laying down my life... or maybe just $100 or an afternoon a week tutoring and befriending an immigrant.

Any fool can recognize evil. Any fool can rant about it. Talk is cheap.

I am commanded to be a doer of the word.

I have little patience with anyone who can talk a good game but shows no personal investment in it, has no skin in the game. Until I have actually known and loved a Muslim myself, helped an immigrant, sought to understand, I am not in the game.

I am just part of the crowd in the stands screaming at the exhausted players to do better.

I have forgotten the story that Jesus told to give an answer to the question:

"And, who is my neighbor."

Day 310
Hope

So... I put on an old faded ball cap today. Used to be vibrant royal blue. Not any more. The brilliant hue has been washed right out of it.

Faded. Hat. And then I heard something and listened... now abide these three: faith, hope and love. These three. 1 Th 5:8 says that faith and love protect my heart making it both strong and right within me. But hope... what is hope? Why is it one of the big three?

1 Th 5:8 says that real unfaded hope, is a helmet - to protect my mind and my emotions; to steel my will... my soul. Do I fear I am losing my sanity; my way in life; destitute from the passing of a loved one? Does my mind race from imagined calamity to envisioned failure to presumed loss?

Maybe my hope has faded; has lost its meaning to me; its power to protect me. While faith is about receiving now, hope is about the future. It is this unreasonable yet full assurance that things will, in point of fact, be all right. That no matter what I will be fine. That no matter what I am loved by God and nothing is beyond hope, outside its reach. It is a calm assurance that God is both willing and able to help me. It is willing to be patient and wait.

It makes hopeful Christians seem crazy and out of touch with the world; in denial. *"This hope we have as an anchor of the soul, a hope both sure and steadfast and one which enters within the veil."* (Heb 6:19) Hope puts me IN TOUCH with something greater than the world. I am denying the lie of hopelessness the right to overwhelm me.

This hope anchors my soul to the one place that is unshakeable, the one place that is the epicenter of peace. When my soul wants to quake within me I follow my anchor line right into the most quiet and holy place ever created... and there I rest in perfect peace. What can men, what can circumstance really do to me in the end?

And hope, unfaded and glorious, allows me to smile even through tears as I understand that someone's passing is simply a transformation of nature, a change of location, a fullness of arrival. They have for ever followed that anchor line through the veil to that holy place where hope is overwhelmed by sight and sorrow washed out by the light of the heaven.

Unfaded glory.

Day 311
Mis-takes

So... one time I brought smoked pork to a Shabbat dinner. OK, that would be last night. What was I thinking? Well, not about that. It was in the freezer and I knew it tasted great so...

There is a concept throughout scripture of the "stumble", the "lapse", the "blind spot", the "misstep", the "blurt out", the "schmutz on the tzitzit" (see I know some Jewish stuff!), the "pork at Shabbat". James says, *"We all stumble in many ways"* (Ja 3:2). So what happens when I do? Well, normally nothing...at least nothing clear and direct. There might be knowing looks, averted eyes, cooling relations, smirks, grimaces, false flattery, even whispers later on. I might feel like something is wrong but I am left to my own damning imagination. This is church.

Polite society is killing us. God is clear. If I act that way I am, in point of fact, the deceitful enemy of this person - God's child: *"Faithful are the wounds of a friend, But misleading are the kisses of an enemy"* (Pr 27:6). I made a mistake in something... a "mis-take", and I need another try at it, another take. "Quiet on the set. Doing Life...take two...ACTION!"

Here is His expectation for me, the friend of the stumbler: "Brethren, if someone stumbles you who are spiritual restore such a one gently...gently. Watch yourself! Don't be tempted to act wrongly toward them." (Gal 6:1). Restore is pretty different from "expose" or "ignore". In another place He tells us to reprove gently. "Reprove" means to "prove again". To reprove to help you improve is to prove I love you.

"Two are better than one because they have a good return for their labor. For if either of them falls, the one will lift up his companion. But woe to the one who falls when there is not another to lift him up." (Ecc 4:9-10)

What would it be like if we each lived in a net of friends who really, really, really had our back? Who mutually agreed that we would never ever, ever let the other one stumble without rushing to their aid, without partnering with them to help them grow in grace and wisdom. *"He who reproves a man will afterward find more favor Than he who flatters with the tongue."* (Pr 28:23)

First of all I would welcome it so others would not be afraid. Second, we would all grow very strong very fast. Last, about 90% of the dark one's ammo would be taken out of his hands. This is actually church.

Day 312
Religion and Science

So... religious leaders making declarations about what science will prove or disprove is just as bad as scientists making pronouncements about whether God exists or is like based on scientific measurements.

Problem is when I, speaking as a representative of God (even if somewhat self-appointed), say something that is sweeping and demonstrably wrong, then all believers to some extent get painted with the buffoonery brush and it ends up being a net kingdom negative. Note that Jesus was tempted to speak knowingly about taxation and politics, to adjudicate an inheritance argument, and to speak to the Greeks. He demurred in every case - so should all who are tempted out of their zone of authority and revelation.

Scientists seem to be able to get away a bit easier with spouting knowingly about God. At least for now.

Here is scientific proof... wink wink

"He who believes that the sun does not move and that it is the earth that moves is stark raving mad and possessed by the devil." John Calvin

"There is mention of a new astrologer who wanted to prove that the earth moves and not the sky. This fellow wants to turn all of astronomy upside down. I believe Joshua told the sun to stand still." Martin Luther

"There can be no such thing as global warming. Man does not have that much power over God's creation." Pat Robertson

"We don't have to protect the environment, the second coming is at hand." James Watt

"The Earth is degenerating these days. Bribery and corruption abound. Children no longer mind their parents, every man wants to write a book, and it is evident that the end of the world is fast approaching." Assyrian Stone Tablets 2800 BC

I rest my case.

Day 313
Be a Giver

So... be a giver.

Giving seems to be of two kinds.

Kind one is to give out of an intentional relationship; it is to choose to walk with someone helping them across the rough patches - giving time, love and resources.

They need a friend they can see and call and hear love from. It is a ligament relationship - unbreakable but flexible. It is what causes the ACTUAL body of Christ to grow (Eph 4:16) as opposed to simply growing numbers of mutual strangers in attendance at some meeting.

We have time for only a few of those at one time. Not all my body parts are directly connected to each other even while they are all part of my body and suffer or compensate in some way if one part is injured. But if we all do it a relational web grows like an unbreakable net - the ACTUAL social safety net God has in mind. Politics may or may not be local but relationship always is (Pr 27:10).

And they will smile.

And God will smile.

The second kind is to give once anonymously to someone who is already walking and hits a tough patch (Mt 6:3-4). Even a cup of cold water (Mt 10:42) or paying for the cup of coffee of the car behind you in the drive through.

They will probably know well enough who to thank and it won't be you or me. Or they might figure it out.

And they will smile.

And God will smile.

Day 314
Enemy Territory

So…theotokos

Enemy-occupied territory---that is what this world is. Christianity is the story of how the rightful king has landed, you might say landed in disguise, and is calling us to take part in a great campaign of sabotage.

CS Lewis

There is often confusion about this point. Is this God's world or Satan's? Scripture tells us that while ultimate ownership of all goes to the Supreme Being, this world has been handed over to the evil one.

"We know that we are children of God, and that the whole world is under the control of the evil one." (1 Jn 5:19)

Jesus never disputed Satan's claim that he could give any kingdom to Jesus, or all of them.

"And he said to him, 'I will give you all their authority and splendor; it has been given to me, and I can give it to anyone I want to.'" (Lk 4:6)

Mary the mother of Jesus is called "*theotokos*" in the Greek language. There are many understandings of what that means – none of them very exact because the word is so multi-dimensional and English flattens it out.

It always means "the one who brought the One who is God" into the world.

But it also has the connotation in this setting of being smuggled, operating in secret – coming in by the side door. God smuggled Himself into the world through a brave and faithful young woman protected by a devout man who risked everything about his reputation to stay with Mary and to believe her.

And one step ahead of Herod they flee to Egypt and save the child.

This world is a dark place, do not be surprised. But the one who was smuggled into the world is now proclaimed from housetops without fear – because death has been destroyed by this One.

Day 315
Forgive From the Heart

So... Matt 18 talks about God's prime directive to forgive someone from your heart. From your heart. Wonder how you do that?

Here's how.

Forgiveness involves three distinct things - each is important. Speak it with Papa God or Jesus (who are you most comfortable with?) in the room, and maybe a friend. Close your eyes and vision them before you. Take your time. Cry all you want.

First forgiveness is about debt cancelled. A quick, "OK, I forgive you," does not go to the depth of the heart where the IOU for has been stored. Take the time to recount and enumerate the debt owed. Even write it down. Speak as if to the person slowly and deliberately saying, "You owed me___ and ___ and ___ and you did not pay. But today... today... I forgive the debt... all of it. All. Of. It. You do not owe it to me anymore."

Breath. Pause. Feel. Tear it up. Let it go.

Second forgiveness is about giving up my right to judge the person, to impugn motives as if I am omniscient. I am not. I do not know why the person did what they did. I do not know the full story. God knows. Speak again, "Today I give up my right to know why you did what you did and I release any judgment I feel toward you. It is not my place and I give it up now. I ask you Papa God to be the judge and... I ask you to please have mercy on them."

Slowly. Breath. Pause. Feel. Let them off your hook.

...*continued*

Finally, forgiveness is about giving up my right and expectation, once and for all, that that person will or can ever fulfill the legitimate need I have - even if they are the one who should be responsible for doing so. If I keep expecting a different outcome I may only be hurt and disappointed again and again. Speak like this, "Today I release you from my demand that you meet this need I have. No matter how much I need it met, you are no longer responsible for doing so. You are not responsible to meet my need."

[For bonded relationships (husband-wife, parent-minor child) the last step should be modified to include help in working through how legitimate needs get met within the relationship.]

Very slowly. Breath. Pause. Feel. Let them go.

Then turn and face God.

"Papa (Jesus) is there anything else? Is there more? Will you show me?"

If there is go back and give that away too. Then.

"Papa (Jesus), I ask if you; would you be willing to cleanse me, free me, and would you be willing to meet this need is feel so strongly now?"

Then just stop and listen. Breathe in. Pause. Feel. What do you first see, sense or hear?

Never let go.

Day 316
Silver Tongue

So... a presidential sick burn (ask your 20-something friends).

In his state address the president remarked, *"I have no more campaigns to run,"* which met with applause from some. Then Obama quipped, *"I know because I won both of them."*

Off the cuff. Off script. But in his heart. I both smiled and winced. They had it coming but it seemed like a great opportunity for our silver-tongued leader to be merciful, wise and impacting (even presidential) missed. Cute, funny, touché. But... he just helped to insured two more years of hell by answering a fool according to his folly, shaming them, and all on national TV (Pr 26:4,5).

"Silver tongue" comes from this verse: *"The tongue of the good man is as choice silver, but the heart of the wicked is worth little."* (Pr 10:20) Without calling someone good or wicked (look in the mirror Andy!), let's think on this. Note the relationship between tongue and heart here - it makes all the difference - all the difference. When I go off script, lose composure, blow my cool, blurt out, I never say what I WANT to say, I say what I NEED to say. And those needs are found in my heart. Jesus said it best, *"Out of the heart the mouth speaks"* (Lk 6:45). I put those needs there, or I let them invade and take root. And when the pressure builds I boil over with what is in there. If pain, jealously, anger, arrogance, frustration then... *"The plans of the heart belong to man, But the answer of the tongue is from the LORD"* (Pr 16:1). It is my responsibility to tend the garden of my heart - water it, pull weeds, plant good seed. If I do then when I need it, out of my mouth will come wisdom, love and the silver-soft response that can break the bone (Pr 25:15).

Silver tongued does not mean articulate and compelling only. Silver has a peculiar property... it is sonorous. Silver bells. It makes a beautiful note when struck. Unexpected love and wisdom; reaching out with humble grace. Like Steven being stoned and Christ being crucified - a silver tongue speaks words of life and it makes all the difference - all the difference. I can be smarter than I am wise. My smart compelling words can embarrass someone, even convince them they might be in error. But only my vulnerable loving gracious silver-tongued wisdom can convince them of what is right. Then I can be more concerned with what is right than being right. And it makes all the difference - all the difference

Day 317
My Famous Friend

So... I live in Nashville and years ago became close friends with a very famous person. You would know the name. We talk all the time.

His writings become very widely read... best sellers. In fact in some places groups formed and had sort of rave parties where they listened to bands, read his stuff and just sort of celebrated. He attended a lot of them at first... not so much anymore. They took on a life of their own and he found he was almost an intrusion into the festivities. Others formed book clubs where someone learned in his works gave a talk on their take on some aspect of what he said. Some speakers grew very influential. He told me early on he attended a lot of them but not so much anymore. When he tried to speak up to help them understand what was really meant or how to apply things to today's issues, he found it awkward. It seemed that they were more comfortable listening to a good speaker talking about his ideas than engaging in conversation with him. A few leaders were sometimes not that happy to have him in the limelight. He mentioned that when he went few recognized him, like they never actually knew him but were mainly interested in the club. That made him sad. He would talk to one or two, even want to get together, but they looked past him to the action on stage.

Not everywhere of course.

Lately it seems a lot of the members of these different clubs are drifting away from them, maybe finding them increasingly irrelevant to their daily lives... not as enticing as the newer things of science or mysticism. Other writings are taking the place of his. And not experiencing his close friendship, the information about him seems not all the interesting any more...passé. I asked him if that made him sad, if he felt sort of "washed up". His eyes glistened and he looked away. "I know them so well," He whispered, "I wish they knew me too." He asked me why I didn't too drift away. I thought for a moment about all our years together - through all sorts of things; his sound advice, helping hand, even his rescue a few times. And our daily chats, his warm and happy love. My eyes glistened too. And I told him, "I know you, and you are my best friend. You are more important to me than anything. Why in the world would I leave someone who loves me so well?"

And, honestly, where else would I go? you have the words of life.

Day 318
Chess

So... I can't tell you I know why it happens that someone passes from this earth before I am ready for them to.

And I can't tell you I like it.

But I can say that God is a far better chess player than His opponent...

... and at the end of the game when He calls "checkmate"

... all His white pieces will be found placed with love in a velvet bag on a silver cord hung close to His heart.

All.

Day 319
Opposite Conclusions

So... all 12 spies saw the same giants dwelling in the Promised Land.

Ten said, *"we became like grasshoppers in our own sight, and so we were in their sight."* Two said, *"we should by all means go up and take possession of it, for we will surely overcome it."* (Num 13:33)

Saw the same thing; came to opposite conclusions.

Only those two lived to take the land.

Peter saw the same waves and wind when he was walking on the water in obedience to Christ's command, and when he was sinking beneath the waves.

Saw the same thing; but came to opposite conclusions.

When Jesus asked Peter, "why did you doubt?" He was not asking because He wanted to know. He was asking because he wanted Peter to know. (Mt 14:30)

The size of the issue is never the issue. Grace abounds all the more. (1 Cor 10:13, Rom 5:20)

A Pastor named Bill Johnson says, "Sometimes our breakthrough begins when we refuse to be impressed with the size of our problem."

Come to an opposite conclusion.

Day 320
Let's Not Bow in Prayer

So... let's all bow in prayer. On second thought...don't.

Did you ever notice how Jesus prayed? No, not the words... but HOW He prayed?

"After Jesus said this, He looked toward heaven and prayed: 'Father...'" (Jn 17:1)
"So... they rolled the stone aside. Then Jesus looked up to heaven and said, 'Father...'" (Jn 11:41)

Did you see it?

Let me be bold to say that the next time you pray try it. See what it does to you. See what it stirs up in you. In some it will feel overly familiar and pushy. In some it will seem irreverent. It flies in the very face of: "Me...why... I'm just a sinner saved by grace...".

It is true that we bow before a king. But it is more true that: *"Let us therefore come boldly to the throne of grace, that we may obtain mercy, and find grace to help in time of need."* (Heb 4:16)

"Because of Christ and our faith in him, we can now come boldly and confidently into God's presence." (Eph 3:12)

Yes, it is true we bow before a king. But it is more true that we are told to seek the face... the face of our Abba, our Papa. Can you see His face? Ask Jesus to help you. Enter with thanksgiving that you can...enter in.

Your mama told you to mind your posture - walk like a princess, stride like a king, strong handshake and look 'em in the eye son. Listen to your mama. And listen here...

Let me say boldly that it is the difference between son ship and slavery this way we pray, this way we enter the throne room. It will make all the difference tomorrow morning. You may never leave. Why not?

Try it. Boldly.

Day 321
Encourage

So... this is my bid to lose followers. :)

We hear a lot about the harmful violent or sexual content of media and should gatekeep our hearts because what repeatedly enters it eventually and invariably helps define who I am.

But I think there is a more insidious problem.

Consider this: Social media companies hire PhD "behavior designers" to find ways to lure and lock me with their application or media. They do this through rewards of three types: (1) social validation - followers or likes, pictures pinned, comments; (2) the "Easter Egg" reward for being the first to find and post the cool YouTube video, LOL cat, or "ten things..."; and, (3) achievement by reaching the next level in...

Most check their smartphone upon waking and more than 150 times a day, sitting at a table with friends each lost in texting those who are not there while overlooking those that are. Day after day.

I binge day after day on a shallow rat-a-tat-tat stream of sound bites, pictures and cute videos; stuffing my heart with shallow junk food and wonder why I feel shallow and junky. That is why.

God has something to say about all this: *"Be careful how you walk, not as unwise men but as wise, making the most of your time, because the days are evil. So then do not be foolish, but understand what the will of the Lord is. All things are lawful for me, but not all things are profitable, I will not be mastered by anything."* (Eph 5:15, 1 Cor 16:12).

Am I growing into what I was put on this earth do do and be; the thing that will fill me fully with life and wisdom? The question is not content but time, not participation but addiction. Its OK sure, just not wise, just not beneficial.

God suggests there is something else I can do day after day: *"Encourage one another day after day, as long as it is still called 'Today,' so that none of you will be hardened by this deceit."* (Heb 13:3).

Encourage each other to be their best. Day after day.

Day 322
Flip, Chop, Kick

So...my New Year's resolution is to quit trying to change myself and just try to be myself.

Before that becomes a bumper sticker I should say more.

Our most pernicious failings, the things we want to change forever seem to want to stay forever. Here is why. The most tender and precious parts of us, the things we were made to be and do - these are the things that are ground zero for dark assault. They get hijacked, damaged and perverted for dark purposes. So... the more we try to stifle or cut off these things we dislike about ourselves the more we find we are battling against our very selves... and fail eventually. They are part of us...just a very bruised, tattered, and distorted part.

The secret of jujitsu is to use the enemy's momentum against him. He is attacking and pushing in one direction and the idea is simply to go with him but let his work carry him past his intention and into ours - and with a flip and a chop and a kick he is done.

It's a Godly great approach. It works like this: *"No push has come at you but such as is common to man; and God will not allow you to be pushed beyond your ability to defend yourself, but with the push He will provide the way of escape. So count it joy - as you become a perfect you, lacking nothing."* (1 Cor 10:13, James 1:2-4)

God says that He is faithful to use the very push of a temptation, test or trial to be the very thing that perfects us - the real us - that is under assault. We can find the good and wonderful intention of our Creator for each hard area and say 'yes" to that intention.

As we learn God's jujitsu and work with Him that thing becomes firm and pure, our identity, our weapon against darkness. We find those places we annually resolve to cut off become the very strength of our lives and we become...well...

...we become ourselves. Flip. Chop. Kick.

Day 323
God's Choices

So... I have had noted charismatic prophet Bob Jones give me a personal word...twice...the second to fix the first I think! Noted charismatic heavyweights Bill Johnson and Kris Vallotton too. James Goll sang a song over me - accurately foretelling a coming event. Prophetic singer Kimberly Rivera too, deep and meaningful. So many more great names over 35 years, I forget them mostly, but each has spoken encouragement to me. So many somebodies... faithful giants. Well known. Names often dropped. Good words. So many. So blessed.

But today a nobody, a young woman who was unbelievably tormented and tortured as a young child, broken into pieces, looked at me after I had witnessed in anguish her riveting relived brutal pain and said, "Jesus said He wants you to know something..."

So I agreed to listen for a minute. Somebody pushed a record button. Why, I wondered. Such arrogance.

This little one, who nobody knows, then proceeded to reveal my deepest dreams and recent prayers, with details nobody could know...nobody; and then spoke the very thoughts of God with detailed uplifting encouragement and direction like nobody could give...nobody.

And I wept.

"For consider your calling, brethren, that there were not many wise according to the flesh, not many mighty, not many somebodies; but God has chosen the foolish things of the world to shame the wise, and God has chosen the weak things of the world to shame the things which are strong, and the nobodies of the world and the despised God has chosen, the things that are not, so that He may nullify the things that are." (1 Cor 1)

The encouragement I needed nobody knew... but Nobody knew.

It has always been so... this season reminds us of Mary, Joseph, Bethlehem, the Magi, Anna and Simeon.

I hope someday to qualify for that position.

Day 324
Capitalism on its Head

So…this should scare every capitalist who is also greedy. Everyone who has subscribed to the Godless singular rule of maximizing profitability.

Your gold and your silver have rusted; and their rust will be a witness against you and will consume your flesh like fire. It is in the last days that you have stored up your treasure! Behold, the pay of the laborers who mowed your fields, and which has been withheld by you, cries out against you; and the outcry of those who did the harvesting has reached the ears of the Lord of Sabbath. You have lived luxuriously on the earth and led a life of wanton pleasure; you have fattened your hearts in a day of slaughter." (Jas 5:3-5)

So…here is what some young energetic smart person should do.

Let's turn capitalism on its head.

Start a certification program where a company can be certified that it pays all its workers $15 per hour or more AND that it is not enforcing job share to reduce benefits.

IF they are found to be telling the truth then they get window stickers saying they are "certified fair labor" and a listing on the "fair15" web site.

All the rest of us will ONLY buy from them - only if they are certified - only.

Let's let the very capitalism that is propelling and compelling the low wages drive some out of business. Can it be we can align capitalism with justice?

The certification must be done by an impartial attorney for free. We must all get used to paying about 35% more for fast food. Is that OK with you?

OK go do it somebody.

Day 325
Thanksgiving Traditions

So... here is a thought about thanks giving Thanksgiving conversations coming up in a few weeks... maybe even a new tradition.

Paul said, *"I thank my God in all my remembrance of you, in view of your participation in the gospel, and that He who began a good work in you will perfect it until the day of Christ Jesus, and it is only right for me to feel this way about you all, because I have you in my heart."* (Phil 1;3)

I think that Papa likes it when we speak to each other about what we are thankful for in each other;

when we thank God specifically in the presence of those we love for what He has done and is doing; our joy in what they have done, have become, how dear they are; something we really like about them.

The bible calls that prophecy (1 Cor 14:3) but why be so religious sounding on that day huh?

When I speak words of thankfulness for someone in their presence then the words are

double-blessed,

double-thankful,

double-life giving.

A second helping.

Those words are truth... in love... in life.

They will be remembered long after the memory of the corn bread stuffing and pumpkin chiffon pie fades.

Day 326
Caricature

So... a caricature is a picture, description, or imitation of a person or thing in which certain characteristics are exaggerated in order to create a comic or grotesque effect or to make a point. It takes something true about a person or situation... something real... and exaggerates it out of proportion to actual reality. It still looks like the thing - but it is all wrong, out of perspective, too big and attention demanding.

It is the evil one's stock in trade.

He hisses to Eve "hath God really said...?"; and the proceeds to misrepresent God. He whispers to Jesus, "If you are the Son of God throw yourself down. For it is written: 'He will command his angels concerning you, and they will lift you up in their hands, so that you will not strike your foot against a stone' " (Gen 3:1, Mt 4:6).

It is a young mother overwhelmed, a teacher unappreciated, a worker stuck, a mate wondering about their choice, a talent diminished, an effort overlooked, a temptation looming large, a persistent and insistent thought, a personal slight magnified. It is Job wondering.

In the midst of these things Papa says, "No test, trial or temptation you encounter today is strange and huge. You are not the only one. I AM faithful to you in this. I know you. I will not allow it to be bigger than your faith and your ability. When it comes along I will send grace to endure and to be strengthened, and a means of escape. Trust Me." (1 Cor 10:13)

Papa seems ever to give loving truth and real perspective. He says, "It is written...", and "I AM", and "nothing can separate you from My love." He says, "Nothing today is larger than Me, and I have made sure that nothing you encounter today is larger than you."

Today, I won't let the master caricaturist make it seem larger than God... or larger than God in me.

Maybe I will even laugh at the comic nature of the caricature.

Day 327
Guilt and Shame

So...feeling guilty?

Guilt is about what I have done.

Shame is about who I am.

Guilt can be healthy and leads me to repent and move on feeling light and relieved. If I have actually done something to be guilty for.

But when I feel ashamed of the man in the mirror there is NO escape.

So I try to hide it behind my back and people around me experience the poser, the fake. They cannot connect with that person, no one can.

So I feel lonely too.

The mirror is no help.

But God says: *"Those who look to ME are radiant; their faces are never covered with shame."* (Ps 34).

Humility is me looking to God, and God helping me to be precisely who I am before Him and before men...

in that order.

Day 328
Storage

So... the NSA opened a facility to store five zettabytes of spy information - 1.25 trillion DVDs, 100 years' worth. But at some point they still need someone wise and watchful to interpret some piece of it; even just a single hovering sentence, to decide what to do.

Many years ago I had Cosmic Top Secret clearance and must have known some stuff found in that drawer. One night in a restaurant in Europe I was approached by a waiter and asked all about why I was in this small German village - very friendly. When I persisted in dumb answers the conversation became a bit icy - not all that friendly. He then moved on and disappeared.

The next morning I asked the owner about the waiter. "We have no such waiter", he said, and strolled away. Ahhhh... that is what spies are like. I wished I were more watchful and wise to decide what to do.

Paul, seeing a devil-trap, encouraged the Corinthians to forgive someone *"so that no advantage would be taken of us by Satan, for we are not ignorant of his schemes, his devices"* (2 Cor 2:11). Peter, the "get-thee-behind-me-Satan" apostle, said not to be trapped in anxiety but to: "be on the alert; your adversary, the devil, prowls around like a roaring lion, seeking someone to devour" (1 Pet 5:8).

Our head takes in "zettabytes" of information, impressions, and thoughts daily. In that stream there is surely bad intel... trials, temptations, targeted cyber-attacks. But we cannot process it, judge it, sort it fast enough. It sometimes just looks like a nosy waiter.

But fortunately for me I have, on the inside, a pretty foolproof mechanism and Helper. If my heart is filled with truth and also filled with the Spirit of Truth when something IS bad it also FEELS bad inside of me. It automatically sets off a small silent alarm, a nudge of warning, a "this does not line up" whisper.

We have been given, as a command, truth to be laid up in our hearts as a yardstick. We have been given, as a gift, Someone watchful and wise to help us decide what to do.

Pretty effective counter intelligence operation. Nosy waiters mostly move on and disappear.

Day 329
Bird Flu

So…officials killed 60,000 chickens, 2,000 cows - those terrible men!!

How could they? Senseless slaughter?

Was it because they hated the owners.

Nope… it was wisdom and mercy: bird flu and mad cow would have been pandemic.

We ask, how could God wipe out whole cities… is that justice.

YES!!

And wisdom and mercy too!!

Evil can be a contagious plague - it is catching, spreading. Demonic infestation of a culture, region, or city is the most contagious and perverse cancer on earth.

God sees beyond life into eternity and maybe, just maybe, He was saving many from evil and bringing them home to joy, peace, and protection. He is just and one day we'll all go "Oh…right…sorry for being so judgmental about You being judgmental."

God says to take decisive action within our own lives (Lk 8:18), against our sin (Mk 9:43), who we hang with (1 Cor 15:33), and who influences those in our charge (1 Cor 5:13).

Its deadly… be deadlier!!

Day 330
Just Run

So…Jesus being angry.

The harshest stance Jesus takes is NOT against the Pharisees.

Nope.

In Matt 7:22ff He condemns to HELL those who call Him Lord, Lord and are all concerned about working miracles, giving prophetic words and casting out demons

but not equally about obedience - specifically toward the poor, imprisoned, widows, orphans and the other helpless and hopeless.

He calls them false, SWINDLERS!

Is 58:2 condemns those who "delight in nearness to God" but actually don't know Him, as proven by their lack of concern for the needy.

Any church or person that is all about God "showing up" but whose practice is not characterized by active concern for the poor, justice, the needy, for discipleship - if those things are an afterthought, a hobby, a sidelight - don't judge, just run!!

Something of eternal worth is at stake.

So...follow your path-ways very carefully.

Proverbs 4 is chock full of life verses.

A favorite: *"Watch the path of your feet and all your ways will be established. Do not turn to the right nor to the left."* (Pr 4:26)

A "path" is where you go, a "way" is how you go - what you do and who you are.

The straight path and narrow way has a ditch on either side.

The devil doesn't care which you fall into, left or right, either extreme is fine.

Control or rebellion both work, legalism or lack of restraint, love or discipline, word or spirit.

Watch your path, watch your way...where you go and who you are.

It makes all the difference in both the trip and the destination.

Day 332
Filled with the Holy Spirit

So…I was a product of the 70's charismatic movement –

Holy Spirit seemed to come time and again.

Been decades since I thought about that.

A year ago I prayed with two pastors in back to back ministry and both ended asking about that "Holy Spirit stuff".

I shared and they asked and drank. One shook and cried for 20 minutes. The other spoke a new language, tears trickling down his cheeks. I was amazed and happy. Been a while. Both changed in many ways from that day to this.

Saw one last week and he hugged me and teared up saying, "That changed my life more than anything except salvation. Everything. Thank you for your part."

I get forgiven because Jesus was crucified.

I get new life because Jesus was risen.

"He who believes in Me, as the Scripture said, 'From his innermost being will flow rivers of living water.' By this He spoke of the Spirit, whom those who believed in Him were to receive; for the Spirit was not yet given, because Jesus was not yet glorified. Therefore having been exalted to the right hand of God, and having received from the Father the promise of the Holy Spirit, He has poured forth this which you both see and hear.'" (Jn 7:39, Acts 2:33)

And I get the Spirit in and on me because Jesus was glorified.

Three volume set, don't forget the third - its paid for. All God's doing.

Love those oldies!

Day 333
Competition

In Gal 5 God tells about the competition He is against:

"Let us not become boastful, challenging one another, envying one another." (Gal 5:26)

In Rom 12 the kind He approves:

"Love one another with brotherly affection. Outdo one another in showing honor." (Rom 12:10)

It's not in me to do that.

But *"I can do all things through the One who strengthens me."* (Phil 4:13)

I'm not trying to be better than my brothers.

I'm trying to be better than myself.

Day 334
Might Just be You Honey

Andy: *"Doesn't seem fair to some waves that they finally get a chance to crash on the shore and some previous wave running back keeps them from splashing way WAY up on the beach?"*

Susan: *"Is it really about how far up the beach your wave runs?"*

Andy: "What ELSE would it be about?"

Susan: "Maybe the fun of the crazy currents when two waves come together."

Andy: "Is this a man-woman thing or...?"

Susan: "Might be just you honey... oh look at the gulls, how beautiful!!"

Out of the mouths of (good lookin') babes...

Day 335
Be Free, Be Great

So...Gal 5:1-3 frame freedom for us.

It was for freedom itself that Christ set us free,

but be careful.

I think true freedom is NOT the carefree and careless indulgence of the flesh in any whimsical desire - the end of all that is being imprisoned in a low life existence.

The most free people I know have made a choice that to some seemed like constraint, like hard discipline.

Why!?

The great pianist or business man, farmer or teacher voluntarily chooses limitations on their focus, self-denial in favor of hours of study or practice to pursue their passion and to chase hard after God.

"Do you see a man skilled in his work? He will stand before kings; He will not stand before obscure men." (Pr 22:29)

That choice leads inevitably being who I was made to be doing what I love to do...

...and a freedom without regret.

And so I will stand before kings.

Be free.

Be great!

Day 336
Walking Straight

So…Jesus seemed to have clashes with people.

Religious leaders (Mt 23:33)

Family (Mt 12:48)

Disciples (Jn 6:66)

Merchants (Mk 11:15)

He seemingly zig zagging through life.

But on careful observance I see that He was neither pulled into the control of men nor repelled by their sins, neither a sycophant nor a merciless critic.

He seemed wonderfully and uniquely demagnetized when it came to those around Him.

He walked a straight path and had a wise way about Him - where He went and how He went.

Maybe it was He who walked straight and it was the world around Him that was crooked.

When I walk straight in a crooked world there will be clashes.

Day 337
Two Lies

Every issue I ever had or have now is derived from the two big lies attempted to be set into the heart of every child of men before or soon after birth:

The world is not safe and

I am not acceptable.

It takes many forms, speaks in many voices with one evil intent. Torment and destruction – stealing, killing and destroying.

But God speaks with a quiet whisper powerful to break the chains, shatter the rocks, free the soul.

He speaks about you beloved with truth far higher, deeper and wiser than the lie:

"I chose you in Me before the foundation of the world, that you would be holy and blameless before Me always. In Me you have obtained an inheritance, having been predestined according to My purpose." (Eph 1:6, 11)

Mmmmmmmmmmmmmm !!

Day 338
Yes Sir

So...I was panicked.

Andy to airport parking helper old black man: *"Somebody stole my car!! - I ALWAYS park it right here."*

Old man: *"Really, stole it?"*

Andy: *"Look I am an EXPERIENCED traveler. It's gone!!"*

OM: *"Bet $10 on that?"*

Andy: *"Of course, its stolen!!"*

OM: *"Get in, this lot can be tricky... for example..."*

Andy: *"We're wasting time and... what's that... ummmm, there it is... I must have..."*

OM: *"Stolen huh?"*

Andy: *"I ah, I... OK here is the money."*

OM: *"No, can't take it, was worth it though. Drive safely sir."*

God could not pass this one up: *"Andy you have read 'The way of a fool is right in his own eyes, But a wise man is he who listens to counsel'* (Pr 12:15).

It is not knowing a Proverb in your mind but recognizing it in your life that matters to Me."

Yes sir.

Day 339
Authority

So...History can be seen as a contest for authority.

God gave man authority over the earth (Gen. 1:26).

Eve, through deception, and Adam, through rebellion, gave it to Satan (Luke 4:6; Rom. 5:12–14; Eph. 2:1–2; 2 Cor. 4:3–4; 1 John 5:19). It was theirs to corrupt.

Satan offered it to Jesus in exchange for worship of Satan (Luke 4:7).

Jesus post-death was given all authority and disarmed darkness (Matt. 28:18, Col. 2:13–15).

Sons of God are freed from Satan's earthly authority and come under God's (Rom. 8:37–39; Col. 1:13; 1 John 4:4; 5:18).

Deception and accusation are the tools against us now. We have a diplomatic visa (Jn 15:18).

When Jesus returns He will visibly establish His authority and reign over the earth (Rev. 21:3–4).

Past tense.

Future perfect.

Day 340
Submit to Authority

More on authority.

So... the godly man seeks to find and submit to God-given authority in every facet of life - government, business, family, church, relationships, (Rom 13:1, Heb 13:17, 1 Tim 6:1, Eph 6:1, Eph 5:21).

Jesus rendered to Caesar (Mk 12:17) and recognized a legitimate role for the scribes (Mt 23:2).

But God does NOT give, nor give way to, control, tyranny, or stifling self-willed hierarchy in ANY of those spheres.

Jesus ignored, avoided or strongly opposed authority that had overstepped its boundaries and imposed its perverted and selfish will and way on individuals.

"Woe!!" He said, "woe to you who..."

What He started eventually overthrew Rome, renewed men, rescued from false religious structures, and transformed society.

The first "Arab spring."

Day 341
Rub the Right Way

The way to be an exceptional friend is *to "consider how to stimulate one another to love and good deeds."* (Heb 10:24)

Talk about your friends with God - He loves to brag.

"Stimulate to good deeds" means to rub together causing heat, maybe sparks.

Iron sharpening iron; provoking each other to greatness; to "the thing I was made for", my destiny call.

I am to tell my besties what I love about them, what greatness I see, what God says about them, words of life.

Beyond recovery to purpose.

Who is better to do it than you?

They will be changed forever - you will too.

Rub somebody the right way today!

Day 342
Serving

So...I have been in the company of many great men;

big city mayors,

wealthy tycoons,

anointed "apostles".

I was just with a man of world renown, leader of thousands, who cooked me dinner, sat among his top 100 and took notes when I spoke, and sent me a gift of thanks.

Jesus said the greatest would be your servants, unlike the world's lording self-promoting system (Mt 23:11).

The ancient church got it wrong when it went to robes to admire and rings to kiss.

The modern church has its equivalent.

But he got it right and I would serve him without question because he would serve me without pride.

Day 343
Drifters

So... I was feeling sort of drifty this morning. Ever felt that way? Like you forgot who you were overnight, what you were about... like you lost sight of land.

Like that.

Sat for the longest time staring out the window, sipping coffee. Then I just opened randomly and read these two seemingly unrelated but juxtaposed things about God, what He likes to do, how He thinks:

"He heals the brokenhearted, and binds up their wounds. He counts the number of the stars; He gives names to all of them" (Ps 147:3-4).

And He said, "That's you too you know... that is you."

Ephesians 4 says this about Jesus: *"to each one of us Christ measured out some of His nature"* (vs. 7) -and- *"the whole body fits and functions when we each work within that measure"* (vs. 16) -and- *"when we do the body measures up to Christ - fully"* (vs. 13).

When God describes some other part of Himself He is also describing you... and you... and you. Each one carries a measure of God to display to the world, to live, to thrive in. I love freedom for people and the infinite heavens... love them.

You were made for something too. Your heart beats with it. You do not have to interview or try out for it - you were made for it.

Feeling drifty?

Ask Him - He'll show you your own landfall.

Like Father like son... and daughter.

Day 344
Christ Like

So…be more Christ like?

I sort of thought that that meant a gentle, soft spoken, "lover not a fighter" sort of guy;

not someone to watch football and have a beer with.

Then I took off my stained glasses and lo and behold: I saw Him in a loud shouting, whip cracking, table turning, party breakin' up rage sending hundreds of robbers running (Mt 21:12);

I saw Him whooping and laughing at kids saying the darnedest things (Lk 10:21);

cursing the the hypocrites calling them sons of Satan damned to hell (Matt 23);

and drinking and partying with a disreputable crowd needing a Friend (Lk 7:34).

And ALL without sin.

I'm all in.

You?

Day 345
Being the Difference

So...if the main thing that makes me different from the world is I go to church then maybe the world will never see the difference.

But if I do not take into account a wrong suffered,

pray for authorities instead of criticizing,

seek to be seen with the least instead of the leaders,

spend time and resources on the poor and mistreated,

deal honestly on my taxes even though I will not get audited,

cover someone's sin against me instead of one of the many negative alternatives,

honor my parents,

work diligently even when no one is watching,

or express encouragement and optimism in the face of the daily grind

...then I bet I will leave a wake of blessing, an aroma of life.

And the only One who matters will notice, smile, and tell the angels, *"This is my beloved son in whom I am well pleased."* (2 Cor 5:8)

Day 346
If I Were the Devil

So…if I were the Devil

If I were the devil then I would try to make things complex, mysterious, erudite, and deep.

I would create one-off ceremonies and require "thous" and "thees" when my ministers pray.

They would all need bible degrees and learn to be exegetic.

That is what I would do.

I would not let them read this:

"But I am afraid that, as the serpent deceived Eve by his craftiness, your minds will be led astray from the simplicity and purity of devotion to Christ." (2 Cor 11:3)

I may go for complexity when I should simply move toward a closer and closer experiential knowledge of Jesus and Papa.

In the end I think it may be my pride or fear or both

…that drive me to the soul man's strength

…instead of the spirit man's power.

Day 347
Knuckleheads

So... I was once a top secret army guy in Europe (I know I know).

Waiter: "So Captain, up here for the exercise?"

Me covering: "No just checking the base condition"

Waiter: "come now Captain, lots of activity huh?"

Me: "Not sure".

He: "I'll be right back".

No show.

Next day me to owner: "Who was that new waiter Hans?"

Hans: "We have no waiter".

Me: "Oh!".

Was that a spy? Did I see it at the time? Probably and not at all. Yet I was safe. Why?

I answered based on principle, adherence to security training - NOT because I knew what was up.

2 Cor 11:13-14 talks of both men and devils coming in disguise.

But if I live and respond by godly principle, not drawn in, I will always be OK even when I am not particularly discerning.

That's good news for us knuckleheads.

Day 348
Roaming in Romans

So…upside down on the mortgage?

Spiritually we all were upside down on our mortgage,
over our credit limit,
bankrupt,
indebted to the mob,
and a fugitive from the law,
thought we were going crazy,
without support from anyone,
no plan to get right, and
sick in body.

Penniless, hopeless, helpless.

That is Romans 1 and 2. Now watch this.

God is talking.

Romans 3 and 4: "Sit still and rest. I will pay your past debt."
Romans 5: "I will pay your monthly note and bills."
Rom 6: "I will give you a new identity free from the mob."
Rom 7 first half: "I will settle the legal claims against you."
Rom 7 second half: "Besides, it was not your fault, you were dissociative –
but no longer. I have severed your evil part."
Rom 8 first part: "I have asked Dave Ramsey (on good behavior) to help
you with your daily financial decisions."
Rom 8 second part: "I have a plan for your long term health in the works."
Rom 8 end: "Nothing can interfere with My plan or my love for you my
son…Oh did I forget to say that I have adopted you into my family?"

His love is unstoppable and will go on forever.

OK now?

Day 349
I Have an In

So... today I was rear ended, maybe totaled.

Two others hospitalized, serious. One dead.

Advil, hot pad, paperwork, rental, drug test, doctor, 7 hours, Atlanta, alone.

Today this world sucks.

Waiting I remember what The Man said in Jn 16. He was giving His guys dire warnings then said, *"In the world you will have tribulation. But cheer up, I have overcome the world... in Me you will have peace".*

Two ins: in the world/in Me.

In the world: persecution, affliction, stress, pressure, anxiety.

In Him: eternal blessings, hidden lives, adopted, chosen, redeemed, predestined, lavishly graced, included, sealed, informed.

In the world (and in the car wreck) but not OF the world (Jn 17:16).

I am part of the ultimate in crowd!!

Cheer up... Andy.

Day 350
Breaking the Cycle

Suggestion
Impression
Oppression
Obsession
Revulsion
Repression
Commission
Revulsion

[INTERCEPTION]

Communication
Confession
Remission
Restoration
Rejuvenation
Destination
Glorification

Day 351
Leadership

So...Jesus Christ really was a superstar (Jn 6:15).

Men tried to make him king.

So were Paul and Barnabus (Acts 14:14). Men tried to make them gods.

Humans NEED leaders to humbly serve and equip them, to help them to their destiny (Jn 13:14, Eph 4:12).

Men WANT kings who will provide care and ease.

Humans NEED leaders who will humbly state the obvious - "I am like you, follow God, I'll help show you how."

Men WANT demi-gods, charismatic heroes to display magic, to excite and enthrall.

The leadership challenge is to do the one without falling prey to the other - and to stay pure in the process.

We can help them do it, giving honor without idolatry, obedience without mindless obeisance... for our own good... and theirs.

Day 352
What, Me Worry?

So…I am stuck upside down on the thin crusty surface of a molten lava projectile,

with a paper thin breathing layer,

spinning at 1,000 miles per hour,

falling at 65,000 miles per hour in a spiral around a 10,000 degree thermal nuclear explosive ball 900,000 miles across,

spun out at 500,000 mph among 400 billion fireballs 4,000 GENERATIONS across at light speed,

and all falling into a black hole, one of 125 billion we think.

And I stand before a God who spoke it into being with two words, and who looks DOWN on all this and calls each star by its name (Ps 147:4)… oh, and numbers my hairs and loves me dearly.

What, me worry?

Day 353
Favor for a Lifetime

So... me 1988, a young engineer looking at rivers with county engineer trying to impress.

He is distracted, inner nudge, I ask.

He: "don't know why I'm telling you this, lost an expensive county survey instrument moonlighting, not sure where and when reported I will be fired."

I say something lame. He leaves. I drive to a bridge crossing, looking at... and...wait...whats that floating like Moses in the bull rushes?

An orange equipment case. Could it be!!

YES!!

Roll up suit legs, suit coat on guard rail, wade out, clean it, card and ribbon and box put on his desk.

He calls in tears.

Was my friend and client till retirement... three offices opened from that one event as a toe-hold.

One second of Papa's favor will trump any card, held by anybody, anytime, anywhere.

"For his anger lasts only a moment, but his favor lasts a lifetime." (Ps 30:5)

Day 354
The Lift

So…I have a hidden partner.

The Holy Spirit loves to express herself/himself behind the scenes and we ourselves can miss that influence within us and others - the sudden inspiration, picture, idea, thought, knowing, excellence, favor.

Daniel had an "extraordinary spirit" for government (Dan 6:3).

The craftsmen in the temple were filled with the Spirit for excellent creativity (Ex 31:3).

Each person is given a measure of God Himself to exhibit to the world (Eph 4:7) and nobody does that thing better than you can.

So when you think, wow that seemed easy, that was great, I LOVE doing that - good chance it is you AND your Gentle Partner in the wonderful dance of destiny.

God loves to make you look good.

Enjoy the lift!!

Day 355
Truth Sets Free

So… many look back with loss and regret, forward with anxiety, and live today with low grade depression.

Not always but it is the flavor of their souls.

I was with a man who realized a few years ago he had no good childhood memories... none.

Now he's great.

What happened? This.

It's not what has happened to me, is happening, or will happen, but what I BELIEVE about it that ensnares and imprisons me after the fact.

Against this God speaks living truth to lies - even lies I fully own, that seem me, lives built on them.

Who was, and is and ever will be a help in time of need (Ps 46:1). He has an amazing ability to both speak in a memory (not just at one) and to come to use from our destiny (not our history).

And He is pretty upbeat about our chances. Your chances.

That truth seeps into me and I begin to look back with thankfulness and forgiven-ness for failure, forward with anticipation, and to live today with inner joyous ok-ness.

The truth sets me free... in any circumstance (Jn 8:32).

Day 356
Good and Best

So…I tend to carefully assess and deal with the intrusion of hardship, pain and trial when it comes through the door of my life.

You probably do too. That's a pretty good thing.

And facing it redemptively with God it can make me stronger, wiser, and more compassionate.

But I'm thinking maybe I spend too little effort checking the credentials of the flood of pleasure, fun and free-time-eaters that seek entrance to my life's living room.

I find that indulging uncritically in those can tend to draw my heart to the trivial.

"Therefore be careful how you walk, not as unwise men but as wise, redeeming the time… Do not be foolish, but understand what the will of the Lord is." (Eph 5:15-17)

Choosing between good and bad is not that hard.

Choosing between good and best is the stuff of which greatness is made.

Day 357
Fire on the River

So... long mahogany table, big city, stern powerful director at the far end, key staff debating endlessly.

I listen, unsure, over my head, quaking inside, game face.

He suddenly: "Reese, we've talking, you're not - speak!"

Sudden peace, knowing inside light as a butterfly alighting, why not?.

Me: "Your most precious dream is to save the City's river beauty, rescue its Great Lake front - your fear is it won't happen in your lifetime. My job is to make it happen for you."

Death-like pause in the room. Everybody is silent. Looking at me and then at him. One woman smiles. She knows what I knw.

He: "Meeting adjourned - Andy we're going to lunch."

Today, five years later, the last legal hurdle was crossed - its established - off and running. We are going to save part of the City and no river will ever catch on fire again within its borders.

"For the word of God is living and active. Sharper than any double-edged sword, it penetrates even to dividing soul and spirit; it judges the thoughts and attitudes of the heart." (Heb 4:12).

Day 358
The Secret of Balance

So...sitting on your stool?

Want to be a "balanced believer?"

Years ago God showed me a secret. I will now show you.

"For God hath not given us the spirit of fear; but of power, and of love, and of a sound mind." (2 Tim 1:7)

The Holy Spirit has three components equally balanced - a stable three-legged stool. Each is fully part of the Holy Spirit - when I keep these three in balance I will be balanced.

When I allow one to grow out of balance I will not only be unbalanced but will look through the camera tripod of that imbalance and will see the world askew.

Unfortunately I will rarely know I am blind-spotted, malformed, and undernourished in one area and will not "see eye to eye" with others... having little appetite for the short-legged part of God I lack.

Such is the source of most divisions within the church.

Ask for hunger for that part and see what happens - though the first bite may taste a bit like Brussels sprouts!

Day 359
Trajectory

So…following trajectories?

Jesus predicts a number of trajectories as this age plays out (might be years ok?) growing in intensity like birth pangs.

Here is one: *"Because of the increase of wickedness, the love of most will grow cold."* (Mt 24:12)

What might that actually look like in a CIVIL society like mine?

Maybe: partisanship, lack of compromise, harsh language, mocking political leaders, inaccurate sound bite put downs, factions, strong harsh opinions, and subtle fear mongering. Social media maybe?

Might also include the rise in terrorism, crime, and violence.

Peter says: *"...they are surprised that you do not run with them into the same excesses... the end of all things is near; therefore, be of sound judgment and sober spirit for the purpose of prayer. Above all, keep fervent in your love for one another."* (1 Pet 4:4)

The frog is in the water.

The heat is rising.

Jump to principled and loving living.

Day 360
You are On Something

Anxiety is at pandemic proportions right about now... heart attacks, bad decisions, alienation, breakdown.

Anxiety is temporary atheism.

Against this God says, "Don't worry" which would be unhelpful except He shows exactly how to actually beat anxiety: truth, tactics, strategy.

Matt 6:25,26 gives the real story - what is actually truth: *"I say to you, do not be worried about your life. Is not life more than food, and the body more than clothing? Look at the birds of the air, that they do not sow, nor reap nor gather into barns, and yet your heavenly Father feeds them. Are you not worth much more than they?"*

Phil 4:6-9 gives the other two: *"Be anxious for nothing, but in everything by prayer and supplication with thanksgiving let your requests be made known to God. And the peace of God, which surpasses all comprehension, will guard your hearts and your minds in Christ Jesus. Finally, brethren, whatever is true, whatever is honorable, whatever is right, whatever is pure, whatever is lovely, whatever is of good repute, if there is any excellence and if anything worthy of praise, dwell on these things. The things you have learned and received and heard and seen in me, practice these things, and the God of peace will be with you."*

Tactics are short term countermeasures, and these work every time (in everything, prayer, with thanksgiving, blurt out the truth to Him about your needs and feelings).

Strategy is a life-changing mindfulness-based transformation process (60 days) that modern science now says works best (whatsoever things are... focus on those things, dwell on them). And the result: peace beyond my logical reasons to be anxious, unreasonable tranquility.

Your friends will think you are on something...

...you are!

Day 361
Face Lift

So... a friend asked if we thought she should get a face lift. She was joking of course... mostly.

We 60-somethings have these kinds of conversations when we get together - trying on old age to see how it fits; sometimes wistfully thinking about spring now in the fall.

And I thought... I love it in the spring when the apple trees fill the air with their lovely perfume and attract my gaze with their gorgeous pink and white blossoms.

Love it, the buzzing of bees. But those who understand the real treasure of the apple tree find it not in spring's beauty but in fall's bounty; just ahead of the first frost - apples of gold in settings of silver.

The purpose of the apple tree is to bear much fruit - not just to be decorative. Winesap, Fiji, McIntosh, Honey Crisp, Braeburn, Jonathan, Gala, Granny Smith, Yellow Delicious... lots of variety, but each one a miracle.

And to do so each also shows the scars of years pruning. It is a beautiful thing, that pruning, not in need of a face lift if I value fruit beyond fancy.

"Charm is misleading, and beauty is fleeting, but a woman who fears the LORD is to be praised" (Prov 31:30).

Give her the product of her hands, and let her works praise her in the gates.

Age is unavoidable, but the fruitfulness of a life well lived...

...maybe that is all the lift she needs.

Day 362
Isms

So...been studying the isms – a couple anyway.

Socialism is man's attempt at protecting the masses but historically resulted in squashed/robbed freedom of individual growth/expression and a greedy ruling government elite.

It trusts too much in human nature...which is inhuman much of the time.

Capitalism is man's attempt to free men to grow/express but by defining growth in terms of dollars it enslaves workers to the most capable and connected enriching a greedy ruling corporate elite (Jam 5:1-6).

It trusts too much in human capacity to climb toward a goal...which limits it to a few climbing on the backs of the rest.

A dog will never not act like a dog (well, maybe for a treat). A fallen human will rarely ever not act like a fallen human. Over time and with temptation and opportunity we humans devolve to sin and perversity.

Both fail because they have an earth-only perspective and leave God and His morality out - and the flesh in. Mostly they rely on human nature – not transformation to do the work.

It's about salvation and transformation, not philosophical approaches.

After that God intends the poor to be rich in faith (Jam 2:5),

the wealthy to be rich in good deeds (1 Tim 6:17,18),

and all to lay up a retirement in heaven (Mt 6:20).

So say we all.

Day 363
The Breaks

So…rising through the ranks.

What caused Joseph to rise to Pharaoh's side? Revelation!

A dream. Yea.

Pop and sizzle!

But more importantly, what caused Joseph to REMAIN by Pharaoh's side?

Character and competence - with that revelation.

Joseph should have been embittered by life's breaks: sold into slavery (due to immature use of revelation), and accused into prison.

While hopelessly incarcerated he worked hard on character and competence and gained wise perspective and a forgiving heart.

When God saw he was ready He caused Pharaoh to SEE Joseph.

Revelation will take me places character cannot sustain.

"For not from the east, nor from the west, nor from the desert comes exaltation; But God is the Judge; He puts down one and exalts another." (Ps 75:6-7)

But if I prepare my heart - God prepares the breaks

At the right time.

Day 364
Woes and Blessings

So…let me show you a secret.

God has hidden in plain sight a deep and contrasting truth - the push me and pull you of religion versus life. He shows clearly the difference between religion (in its worst sense) and true life in Him.

He does it in two lists that just happen to be the same length and just happen to be addressed to two different crowds. The first is the eight beatitudes (Mt 5:1-12). The second is Jesus declaring eight woes to the Pharisees (Mt 13:23-36).

They match one for one. Exact opposites when you think carefully about them.

Poverty of spirit brings heaven ownership but they shut off heaven;
Morning is comforted but they devour a mourning widows purse and pretend mourning;
Gentleness inherits the earth but they travel the earth trying to make sons of hell like themselves;
Hungering for righteousness is satisfied but the miss it totally with pretense and show;
Mercy obtains mercy but they ignore the weighty things of mercy and justice;
The pure of heart see God but they only clean the outside of the cup and are whitewashed tombs;
Peacemakers are called His sons but they murder the prophets;
The persecuted also own heaven but they themselves are the persecutors from hell.

It is to religious pretense He cries, "woe" …not to the world.

It is that pretense within that keeps me from the "blessings" not the externals.

Day 365
Two Laws

So…there are laws around me, and within me.

Two physical laws around me - the brick and the helium balloon.

Both work automatically, without effort on the brick's or balloon's parts. Bricks fall naturally. Helium balloons rise naturally – lighter than air.

Flapping wings is a fake law and only works while I am, in fact, flapping hard. But in fact it falls to the ground just like the brick without the flapping.

There are two similar spiritual laws within me: (Rom 8:2) *"For the law of the Spirit of life in Christ Jesus has set me free from the law of sin and of death."*

Both work without effort on my part - except to choose which law I will fall under: flesh or spirit. Both work – but the spirit has overcome the downward pull of the flesh – without flapping.

"For the mind set on the flesh IS death, but the mind set on the Spirit IS life and peace." (Rom 8:6)

There is also flapping (Rom 7:23) - the religion of self-effort, the law of the mind but it's not a real law. It only stays aloft like the law of the spirit when I flap.

But who wants to work that hard?!

Today I'll pick only one to focus my eyes on, to be intentional about.

Day 366
The Cup is Half

I don't believe the cup is half empty...

Or half full...

I believe the cup is half drunk...

And I intend to drink the other half before I die!

Blessings to you all

Andy Reese

ABOUT THE AUTHOR

Andy Reese is an Ivy League educated engineer, husband, father of four, church leader, textbook and Christian author, prayer counselor, amateur astronomer, beekeeper and speaker.

He is the co-author of Freedom Tools, a popular book about prayer ministry used in hundreds of churches and in thousands of prayer settings. More at www.freedomprayer.org

None of this, of course, qualifies him to write a book like this. But he is an insightful and wry observer of the oddities and realities of life, especially life with God and each other as Christians.

Also available is Bleats – the first 100 Bleats published. Find it on amazon.

Made in the USA
Columbia, SC
14 July 2019